Words Work

Words Work

ACTIVITIES FOR DEVELOPING VOCABULARY, STYLE, AND CRITICAL THINKING

Thomas Carnicelli

Boynton/Cook
HEINEMANN
Portsmouth, NH

Boynton/Cook Publishers, Inc.
A subsidiary of Reed Elsevier Inc.
361 Hanover Street
Portsmouth, NH 03801–3912
www.boyntoncook.com

Offices and agents throughout the world

The author and publisher wish to thank those who have generously given permission to reprint borrowed material:

"These Are the Days When Birds Come Back" by Emily Dickinson from *The Poems of Emily Dickinson* edited by Thomas H. Johnson is reprinted by permission of the publishers and the Trustees of Amherst College. Copyright © 1951, 1955, 1979 by the President and Fellows of Harvard College. Published by the Belknap Press of Harvard University Press, Cambridge, Mass.

"Fire and Ice" by Robert Frost is reprinted from *The Poetry of Robert Frost* edited by Edward Connery Lathem. Copyright © 1963, 1951 by Robert Frost, Copyright © 1964 by Lesley Frost Ballantine, Copyright © 1969 by Henry Holt and Co. Reprinted by permission of Henry Holt and Company, LLC.

Library of Congress Cataloging-in-Publication Data
Carnicelli, Thomas A.
    Words work : activities for developing vocabulary, style, and critical thinking /
Thomas Carnicelli.
        p. cm.
    Includes bibliographical references (p. 209).
    ISBN 0-86709-565-2
    1. Vocabulary—Study and teaching (Secondary). 2. Language arts (Secondary).
    3. Critical thinking—Study and teaching (Secondary). I. Title.

    LB1631 .C395 2001
    428.1'071'2—dc21

                                                                                2001035895

Editor: Lisa Luedeke
Production service: Denise Botelho, Colophon
Production coordinator: Elizabeth Valway
Cover design: Cathy Hawkes, Cat & Mouse
Manufacturing: Steve Bernier

Printed in the United States of America on acid-free paper
05 04 03 02 01   RRD   1 2 3 4 5

*This book is dedicated
to my mother, Anne McIntyre Carnicelli,
and my wife, Pamela Stone Carnicelli.*

CONTENTS

LIST OF FIGURES

FOREWORD

When I wrote *The English Teacher's Companion: A Complete Guide to Classroom, Curriculum, and the Profession*, I recommended certain books at the end of each chapter. These were books that would allow the reader to go into greater depth about that chapter's subject than I had space for in my own book. As Thomas Carnicelli notes in his introduction, my chapter on vocabulary was the only one that lacked such recommendations. Aside from books of lists and quizzes like *Word Smart: Building an Educated Vocabulary*, and Janet Allen's *Words, Words, Words*, which focuses on the middle-school years, there were no books that address the specific challenges of high school teaching. With the publication of *Words Work*, now there is and I'm grateful for its arrival.

Words Work's table of contents reads like a list of all the areas of language study I want to know more about but do not know how to learn about on my own. *Words Work* offers a series of examples of good teaching that show you what integrated language study looks like. Thomas Carnicelli shows you *how* to do it and, through his examples, you feel confident that you, too, could do that lesson just as he described.

In this era of standards and standardized tests, we all struggle to balance what we want to teach with what we are required to teach. Many of us have worked diligently with our students to examine both the connotative and denotative meanings of words. We've tried to point out the roots, perhaps even study them, but too often such efforts have lacked the depth and satisfaction the close study of language should provide.

This work is especially challenging our era of evolving language. New words like *cyber* stand next to older, more familiar words like *memory*, which take on new meanings in light of these additions to our vocabularies. Thomas Carnicelli gives me a way to understand how language changes and how "words work," and shows me how to integrate such language study into my class.

Integration of such study is at the heart of this book. Some people are so passionate about their area of interest that they want it to displace whole sections of the curriculum. Carnicelli would consider such an approach a tragedy, for he clearly demonstrates that it is through the study of our language as it is *used*—to speak and to write, in the past and present—that we come to understand and appreciate it.

Every day someone—an administrator, a counselor, a school board member or legislator—tells me something else I must fit into my curriculum. Their requests almost never help me teach better and rarely contribute something substantial to my class. This book is different. It offers me the ideas and methods I've long wanted to help my students better understand language and improve their vocabulary. The approach here will benefit them as readers and writers, thinkers and speakers. Such learning will also, I believe, translate into higher scores on the tests my students must take to graduate or attend the college they want.

Someday I will write a new edition of *The English Teacher's Companion*. When I do, it will be a better book thanks to books like *Words Work*, by Thomas Carnicelli, which I will eagerly recommend to readers. Much more importantly, however, I will be a better teacher because this book has allowed my students and me to better understand *how* words work.

JIM BURKE

ACKNOWLEDGMENTS

I would like to thank four English teachers for letting me visit their classrooms to try out my ideas: Donna Bakke of York, Maine, High School; Elaine Burnham of Marshwood High School in Eliot, Maine; Susan Fryling of York, Maine, Middle School; and Mary McIver of Newmarket, New Hampshire, Middle School. It was a privilege to teach alongside such skillful and knowledgeable teachers. I learned a great deal from them, and from their lively and talented students, whose work appears prominently in this book.

I would also like to thank four of my colleagues from the UNH English Department: the late Bob Connors, John Lofty, Tom Newkirk, and the mentor of us all, Don Murray. I have received support and encouragement from these fine teachers and scholars for years, and I deeply appreciate it.

Finally, I would like to thank my publisher son, Matthew Carnicelli, for practical advice and general encouragement, and my editor, Lisa Luedeke, for believing in a book that tries some unusual things.

INTRODUCTION

As an English teacher, I've spent most of my time teaching reading and writing. I've felt that my students would read and write better if they knew more about the English language, but I've struggled to find time for language study in my regular courses. I'd venture to say that my experience has been fairly typical, that many of you would like to do more with language study if you could only find the time. With the exception of grammar, which often gets too much attention, language study tends to get short shrift in the secondary English curriculum. This book is an attempt to right the balance, to help you find more time for language study without diminishing your attention to reading and writing, or speaking or listening or thinking.

The solution I offer is simple enough: activities in which language study, language arts, and thinking can be taught at the same time. In this book, I want to offer English teachers some very practical ways in which language study, specifically word study, can be integrated into the secondary English curriculum. The key is integration. In the activities I set forth in this book, two things happen at once: Students develop their language and thinking abilities by exploring the meanings and properties of words; at the same time, they develop their understanding of particular words and kinds of words by using them in meaningful contexts. Word study, language arts, and thinking are integrated. Knowledge about words and knowledge of how to use words are acquired at the same time, in the same activities.

This book has three main objectives. The first two are, as I've just described them, inseparable: to foster vocabulary development and to foster skills in language arts and thinking. My third objective is a broader one. I want students to examine the cultural values inherent in the words they use, and thus to gain a better understanding of the society they live in.

I started designing and experimenting with these activities some years ago, when I took a sabbatical from my college job and taught high school English. Over the years, I've developed additional activities to use in summer school teaching with high school students and in my own college courses. As I began to put this book together, I contacted four outstanding secondary English teachers—two in middle schools, two in high schools—and asked if they'd be willing to let me try out some of my teaching ideas in their classes. They graciously agreed, and this book is full of examples from their students, who range from fifth-graders through high school seniors. I have added a few brand-new activities while writing these chapters; most of these have been placed at the ends of chapters and labeled "Applications." Almost every other teaching idea in this book has been tried out in an actual classroom, either with my high school or college classes or with the classes of my four secondary colleagues.

While I've based this book primarily on my own classroom experiences and observations, on what I've learned from my own classes and from the classes of my four colleagues, my approach is based on widely accepted ideas within the fields of reading, writing, and language acquisition. There is now a very broad consensus that people learn skills and vocabulary best through meaningful, purposeful language use. I've been studying the research record on grammar and writing for years, and the lesson from this extensive body of research couldn't be clearer: Language study done in isolation from meaningful language use will have no significant impact on student language practice. See Hillocks (1986) for a full summary of the relevant studies. Baumann and Kameenui (1991) reach similar conclusions in their summary of the research record on vocabulary instruction: They find that students learn new words better if definitional instruction is combined with exposure to the target words in actual contexts; they advocate frequent independent reading as a key component in vocabulary development; they recommend regular oral and written composition as a way to make student vocabularies both receptive and expressive. I've taken these lessons to heart in designing the integrated activities offered in this book. There are no passive, decontextualized activities here, no word lists for students to memorize.

A review article by Michael Graves (1987) was particularly helpful in clarifying and organizing my thoughts about vocabulary development. Graves sees instruction as fostering vocabulary development by addressing three goals: Learning Words, Learning to Learn Words, and Learning About Words. He breaks the first goal—Learning Words—into several parts; the parts relevant to this book are enriching the meanings of known words and learning the meanings of new words. I want to emphasize here that my focus is more on the first part than on the second. This book is not one of those vocabulary-builders; it aims more at deep conceptual knowledge of some words than at superficial awareness of many words. Graves breaks the second goal—Learning to Learn Words—into three skills, all of which are stressed in this book: using context clues, learning and using word parts, and using a dictionary. Under his third goal—Learning About Words—Graves lists two practices that I also stress in this book: studying words in terms of their synonyms and antonyms, and learning to recognize and interpret figurative language. I use Graves' three goals, and some of his various subgoals, quite often as I explain what my various activities are designed to do.

At this point, I'd like to run through the book, describing the activities and explaining how they relate to my three main objectives. I should add right at the start that this book is not designed to be used in any one particular order. Some of the chapters rely on other chapters, but most of these activities can be done independently of the others. This is certainly not a book designed to be "covered" in one continuous year. Some of these activities can be used anywhere from fifth grade up; others would be better left for the upper grades of high school. I think of this book as an anthology of activities from which a teacher at any point in the secondary curriculum can draw.

The chapters are grouped into four sections. The first section—Getting Started with Word Study—sets forth some activities that I've used to get classes "hooked" on word study. These activities work well as introductions, but they can also be repeated at intervals throughout the year if you and your class get to like them.

Chapter 1, "Verbal Charades," presents my favorite way to introduce students to word study. It's a verbal equivalent of charades, featuring writing, listening, and reading instead of acting and viewing. In verbal charades, a class is divided into groups of three or four students, and each group receives a secret word, which they must keep hidden from the other groups. Each member of a given group writes a short sketch or vignette that illustrates the word without using it. The group members then read their vignettes aloud to the other class members, who try to guess the secret word. When the secret word has been identified, the whole class goes on to discuss how well each vignette conveyed the intended meaning. The game continues until each group has read its sketch.

Verbal charades provides practice in all of the language arts: in precise writing, in careful listening and reading, and in focused class discussion. The game is not designed to introduce entirely new words; if the secret words were unfamiliar to the whole class, no one would ever guess them.

While verbal charades can lead to deeper understanding of the specific words used, it fosters vocabulary development mainly by emphasizing a key skill needed in Learning to Learn Words—the use of context clues: Students have to rely entirely on context to guess the secret words, because the words themselves are not used. Verbal charades has all kinds of pedagogical value, but it's also a game that students of all ages pick up easily and enjoy playing.

The second chapter, "Verbal Clusters," describes an intensive, week-long study of a group of related words. Students explore the meanings of these words through a variety of language arts and thinking tasks: They discuss them; write definitions for them; write, read, and listen to verbal charades containing them; compare them to antonyms and synonyms; and use them to analyze hypothetical and personal situations. At the end of the week, they apply their knowledge in a test that stresses writing and thinking with the words, not just knowing the names. This activity, with its multiple tasks and repeated exposures to the target words, resembles the intensive instruction method developed by Beck, McKeown, and their colleagues; see Beck, McKeown, and Omanson (1987) for a summary of their various studies. Verbal Clusters is a useful activity in and of itself; it's also a good way to introduce the key terms and concepts in a unit of study, in English or in almost any field.

In the second section, English Words in Historical Perspective, I offer some historical background that should help any teacher feel more comfortable with the activities in several of the subsequent chapters. Chapter 3, "A Brief History of the English Vocabulary," is written for the kind of teacher I was when I first started, a teacher with little or no knowledge about the history of the English language. Because I, too, have the native English Teacher's fear of technical jargon, I've tried to make this chapter as clear and nontechnical as possible. I've also "front-loaded" it to provide the basic, minimal information all in the first few pages. If you like, you can read those pages and choose to go no farther. If you do choose to read on, I've provided a thumbnail history of the English vocabulary, some detailed practice in looking up word histories in a dictionary, and some teaching activities that might interest students in various aspects of the history of English. I hope, of course, that most of you will choose to read the entire chapter. The additional materials therein should make you more comfortable in fielding off-the-wall, but interesting, questions from students. These materials might even entice a few of you to develop whole units on the history of English and/or on the use of a dictionary to figure out word histories—

units I wouldn't mind seeing in an occasional secondary English curriculum.

Chapter 4, "Etymology: Root Meanings and Current Meanings," picks up on the historical information set forth in Chapter 3, but its primary focus is on helping students learn new words and write clear, precise definitions. Graves includes the learning of roots and prefixes in his Learning to Learn Words category. This chapter offers a more active version of the traditional root and prefix method. Students are given a Latin root and a list of common Latin prefixes, and are asked to find as many words containing the root as they can. For each word they find, they are expected to write their own personal definition, using the meaning of the root in the definition. Thus, they are asked to do active writing and thinking tasks, not just memorize words and definitions from a prewritten list. This method can, of course, be repeated with many productive Latin roots, thus allowing students to learn a vast array of significant new words. The focus on root meaning can also lead to deeper understanding of familiar words, and of the conceptual connections between them. The chapter has a section called Roots Across the Curriculum, which shows how students can find the same Latin root in words used in different school subjects, and also in many nonacademic areas that they are familiar with. The effect is to make school subjects less isolated from each another and from the familiar world outside of school.

Chapter 3 also provides historical background for the four chapters in Section III, Exploring Word Choice and Writing Style. These chapters are all concerned with the differences between native words and French–Latin loan words. As a result of the massive borrowing of French–Latin words during Middle and Modern English, the English vocabulary has at least two distinct registers, or levels of style. The French–Latin loan words, which tend to have a more elevated and intellectual tone, dominate in a formal style; the native words, more down to earth in tone, tend to congregate in a common or ordinary style. The tone of a word is knowledge About Words which Graves doesn't happen to mention, but it's something students need to be aware of in order to read, write, and speak effectively in English.

Chapter 5, "Native Words and French–Latin Loan Words: Seeing the Differences," provides some painless, relatively amusing activities that you can use to introduce students to the basic terms and concepts: *native word, French–Latin loan word, formal style,* and *ordinary style.* After doing some warm-up activities like these, your students should be ready to do any and all of the activities in the next three chapters.

Chapters 6 and 7 focus on native words. Chapter 6, "An All-Native Style?", sets forth the challenge of writing a descriptive paragraph entirely in native words. To illustrate what a writer can learn from this challenge, I offer a "movie of my mind" as I try to write a reasonably effective all-native paragraph. Then, I describe how a high school class went about rewriting a paragraph, trying to find native synonyms for the loan words in the original text—a task that can teach students a good deal about the meanings and tones of semantically related words. This chapter offers additional writing challenges for students in its Applications section. The activities set forth in this chapter are designed to improve writing; they provide opportunities for careful word choice and thoughtful revision. In Chapter 7, "What Native Words Can Do," I illustrate what a reader can learn about Ernest Hemingway and George Orwell by analyzing their writing styles in terms of native words and loan words. Students who do this kind of analysis will find that, while both writers rely heavily on native words, Orwell, the patron saint of the Plain Style, has, in fact, "a balanced style," a judicious blending of native and borrowed words. In this chapter and the next, I offer activities designed to show students that such a balanced style is, in most cases, the best way for a writer to exploit the full resources of the English vocabulary.

Chapter 8, "Creating a Balanced Style," sets forth activities in which students explore the strengths of French–Latin loan words. Students are asked to find native synonyms for the French–Latin words in the "Gettysburg Address," in a passage from Thoreau's *Walden*, and in Frost's *Fire and Ice*. These tasks are, of course, impossible to do very well, but they can lead students to a greater appreciation for French–Latin words and for the virtues of a balanced style. The activities in this chapter are designed to foster reading, writing, and analytical thinking. Students are analyzing famous literary texts, but they are also confronting issues they will have to deal with in their own writing.

The fourth section of the book, Word Study and Cultural Values, is concerned mostly with my third objective—fostering greater awareness of cultural values—but my two other objectives get plenty of attention, too. In Chapter 9, "Native and Borrowed Words in American Society," I describe an inquiry in which students explore the distribution of native and French–Latin loan words in seven areas of American society: sports, food, clothing, values and relationships, government, the military, and education. To perform the inquiry, small search groups are assigned to each area; they are asked to collect all the common words used in the area, to determine the historical origins of those words, and to interpret the results. In general, they find that the words with higher status, the words with power and prestige, tend to be of French–Latin origin; they also find significant exceptions, which are extremely interesting to explore. To illustrate the whole process, I've done the dictionary work for all seven areas and identified some issues for discussion in each area. This inquiry is designed to foster greater understanding of American culture. It is not focused primarily on language arts or thinking skills, although discussing the results will certainly involve analytical thinking, and I've provided some Applications with language arts and/or thinking tasks for each of the seven areas. This kind of inquiry can stand alone as a way for students to explore American cultural values. It also can be used as a lead-in to a thematic literature unit or as a source of topics for student writing.

Chapter 10, "Words and Gender," sets forth a variety of ways for students to explore common words used to refer to gender differences, words such as *bachelor, boyfriend, girlfriend, lady, macho, master, mistress, tomboy,* and many more. Students respond in writing to a series of questions involving such words, questions like "Why is there a positive word, *tomboy,* for a girl who is thought to act like a boy, but a negative term, *sissy,* for a boy thought to act like a girl?" As students explore these questions, in writing and discussion, they uncover underlying social assumptions and attitudes about gender. In another activity, students are asked whether a series of words would be considered compliments by males, females, or both genders; words such as *aggressive, competitive, gentle,* and *sensitive* can produce some surprising responses. In addition to fostering greater awareness of social and personal attitudes toward gender, the activities in this chapter foster analytical thinking; they also offer an abundant supply of thought-provoking writing topics.

It's impossible to talk about words used for gender without getting into the topic of homosexuality. Our society has a deep-seated aversion to homosexuality, especially in males: girls can call their female friends *girlfriends,* but boys cannot call their male friends *boyfriends* without being considered gay. In a class I visited last spring, the high school juniors and seniors who worked through the activities in the previous chapter brought up the issue of homosexuality frequently and discussed it quite comfortably. Their mature performance encouraged me to develop a chapter devoted entirely to the topic. Chapter 11, "Homosexuality: The Words We Use to Talk About It," provides a detailed study of common words used to describe homosexual people and behavior. The study starts with fairly neutral words, such as *homosexual* itself and *gay,* and then moves through the rich panoply of negative terms: *deviant, fag, fairy, pervert, queer,* and the like. Students are asked to look up each word's root meaning and its current meaning and status. They are asked to analyze each negative word in terms of its underlying attitude: Does the word describe homosexuality as a sin, a disease, or some kind of biological abnormality? This chapter involves word study, not direct consciousness raising; the focus on the words is intended to keep discussion from degenerating into angry exchanges of opinion. I would hope, of course, that this study might produce more tolerant attitudes, but I've tried to design it as an academic exercise in the analysis of word meanings. It stresses analytical thinking generally and the ability to recognize and interpret metaphorical language, words such as *deviant* and *straight*, for example.

Recognizing and interpreting metaphors is a big part of Chapter 12, "Kinds of Intelligence: Words and Metaphors." In the activity set forth in this chapter, students collect all the common words used for intelligence, and lack of intelligence, in our society. Then, they analyze the words in terms of common metaphors. When they do so, they discover that there are three major metaphors for intelligence in the English vocabulary: Intelligence is associated with brightness, sharpness, and quickness. In the second part of the activity, students are asked to determine how these three metaphors are used in our society: What kinds of intelligence do they refer to? What kinds of jobs or occupations require brightness, or sharpness, or quickness? This is a far-reaching activity that can teach students a good deal about the history and current values of the culture in which they live.

In Chapter 13, "Familiar Quotations: Exploring Concepts in Depth," I offer a way for students to explore a single word or concept in great depth. A class is given a list of quotations that contain the same word, a list compiled from *Bartlett's Familiar Quotations* and/or from similar sources. The students then discuss the quotes as a class, trying to understand them and establish connections between them. In these oral discussions, students share their prior experiences with the word/concept involved as they try to make sense of the various quotes. This kind of discussion can lead students to a much deeper understanding of the word/concept involved, while also providing a good opportunity for meaningful reading, thinking, speaking, and listening. Such discussions are valuable in and of themselves. They also can serve as useful prereading activities to introduce thematic units in literature or Humanities courses; I provide quotations for a literature unit on courage and for a Humanities or Philosophy unit on violence and nonviolence. Finally, because the quotes tend to be famous statements or statements made by historically important people, students can learn culturally significant ideas and information by reading and discussing them. Studying the quotes fosters cultural literacy, an important prerequisite for reading and for informed participation in our democratic society (see Hirsch [1987]).

This is a fairly detailed summary, but there's a good deal more I wish I could mention. The Applications sections at the ends of many chapters have lots of teaching ideas that might appeal to you and your students: activities such as the writing of cynical proverbs (Chapter 6) or the renaming of modern inventions with Old English compounds (Chapter 3). In the figures within the chapters, I've complied tables and hand-outs that you can easily copy for classroom use. In a concession to modernity which should shock those who know me, there's even a section on searching the Internet.

I do hope that the time is ripe for a book like this. Teaching vocabulary has long been one of those things that seem to fall through the cracks. Most English teachers do it incidentally, if at all. In his fine new book, *The English Teacher's Companion* (2000), Jim Burke ends most of his chapters by suggesting one or more key books on the topic discussed. At the end of his chapter on teaching vocabulary, he has no such suggestions to offer. There are, as Burke points out, workbooks on vocabulary building, books that treat words in isolation from the rest of the language arts curriculum. These have their uses, but practicing teachers know that workbooks and crash courses on vocabulary designed to improve test scores won't have any lasting effects on students' ability to use words well. The real need is for a book that can connect the teaching of vocabulary to the teaching of reading, writing, speaking, listening, and thinking. That's what this book aims to do.

Although practicing teachers are, quite rightly, wary of vocabulary builders and crash courses, they are feeling increasing pressure to do "something more" with vocabulary. The pressure comes, of course, from the Standards Movement. All state English standards include at least some attention to the teaching of vocabulary, even though critics like Sandra Stotsky (1997) claim that most states aren't asking nearly enough in this area. I find myself sympathetic to both camps—to the wary practitioners and to those who are pushing for more attention to vocabulary. I, too, would like to see English teachers do more teaching of vocabulary; I, too, hate the notion of teaching vocabulary just to improve student scores on standardized tests. Perhaps this book could give teachers an honorable way out of this dilemma. Nothing in this book involves a sell-out to the testers; everything in it is designed to foster student skills in language arts and thinking. If their skills improve, shouldn't their test scores improve, too? If students' skills improve and their test scores don't improve, then the tests aren't doing their job.

I would, of course, have written this book even if the Standards Movement didn't exist. Like many English teachers, I've been fascinated by words and word study most of my life. I don't expect that all adolescents will become word lovers just by doing the activities in this book. I'd be more than happy if the book could help some of them use the language better and understand their culture more fully. Still, I do have a final, less practical aim, which is more a wish than an objective: I'd like to see the activities in this book convey to students the intellectual fascination of word study and the incredible richness of the English vocabulary.

1
Verbal Charades

A *written* sketch that illustrates the meaning of a word without using that word might be called a *verbal charade*. For those who may not know charades, it is a game in which titles or sayings are acted out in pantomime. A player is given a title (of a book, movie, etc.) or saying on a folded slip of paper and must try to act it out, without speaking or using props, so that the other players can guess it. In verbal charades, reading a written sketch out loud takes the place of acting something out physically; the clues are in the writing, not in the acting.

Three Sketches

Here are three sketches I wrote to introduce verbal charades to a group of high school students. All three sketches are designed to illustrate the same word. I started with this one:

> 1. The score was tied, and there were fifteen seconds left to go. Jamal stole the ball at the top of the key and dribbled down the court, way ahead of the defenders. All he had to do was sink a routine lay-up, but Jamal couldn't resist trying something a little more dramatic. He swirled into his double-twist, slam-dunk move and let the ball go. It didn't go in. It bounced high off the back rim, right into the hands of an opposing player. One jump shot later, and Jamal's team had lost, by two points.

After reading this sketch aloud, I asked each student to write down a word that best describes Jamal. I told them I was looking for an adjective, as in "Jamal is very ___." I asked them not to share their responses until all three sketches had been read. Then, I moved on to sketch 2:

2. Howard dragged into the practice room and slumped onto the piano stool. He was running through a few warm-up chords when he heard a knock on the door. It was his best friend, Buzz-saw.

"Hey, Howard," said Buzz-saw, "let's go get a pizza."

"Can't do it, man. Gotta practice."

"Oh, come on. You can practice later."

"O. K., I'll come," Howard said, jumping up and following Buzz-saw out the door. "I can't play piano on an empty stomach."

After reading this one, I asked the students to find an adjective that could describe Howard here and Jamal in the first sketch. Once again, I asked them to keep their choices to themselves. Then, I read the third sketch:

3. Mr. Plum was having a bad time training his new dog, Frufru. The dog just wouldn't behave. Getting nowhere on his own, Mr. Plum decided to enroll Frufru in the dog-training class held in the high school gym. Things still didn't improve. Every week, Mr. Plum would issue the command "Sit," and Frufru would just keep walking around, sniffing the other dogs. Finally , Mr. Plum was asked to withdraw Frufru from the class, after she had a little "accident" on the gym floor, for the fourth week in a row.

After reading this one, I asked the students to try to find a single adjective that could fit Jamal, Howard, and Frufru. At this point, I encouraged them to share their choices and try to decide on the best choice.

The group went through a process of elimination. For Jamal alone, they had written down *stupid, selfish, self-centered, careless,* and *irresponsible.* For Jamal and Howard, most had narrowed it down to *careless* or *irresponsible;* one student had also written *undisciplined.* With Frufru in the picture, the choice became more complicated, because "human" words couldn't really apply to a dog. If Frufru can't be *careless* or *irresponsible,* then what does she have in common with Jamal and Howard? She lacks discipline, just as they do. After some good discussion, the word *undisciplined* won a consensus, and it was, in fact, the word I had in mind when I wrote the sketches.

Once the group understood what a verbal charade is, they were ready to write their own sketches. I broke them into small groups, gave each group a different word to work with, and they plunged right in. It took no more than fifteen minutes to get this class actively involved in playing the game. I wasn't surprised. I've introduced verbal charades in many classrooms, from elementary school through college, and the students always pick it right up. Here, in more detail, is how the game is set up.

Setting Up Verbal Charades

1. A class is divided into teams of three or four players. Each team is given a mystery word, which it is careful to conceal from the other teams.

2. Each member of the team writes a charade illustrating the word. The team members then read each other's charades and suggest revisions. After revisions are made, the team decides on the order in which their charades will be read aloud to the whole group. The game works best if the charades are read with the least obvious one first and the most obvious one last.

3. After all the teams are ready, the first team reads their charades aloud to the rest of the class. After each charade is read, the listeners write down the words that it suggests to them. It's important that this guessing be done in writing, not out loud, so as not to influence responses to the next charade.

4. After all of the team's charades have been read, the whole class shares their guesses and tries to reach a consensus. Then, the team reveals its mystery word.

5. Before moving on to the next team, the current team and the class discuss how the charades worked: What details clued the class in? What details threw the class off? In terms of reading and writing, this focus on key details is probably the most valuable part of the whole activity.

6. Then, the second team reads their charades. The process continues until all the teams have finished.

More Sketches

Let me provide a full illustration of how the game works by describing what Mary McIver's eighth-grade English class did with it. It was a regular class of about twenty students. I introduced the activity by reading three charades aloud from a written handout, a copy of which had been given to each student; thus, they were reading along while listening. Mary added a neat touch by asking them to underline the details that served as important clues. Because Mary had told me the class was reading Chris Crutcher's *Staying Fat for Sarah Byrnes*, I introduced Sarah Byrnes into the first sketch. Here are the three charades:

1. Johnny and Bill were sitting at a round table in the cafeteria. It was 12:30, the beginning of lunch period.

Johnny spoke first: "That Sarah Byrnes is so gross-looking. How can you stand to be in the same room with her?"

Bill replied firmly, "How can you be so cruel? She can't help how she looks—she had an accident. Actually, I like Sarah Byrnes. She says neat things in class."

As they were talking, Sarah Byrnes took an empty seat at their table. Both boys jumped up, stammering "Uh . . . Oh, hi, Sarah. We've gotta get to class."

As they were walking off, Johnny asked Bill, "How come you didn't stay with your friend Sarah?"

"Oh, I, I . . . gotta get something in my locker before my one o'clock class," said Bill.

2. "No food in the library—that's the rule," Mrs. Grundy, the librarian, said as she made Mary throw a half-eaten chocolate bar into the trash basket.

Mary didn't really complain: she knew she'd been caught.

Later that day, when the library was empty, Mrs. Grundy opened her desk drawer, took out a hard candy, and popped it into her mouth.

"Hard candies are different," she thought to herself. "They're not messy like chocolate."

3. "How can you eat that stuff?" Sam said as he watched his buddy Hank stuffing a Twinkie into his mouth.

"That junk food will rot your teeth, and your stomach, too. Why don't you eat an apple for dessert, like I do?"

As Sam reached in his pack for an apple, a candy bar fell out on the table.

We asked the class for a single adjective to describe Bill, Mrs. Grundy, and Sam, and the students had no trouble coming up with *hypocritical*, the word I'd had in mind. When asked what details they had underlined in sketch 1, they zeroed in on "jumped up, stammering" and on the fact that Bill had a whole half hour before his next class. They had the word after the first sketch, and the next two simply made the choice more obvious. I'd have to say that these three were too easy for the class, but they did serve to introduce the game in a nonthreatening way.

The next three charades on the handout were a good deal more challenging.

1. Johnny loved to climb trees, and the tall maple in the front yard was just too tempting to resist. He climbed quickly through the thick, lower branches, but he began to slow down as he got closer to the top and the branches got thinner and thinner. The thin branches trembled beneath his weight and began to sway back and forth when the wind picked up.

Johnny climbed a little bit higher and then perched there, thinking, "Maybe I've climbed high enough for now."

2. The score was tied when Mary, the star player, stepped to the foul line. Mary was good at foul shots. She practiced every day and usually hit 8 out of 10. She had already hit 3 out of 4 in this game. She bounced the ball slowly and stared up at the basket. Expecting another victory, the crowd was all ready to celebrate. "I can't let them down," Mary thought to herself.

3. Sarah was the girl who had everything: nice family, nice clothes, lots of friends. She was a top student and a star athlete. Everybody expected her to do well at everything she tried. And she always did do well, but still she had her doubts. "I'm not as good as they all think," she thought, "and someday they'll all find out."

The class struggled with these sketches. Most chose fairly generic words, such as *scared*, *afraid*, and *frightened*. Quite a few picked *pressured*, which works for the last two sketches but not so well for the first one. The guesses I liked best focused more on the particular mental states of these characters in these particular circumstances: *uneasy*, *lacking self-confidence*, *unsure of themselves*. Those who chose these words tended to underline the inner thoughts of the characters: "Maybe I've climbed high enough for now," "I can't let them down," "I'm not as good as they all think." Nobody guessed the precise word I'd had in mind, *insecure*, but they could see how well it fit the three sketches: I explained that I was trying to convey that all three characters are in a high position but don't feel entirely comfortable there. We compared *unsure* and *insecure* and found them very close in meaning, as well they should be, because both derive from the same Latin adjective, *securus*, meaning "without care or worry."

Students Write Their Own

After these two warm-ups, the class was ready to write their own sketches. Mary and I put the students in groups of three or four and gave each group a word to work with. Because we were experimenting, we tried quite a variety of words: *energetic*, *responsible*, *intense*, *wise*, *manipulative*. The students wrote nice, detailed sketches for all of the words. The ones for *energetic*, *responsible*, and *wise* turned out to be rather predictable and easy for the class to guess: We were hoping for some personal examples of *wise* but got wizards with glowing eyes instead. The three sketches for *responsible* drew much more directly from personal experience:

1. Omar and his friend Devan were playing Playstation up in Omar's room. Omar's mother yelled up to him, "Omar, feed the dog."

"Yes, Mother," answered Omar. Ten minutes went by before his mother called up to him again. "Omar, feed the dog *now!*" shouted Mom.

"Yeah, whatever," Omar mumbled to himself, although he made no indication of doing so. Finally, Devan got fed up with Omar and went and fed *his* dog for him.

"You poor dog, you must be starving," said Devan kindly.

"Thank you, Devan, you are so kind," said Omar's mom nicely.

How would you describe Devan ?

2. It's Thursday afternoon and Jeff has to work, but Bobby wants him to play a football game. "Oh, come on, Jeff, just come to the game and blow off work, just once," said Bobby. "No, I can't. I promised that I would be there and I'm going, so don't try to change my mind," said Jeff, and he walked away to go to work.

3. Jessica went to a party. At the party there were drugs and alcohol. Jessica's friends all got drunk and stoned. Jessica was the only one who didn't drink or smoke. When it was time to leave, Jessica was the designated driver.

The words *intense* and *manipulative* produced the most interesting results. When Mary and I gave out *intense*, I doubted it would work. I've had the most success using words that describe people's feelings and attitudes. *Intense* is used to describe a kind of experience or situation, not how a person might feel in such a situation. Nevertheless, Mary wanted to try it, because it is a word that her students knew and used all the time. When she gave it to a group of three girls, they wrote three vivid sketches quite quickly. They read them to each other, made some minor revisions, and then decided to read them in the following order.

1. Fred was walking through the jungle. He was looking for a special type of snake, when all of a sudden, a lion popped out from behind a tree. All of Fred's muscles tightened, and he dropped to the ground. He was very scared. The lion thought he was dead and walked away. Fred got up, with his heart beating a mile a minute, and went home.

2. As Rebecca sat by the window, during the rain, she got frightened. She heard the thunder and saw the lightning. She felt afraid, as she backed away from the window. Rebecca felt her hair start sticking up on its edge, and she dropped to the ground.

3. As Sally got on the rollercoaster, she sat on the seat and tightened her muscles and gripped the bar that would be holding her in the seat.

The rollercoaster "clicked" up the hill. When they reached the top, they stopped for one brief second. And Sally gripped the bar as hard as she could and let out a blood-curdling scream of both horror and delight.

After these three sketches were read aloud, the class compared their guesses of the intended word. Their initial focus was on the feelings of the characters involved, and words such as *terrified*, *afraid*, *shocked*, and *horrified* were the common choices. Then, Mary and I framed the question more sharply: What kind of experience is each character going through? One boy offered *tense* and then, with another nudge from us, *intense*. When we asked him what clues he'd used, he recalled the tensing of Sally's muscles in the rollercoaster. Some of the other students then mentioned how Fred's muscles tightened, too, in the first sketch, and how Rebecca felt her hair stiffening in the second sketch. These physical clues led them to the word for the kind of emotional experience, and, without realizing it, they were using etymology to make the connection: Both *tense* and *intense* (and *tension*, too) are derived from the Latin root *tendere*, *tensus*, meaning "stretch, tighten." Using the word *intense* had provoked a valuable classroom discussion.

The word *manipulative* proved even more valuable. The three students who received it had never heard it before. Mary and I had to explain it to them, an easy enough task since they did know and understand the verb *manipulate*. I listened in as the three of them worked on their sketches. They read them aloud to each another, asking whether the details really captured the meaning they wanted. They all made revisions after sharing their initial versions. When they were satisfied, they decided to read their sketches in the following order.

1. Priscilla walked into the living room.
   "Hey, Mom, I was thinking we haven't been shopping for clothes lately."
   "What are you trying to tell me?" Priscilla's mom Shirley asked.
   " Shirley—I mean Mom, I just wanted to get some new clothes for school to be cool."

2. Dude walked into the kitchen, taking a break from studying for finals. His mom was there making dinner.
   "You know what, Mom?" He said.
   "What?" His mom said without looking up from the food.
   "Well, we haven't gone to a movie for a long time. I think it would really take my mind off the finals. I would relax and wouldn't be so stressed out any more. Anyway, you could have fun, too."
   "That sounds like a good idea," his mom said.

3. "What's for supper tomorrow?" Gertrude asked her mom. "Could we have steak?"

"Um, I don't think we have any."

"Could we go and get some?"

"I don't want to go to the grocery store, though."

"O.K., Mom, put it this way. Tomorrow night, let's go get some steak, not from the grocery store, from some other place."

"Oh, Hun, we could go to that new steak house you were talking about, if you want."

"Oh, thank you," Gertrude said.

To be perfectly honest, I don't find these sketches particularly effective. I'm not at all sure I would have come up with *manipulative* after hearing them. They did, however, provoke a lengthy and fruitful whole-class discussion after they were read aloud. Mary and I had asked each student to write down a word or two after each of the charades was read aloud, and to choose one word that would best fit the children in all three sketches. We then went around the room, asking all the students to give and explain their choices. *Selfish* was the most common choice. Others were *nagging, begging, persistent, spoiled, demanding,* and *greedy.* The students carefully pointed out that, in each sketch, the child "wants something" from the parent and is trying to get it. After a while, we suggested that the students focus more on *how* the children go about getting what they want. One boy said they were *sneaky*; a girl said they were being *clever.* We urged them to put *selfish, sneaky,* and *clever* together into one word, but they couldn't quite come up with it. They sure did try, though! The whole class was determined to come up with the perfect word to fit those three sketches. When we gave them *manipulative,* they all said they hadn't known the word before, but they could see right away how well it fit. To solidify their understanding of this newly familiar word, Mary wrote it on the board and showed them how it contains the word *mano,* which is Spanish for "hand." This entire discussion took twenty-five minutes, and every student contributed to it. Twenty-five minutes might seem a long time for a group of students to learn one word but I'd submit that they really came to understand that word and that they developed their skills in speaking, listening—and thinking—in the process.

Mary's class spent two full forty-five-minute periods on verbal charades. I think they did very well and learned a good deal from it. They were very much an average class, with a wide range of abilities, yet all of them were able to produce a piece of writing and contribute to a truly remarkable whole-class discussion. I've described verbal charades as a game, as it surely is, but it's a game with enormous educational value. It can teach students new words, but that's not its primary purpose. Verbal charades gives students practice in all of the traditional language arts. It promotes writing by giving students the chance to see how their writing affects a real audience; it shows them the value of using specific details to communicate a general impression. Verbal charades promotes comprehension skills as well: As students read or listen to what their peers have written, they learn to look for the key details, the context clues, that will enable them to understand the focus of the sketch as a whole. Obviously, verbal charades also promotes speaking and listening, in both the small groups and in the whole-class discussions. The lively yet focused conversations this activity can generate may well be its greatest benefit. These conversations are so valuable because they involve precise and rigorous thinking, the making of fine distinctions between several possible words. This kind of thinking is a key to effective performance in all of the language arts.

As I stated earlier, verbal charades can work well at all levels of schooling. To support this claim, here's a description of how it worked when I visited Sue Fryling's fifth-grade class. This was, Sue told me, an exceptionally bright class, and the students certainly seemed bright to me. I introduced verbal charades to them by reading the three sketches introduced at the start of this chapter—the ones describing the undisciplined Jamal, Howard, and Frufru the dog. I felt these might be a big stretch for Sue's students, but I was curious to see how they'd do. After I read each sketch aloud, Sue and I asked the students to write down words to describe the behavior of the main "characters." The students worked in teams, and they generated a great barrage of adjectives. When it was time for them to choose one adjective that would fit all three sketches, though, they were clearly frustrated. To help them, I made up a fourth sketch right on the spot, about a boy named Johnny who couldn't sit still and kept disrupting his class. There were seven groups of students, and these were their final choices: *lazy, ignorant, irresponsible, selfish, careless, distracted,* and *stubborn*. None of these quite worked, although *distracted* did fit the three boys and the dog pretty well. Sue and I then tried to lead the students to the word *undisciplined* by getting them to discuss the four sketches. After a while, someone said that Jamal and Howard "couldn't resist" doing what they were supposed to do. "Why not?" we asked, "What do they lack?" Still no clear answer. We told them to think of a word beginning with *self-*, and they were still stuck. Finally, we gave them the words *self-discipline* and *undisciplined*, which none of them knew. They did know *discipline*, but only as a punishment imposed by someone else. The concept of *self-discipline*, of self-imposed restraint, was not something they'd really thought much about: After all, I realized, they were only fifth-graders and were used to doing what they were told to do. Nevertheless, they did seem to understand the concept after we discussed it for a while, and one student came up with a fine definition of it: "forcing yourself to do what should be done." This discussion took up much of the forty-five-minute class period. There was, however, time for me to read them three somewhat easier sketches, which they handled with ease. By the end of the period, I felt that they'd done some good thinking, acquired a valuable new word, and learned what a verbal charade is.

In the next period, we had the students write their own charades. Sue kept the students in the same seven groups, and we gave each group one of these mystery words: *conceited, obnoxious, courteous, irritated, frustrated, humiliated,* and *unsatisfied.* We wanted to give them words they would know and be able to illustrate from personal experience. The group members worked together closely, sometimes collaborating on one piece, rather than developing a different one for each member. Not surprisingly, the sketches tended to be shorter than those written by Mary McIver's eighth-graders. The ones from the *conceited* group were quite typical.

> 1. Sarah came to school today and showed off her new bracelet. She thought it was the best, and she was the coolest! How would you describe the way she acted today?

> 2. Steve was playing soccer and made the winning goal. For the rest of the week, he said he was the best on the team. Steve was acting so ___!

> 3. It was Jill's birthday and she had gotten a brand new 5-disk holder, portable C.D. player from Jack. She was the only one who had one of those and she said "This is the coolest birthday present ever and none of you have one. That's because I'm the coolest and you're so lame."

> Question: How was Jill acting about her new gift???

The sketches developed for *irritated* and *frustrated* were more developed, perhaps because they were collaborative efforts. Each group had four members but produced only two sketches. Because the words are very similar in meaning, the sketches are hard to tell apart, and the other students chose *frustrated* for all of them. Here they are.

> 1. Last night Herby woke up 5 times, at 10:00, 12:00, 2:00, 4:00, and 5:00. He stomped out of his room. When he had breakfast, his toast was burnt and his cereal was soggy. If anything else had happened, he would have burst out screaming. Every little thing bothered him. When he went to school, he spilled his juice on him at lunch.
> He was so ___.

2. There was a boy named Joseph. He was on a hockey team. Even though he was the best, he was a puck hog. Every game, he scored at least 2 goals. All the teammates were mad because he wouldn't pass the puck. When his coach tried to take him off the ice, he wouldn't listen.

All the teammates were so ___.

3. Sally was packing her lunch for school. She was home alone. She decided to make a peanut butter and jelly sandwich. She got out the jelly jar and tried to twist the top off. She pulled and tugged until she was red in the face. All of a sudden out of rage she threw the jar as hard as she could against the wall. It shattered into little pieces and glass flew everywhere.

Sally felt very ___.

4. It was Nick's turn up at bat. Here comes the first pitch: STRIKE ONE. Here comes the second pitch: STRIKE TWO. And now comes the last pitch: STRIKE THREE. YOU'RE OUT!

Nick was very disappointed. He threw his cap on the ground and spat on it. Now it was his team's turn to play in the outfield. The first hit was a pop fly, and it came right at Nick; he missed it, and was feeling low. The batter got a home run because of him. No matter how hard he tried, he was convinced that he could not do anything right.

Nick felt ___.

The first two were meant to illustrate *irritated*, and the last two to illustrate *frustrated*. I'd say that sketch 3 is a perfect illustration of frustration: You try to do a simple task, and something prevents you from doing it. I also find sketch 1 to be a pretty good illustration of feeling *irritated:* A lot of little things add up to ruin your mood. The other two sketches are perhaps not as clear. I find *frustrated* to be the word I'd choose for sketch 2, and *discouraged* or *frustrated* to be the word I'd choose for sketch 4. Sue and I were probably asking too much of the students here: Distinguishing between *irritated* and *frustrated* is difficult for anyone, myself included. Still, the students produced nice, detailed sketches when trying to illustrate the two words.

The *courteous* group also produced some nice sketches, although Sue and I didn't think any of them quite fit the meaning of the word. All four members of the group wrote a separate sketch.

1. Dave and his friend were playing frisbee when they saw a kid looking lonely, so they asked him if he wanted to play.

2. True Life Story. Evan was walking into Ruby's restaurant, to get a Red Sox game schedule. Evan asked the waiter where they were. The waiter said, "Well, I'm new here, so I don't really know where they are, so here, have mine."

3. After a hard track practice, Bobby was about to get driven home by his mother. He saw another team member walking home on a *very* hot day, so he asked him if he wanted a ride home.

4. Gerald, his brother, and his mother all went to go get ice cream after a real hot baseball game. Gerald's little brother dropped his ice cream, so Gerald gave him his.

After these four sketches were read aloud, the class chose *kind, generous, considerate, nice, thoughtful, unselfish, friendly,* and *helpful.* No one chose *courteous.* Sue and I agreed with the choices the class made; we felt that the sketches did illustrate kindness or generosity more than courtesy. We gave them the word *courteous* and gave them our views on what it means. As I see it, *courteous* can include all the positive qualities the students listed, but it must also involve manners, a gracious way of acting toward people in a social situation. For my money, the person who is closest to *courteous* in the four sketches is the waiter in sketch 2. Sue and I shared our thoughts with the class, as was appropriate. The charades that students write won't always match the word they're supposed to illustrate. When that happens, the teacher needs to point it out and help students to see and understand the problem. The teacher also needs to write the more accurate word on the board so that all students can see it. That, apparently, we failed to do, because one group wrote, "We didn't get *curdious* for this one."

Acting out Sketches

Writing, reading aloud, and discussing these charades took all of my second day in Sue's class. The students did these activities with enthusiasm, but what they really wanted was to act out their sketches. We worked on other things for the next few days, but they kept begging Sue to let them do it. She was more than willing, and so was I, because I felt it might add a new dimension to the activity. On the appointed day, the students formed their groups on their own, chose their own word, and collaborated to write a sketch for it. There was a certain amount of hilarity involved in some of them. In the following one, for instance, Ryan's spectacular fall was somewhat more impressive than the written text:

"Hey, look! There's Ryan. Let's go sit with him."
 (Ryan falls off the chair. Everybody laughs "Ha, ha.")
 "Look, everybody, Ryan fell off his chair!"

—How did Ryan feel?

The answer was *humiliated*, one of the original group of mystery words, and I was pleased to see that the class guessed it right away. A second memorable sketch was a rather chilling dialogue between two girls, who stood in front of the class whispering audibly to each other:

MICHELLE: You know that new girl. Well, after second period we will trip her on the stairs.
LINDSAY: So then everyone will see her fall.
MICHELLE: Then we can pour water on her, and say we tripped.
LINDSAY: No, ya know what we can do? We can lock her in the closet. We can tell her there are towels to wipe the water with, and lock her in.
MICHELLE: But we can't tell anybody about this.

The girls wanted to illustrate *scheming*, and they did it very convincingly, but they didn't ask the class to describe what they were doing. Hence, the class focused on their attitudes and chose *mean* or *obnoxious*.

My favorite dramatization involved a young man named Evan strolling along and talking to four friends along the way.

Evan was walking, and he was talking to everybody.
Evan says to Chris, "How's your mom?" Chris says, "She's good."
Evan says to Ryan, "How about that new Star Wars movie?"
Ryan says, "It was cool."
Evan goes up to Mitchell and says, "How about that grand slam Garciaparra hit last night?" Mitchell says, "That was awesome."
Evan goes up to Andy and says, "How's your go-cart running?"
Andy says, "It goes thirty."

The class really enjoyed this one and came up with some good guesses: *conversational, talkative, polite, friendly*. The word the group had in mind was *sociable*, of all things. I wouldn't have expected them to know this word, but they did, and they illustrated it perfectly. Although several of the dramatizations were, frankly, a little silly, there were enough promising ones for me to suggest that teachers might want to consider making dramatizations part of verbal charades on occasion. I don't recommend using dramatization all the time; it promotes only one kind of writing—dialogue—not the richly detailed writing that composing full sketches can produce. Still, it does promote other skills, and it is fun to do. After all, dramatization is what has made the original game of charades so popular for so many years.

As I hope I've demonstrated, verbal charades is an enjoyable activity with great educational value for classes at just about any grade level. I've even had success with it in my wife's first- and second-grade classes, although you'll have to take my word (or hers) for it. As a self-standing activity, verbal charades can be plugged into a spare hour whenever a class needs a change of pace or a special treat. I feel, however, that verbal charades can also serve a larger curricular purpose. I wrote this book to encourage teachers to incorporate more attention to words and word study into their courses. For any teacher who wants to do that, verbal charades is an excellent way to begin. It can be introduced early in the year, with no special preparation. If it works, and I think it will, it will get students interested in words and prepare them for some of the other, more demanding types of word study set forth in this book. It provides a perfect lead-in to word clusters, the activity described in the next chapter.

2
Word Clusters

Verbal charades can be combined with other forms of word study to help an entire class become familiar, or more familiar, with a group of related words in the course of a week. In this chapter, I outline what the full sequence of activities looks like, using a traditional five-class week and taking examples from Donna Bakke's ninth-grade general class.

Introducing Clusters

On Monday, a list of words is introduced to the whole class. Lists of related words, *clusters* of words in the same category, are more meaningful to students than words collected at random. Lists of roughly paired synonyms are particularly useful because they encourage students to make fine distinctions. I like to start with words about people, their personalities and attitudes, because students can use such words right away to describe or make sense of their own relationships. Here's the list of words we used in Donna's class:

    assertive/arrogant
    cruel/inconsiderate
    cynical/indifferent
    deceitful/dishonest
    idealistic/naive
    impulsive/spontaneous
    sympathetic/tolerant
    reasonable/rational

The list can be distributed to the students at the start of the Monday class. The best format is to list the words, one by one, at the left margin, so that the students have room to make notes about each one. After the list is distributed, the class is invited to discuss the words for a while. I suggest that the teacher try to draw out what the students already know about the words, rather than provide them with prepackaged definitions. Some of the class members will know some words; others will know other words. With a few timely questions from the teacher ("Where have you heard this word used?" "Can you give me an example of someone being *assertive?*"), the class may have quite a long and fruitful discussion. Donna's class discussed the words for almost half an hour, with very little prompting from us.

Every student is responsible for knowing every word on the list—you might want to announce that there will be a class test involving all the words on Friday. Each student is also responsible for performing an intensive study of one particular word from the list. Hence, after the initial discussion dies down, you need to assign each word on the list to an individual student, perhaps by having students draw numbers out of hat. It's always a good idea to have students work on their words in pairs, especially if the list consists of paired words. Thus, if number 1 stands for *assertive* and number 2 stands for *arrogant*, the students who draw those numbers can find each other and work together. It's important that the pairs keep their words hidden from the rest of the class, so that verbal charades can be properly played later in the week.

Steps for Intensive Word Study

Intensive study of a particular word involves the following five tasks, which can be typed on a work sheet that each student can use during the week:

1. Write a personal definition of your word, using a dictionary and your partner for help.
2. Use your word in three sentences that clearly illustrate its meaning.
3. Write a sentence in which you contrast your word to an antonym, a word that has an opposite meaning.
4. Write a sentence in which you compare and contrast your word to a synonym, a word that has a similar meaning (use the word it is paired with).
5. Write two brief sketches for your word. In these sketches, try to illustrate your word without using it. Try out your sketches on your partner and pick one to read to the class.

Depending on the past experience of the class, the teacher may need to illustrate how to perform some or all of these tasks. After Donna's class got their words, partners, and work sheets, I read them a sample sentence or two for each of the first four tasks. Because the students had never played verbal charades, I took more time for task 5, reading them two sets of sketches and having them guess the words and then identify the clues they used.

In the Tuesday class, the students can work on their words with their partners. A class that has done this activity before could do their work sheets as homework, but, for the first time, it's best that the students work on them in class: The teacher is there to answer questions—there will be a lot—and monitor how the students are doing. Each of the five tasks can foster student learning, but only if they're done in the right way.

Task 1, writing a personal definition, is more valuable than it might appear. Students can profit from using a dictionary, but they should be discouraged from simply copying a dictionary definition. They should try to compose their own definitions, using words from the dictionary *and* words of their own. A student who can create a definition in his or her own words is on the way to owning that word for good. In Donna's class, only one or two students seemed to be copying definitions verbatim from the dictionary. I'd like to believe that the long and fruitful initial discussion gave most of the class members some personal connection to the words.

Task 2, writing sentences that "clearly illustrate" a word's meaning, requires students to provide telling details, or context clues, that would help a reader figure out the word's meaning, even if the word were unfamiliar. Donna's students came up with some good, specific sentences: "The boy's parents were deceitful when they told him his party was for somebody else" and "The impulsive child talked without raising his hand in class, so the teacher kicked him out." In performing this task, however, students often do not write enough detail. When we noticed too many sentences like "People in this town are not tolerant towards different ethnic groups," we decided to address the issue of specificity. One way to do that is, of course, to ask students who have nice, detailed sentences to read them aloud. Another good way is for the teacher to compose some sentences with the class, drawing in details from class members. I tried doing that with Donna's class. To illustrate *impulsive*, I wrote this sentence on the board: "Driven by a sudden urge to swim, Sam jumped impulsively into the pool." A student pointed out that Sam would look a good deal more impulsive if he jumped in with all his clothes on, and I added that detail to make a much more telling sentence: "Driven by a sudden urge to swim, Sam jumped impulsively into the pool, still wearing his clothes and shoes."

Task 3, contrasting a word to an antonym, is generally an easy thing for students to do. I've seen fifth-graders do it easily. Donna's class wrote some very powerful sentences, including this one, which is my favorite: "My friend John is the exact opposite of my arrogant friend Mike; John is so insecure that he hates himself." *Task 4*, however, is another matter entirely. Comparing and contrasting a word to a close synonym is an extremely challenging mental operation; it is, in fact, two operations in one: defining a point of similarity and a point of difference. Only one of Donna's ninth-graders, the same student who wrote the sentence just quoted, could do this task successfully: "Being assertive means to be confident of yourself but not to the point of being arrogant, which means you brag about yourself." Most of the time, students simply put two words side by side, without clearly establishing a point of similarity or of difference: "*Spontaneous* is doing something without really knowing why, and *impulsive* is acting on a sudden feeling."

A couple of little devices could have helped the latter students. I chose not to introduce these devices to Donna's class on Tuesday, when they were writing their sentences. Because the students were going though the whole activity for the first time, I didn't want to bombard them with too many prior instructions. Also, I was experimenting, and I wanted to see how the students would do on their own. In retrospect, I recommend that teachers introduce these two devices before their students tackle task 4. Following are descriptions of these devices.

One way to distinguish between two roughly synonymous words is to insert them into the following sentence frame:

"She's not ____; she's just ____."

If the words really differ in some way, use of this device will bring out the difference. In Donna's class, the two students working on *spontaneous* and *impulsive* did a fine job, but they never really distinguished clearly between the two words. If they had used the sentence frame, they might have seen that *spontaneous* has a much more positive connotation than does *impulsive*. "She's not impulsive; she's just spontaneous" means that she is following her natural, true feelings, not just acting irrationally. "She's not spontaneous; she's just impulsive" is a more negative statement, meaning that she is not following her true and genuine feelings; she's just acting on whims. After experimenting with this sentence frame, the two students might well have decided that *spontaneous* and *impulsive* are not so close in meaning after all: *Spontaneous* shades positively toward *natural*, and *impulsive* shades negatively toward *irrational*.

This device works equally well for most of the paired words on the list. The basic principle is that the second word is less than the first: less positive, as in "She's not sympathetic; she's just tolerant"; or less negative, as in "She's not naive; she's just idealistic." A minor variation is to place the words *not just* in the first half of the frame. In that arrangement, the second word is more than the first: more positive, as in "She's not just tolerant; she's sympathetic"; or more negative, as in "She's not just inconsiderate; she's cruel."

Another clever device for uncovering shades of meaning was reputedly invented by the British philosopher Bertrand Russell. It involves the "conjugation" of "irregular verbs," as in

I am firm.   You are stubborn.   He's close-minded.

One starts with the most positive term, applied, of course, to one's self, then becomes increasingly negative when describing the same sort of behavior in others. I introduced this device to Donna's class, but only on Thursday, after they had already completed their five tasks. I explained it by describing the second column as "too ___" and the third as "too, too" or "way too." I put "I'm cautious" on the board, and the students came up with "You're timid" and "He's a coward." When I wrote down "I'm spontaneous," they came up with "You're impulsive" and "He's irrational." The students picked up this device quite readily and used it well on the concluding test.

In a typical weekly sequence, each student should come to class on Wednesday with the first four tasks on the work sheet completed, and with one or two draft charades (*task 5*). You may wish to allow some time at the start of the Wednesday class for students to try out their charades on their partners. Then, it's time for all of the charades to be read to the whole class. For the first time at least, I'd suggest having the students read their charades in random order. If a class is experienced at making fine distinctions, the two students with paired words could read their charades in turn, and then the class could decide which charade fits which word. Donna's class chose to read in random order and also chose to disguise the pairings by having students switch papers around and read someone else's—a neat suggestion. Since I already discussed verbal charades at length in the previous chapter, I won't do so here. Suffice it to say that every student wrote an acceptable sketch, and that the sketches were generally much more detailed than the sentences written for tasks 2 through 4. (Writing charades does seem to foster detailed writing!) The students were able to guess the words illustrated by each charade, thus getting some additional familiarity with every word on the list.

The last component of this sequence of activities is a vocabulary test. The test can be designed to involve one class period or two. Because I was

FIGURE 2.1
Cluster Test 1

These questions involve the words we've been studying this week. Here's the full list: *assertive/arrogant, cruel/inconsiderate, cynical/indifferent, deceitful/dishonest, idealistic/naive, impulsive/spontaneous, sympathetic/tolerant, reasonable/rational.*

1. Imagine a scene involving Mr. Smith, who is wearing a business suit, and a beggar on a street corner. Write the scene in two different ways: first, to portray Mr. Smith as *indifferent;* second, to portray the beggar as *deceitful.*

2. Who is more likely to be *inconsiderate*—an *arrogant* person or an *impulsive* person? Please explain why you think so.

3. Read the following sketch carefully. Then, pick from the list *two words* that describe Mrs. Taylor, the teacher. What details led you to your choices?

> After the bell rang, Mrs. Taylor let Jane talk to her friend Sarah for a few minutes before asking the girls to get down to work. Jane made a wise remark, but Mrs. Taylor chose to let it pass.
>
> "Why don't you just send me to the office again?" Jane asked.
>
> "I'd rather you stayed here and did some work for a change. You could pass if you just put your mind to it. I know you could," Mrs. Taylor answered.

4. Pick from the list *two words* that are close in meaning to the word *natural.* Give reasons for your choices.

---

experimenting with different kinds of questions in Donna's class, I designed a test for two days, Thursday and Friday. Vocabulary tests need not be mechanical exercises of the memory. A good vocabulary test lets the students use the words in a variety of ways. It encourages students to explore the relations between words, and the relations between words and the world of experience. The test for Donna's class was based on these principles. I'll show you the test first, in Figure 2.1, then comment on the questions and the results.

5.   Make three pairs of words. Each pair must have one word from the left list and one from the right list. Then, *write a sentence with each pair*, showing how the two words can be related. For instance, if the paired words were *confident* and *insecure*, you could write something like this: "Confident people are so sure of themselves that they rarely feel insecure." Here are the two lists. You can choose any three words from each list:

reasonable	sympathetic
arrogant	cruel
dishonest	tolerant
rational	indifferent
impulsive	cynical

6.   A good way to see shades of meaning is to play the "I-You-He" game. Take the same basic idea and describe it in three different ways: Describe the "I" in positive terms; describe the "You" in less positive terms; describe the "He" in even less positive terms. For example, you could write "I'm firm," "You're stubborn," "He's pig-headed." Fill in the gaps in these three sets. The missing words will *not* be from the list; you'll have to think of some.

I'm idealistic.	You're naive.	He's ___ .
I'm assertive.	You're ___ .	He's aggressive.
I'm ___ .	You're cocky.	He's arrogant.

7. Which would you rather be—*cynical* or *naive*? Please explain your choice.

In Figure 2.1, the first question worked well. The students were familiar with illustrative sketches, and they enjoyed writing them. Here are some of the better ones:

1. Mr. Smith was walking to work when a beggar politely asked him for some change. Mr. Smith ignored the beggar and just walked on by.
2. Mr. Smith walked down 32nd Street. As he looked down the street, his eye made contact with a beggar's. He walked by with his nose in the air and dropped a single penny in the beggar's cup.
3. As Mr. Smith walked down the street, he snickered at the beggar as he walked by.
4. A beggar saw Mr. Smith coming. He quickly put a bandage on his head and made a horrible face. He asked Mr. Smith for money, but Mr. Smith had seen him put on the bandage and walked right by.

5. As Mr. Smith walked by, the beggar asked him for money, so Mr. Smith gave him some. "Huh, he really thinks I'm poor," laughed the beggar.
6. As he turns the corner, Mr. Smith sees the beggar he recently gave money to driving a Lexus away.

The second question is in a format I've had lots of success with; it requires students to explore the connections between three related concepts. This one, however, was too skewed toward one answer. Most of the students seemed to assume that being inconsiderate requires conscious, deliberate action; this well-developed example reflects their general view: "An arrogant person is more inconsiderate than an impulsive one because he knows what he's doing but doesn't care." I would see an impulsive, unthinking person as likely to behave in an inconsiderate way, too, but the students were probably right in their view that the arrogant person is "more likely" to be inconsiderate.

The third question is the obverse of the first, in that it requires students to interpret details in a sketch rather than provide them. There were many thoughtful responses to this one. Every student described the teacher as "tolerant." Choices for the second word were equally divided between "reasonable" and "idealistic." Here are some typical answers:

1. Mrs. Taylor is tolerant and reasonable. She is tolerant of Jane's wise attitude, and she reasons with the girls to do work.
2. Mrs. Taylor is idealistic and tolerant. She is idealistic because she thinks she can help every one she can. She is tolerant because she takes a lot of b.s. from students.
3. She was tolerant—she put up with Jane's actions—and she was idealistic—she chose to stick to her beliefs.

The fourth question didn't really work. I was hoping for choices such as *naive* or *spontaneous*, perhaps even *cruel*. A slight majority picked *naive* as one of the words, but there was no clear choice of any other word. The reasons given for any choice were not clearly developed. I suspect that, because *natural* wasn't on the list and we hadn't discussed it as a class, the students weren't comfortable using it. The fifth question yielded a lot of thoughtful answers. I've had a lot of success with this format; it's open-ended enough to encourage individual thinking, and it's structured enough to pose an intellectual challenge. It also works well with much younger students, as I've found when testing it with fifth-graders. Here are some interesting examples from Donna's class:

1. Dishonest people are indifferent to the law.
2. The cruel child was dishonest about what he had done to his little brother.
3. The quarterback was very arrogant but everyone was tolerant of him because he was an excellent player.
4. I respect someone who can listen and be reasonable and sympathetic with people at the same time.
5. My Mom was tolerant with my dishonest ways.
6. Arrogant people can be cruel without even knowing it.

The students did quite well on question 6 of the cluster test, even though we'd spent very little time on the "I-You-He" format. The most common choice for the first triad was *unrealistic*, distantly followed by *stupid*. *Pushy* was the top choice for the second triad, with *competitive* coming in second. Just about every student chose *confident* for the third triad; one chose *cool*, which fits well, too. These results were more unanimous than I had anticipated they would be, probably because one-word answers are easy to copy and the whole atmosphere was casual and collaborative, anyway. I try not to ask questions that have one-word answers very often. It's much better to have students use words in sentences that they themselves compose.

Question 7 of the cluster test is the kind of philosophical finale I particularly like. I always try to get students to apply the words they're studying to their own lives, hoping the words will acquire a personal meaning for each student. I'm sorry to say that *cynical* nosed out *naive* as the word of choice—or should I be pleased?—but the various reasons given were quite revealing:

1. I'd rather be naive because I would float through life being happy and not knowing about the bad things that happen.
2. I'd rather be naive so at least that way I would be happy.
3. Cynical, because that's the way I already am.
4. I hate to say it, but I would rather be cynical and intelligent than naive and unknowing. I would rather have a darker outlook, but at least I would be educated in the harshness of society, and not just the good.
5. I would rather be cynical because, if you are naive, you are almost in your own little world but, if you're cynical, you see things in a more real sense, which sometimes happens to be a more negative sense.
6. I would like to be a little bit of both. It's not good to see all the bad but it's also not good to be happy all the time and not see the reality.

FIGURE 2.2
Cluster Test 2.

This test will involve the following word pairs: *apathetic/indifferent*; *assertive/aggressive*; *conventional/traditional*; *cynical/skeptical*; *immature/ sophomoric*; *introspective/introverted*; *insensitive/callous*; *pensive/reflective*; *reserved/detached*; *sophisticated/experienced*; *spontaneous/impulsive*.

1. Who is more likely to be apathetic—a cynic or a skeptic? Explain your answer.

2. Who is more likely to be introspective—an assertive person or a conventional person? Explain.

3. Who is more likely to be spontaneous—a sophisticated person or a sophomoric person? Explain.

4. "I don't want to hear about women's rights. A woman's place is in the home." Characterize this speaker's attitude with three words from the list, and explain your choices.

5. "Anybody who still thinks a woman's place is in the home is an idiot." Characterize this speaker's attitude with three words from the list and explain your choices.

6. "She's not immature; she's just ___." Fill the blank with a word from the

---

This has been an account of a general ninth-grade class doing this sequence of activities for the first time. Keeping this context in mind, if you want to try this activity, you can use this account as a basis for comparison with the efforts of your students. To provide another basis of comparison, the following is a vocabulary test I gave to a tenth-grade honors class. The cluster of words this class studied was somewhat more demanding:

apathetic/indifferent
assertive/aggressive
conventional/traditional
cynical/skeptical
immature/sophomoric
introspective/introverted
insensitive/callous

list, and describe a context in which the sentence would make sense. Then, do the same thing again, with another word from the list. Note: Do not use the word *sophomoric* for this question.

7. It's possible to have "too much of a good thing." Take three good qualities from the list and explain why "too much" of each one of them might be undesirable.

8. Make three pairs of words, choosing one word from each column. Then, write a sentence with each pair, relating the two words in a way that clearly reveals their meanings:

traditional	introverted
insensitive	reserved
impulsive	experienced
pensive	callous
conventional	indifferent

9. Apply two or three words from the cluster list to a person you admire (or, if you prefer, to a person you can't stand) and provide examples of how the words fit the person. The person may be real, a character from your reading, or a character you invent.

10. Using two or three words from the cluster list, give your definition of a mature person.

---

pensive/reflective
reserved/detached
sophisticated/experienced
spontaneous/impulsive

The test (Figure 2.2) was somewhat more challenging as well, but it is based on the same principles and it uses similar kinds of questions. I invite you to try it.

The intensive approach to word study described in this chapter takes a good deal of time—three, four, sometimes even five full class periods. How can spending so much time on one cluster of words be justified? This sequence of activities involves vocabulary development, writing, reading, speaking, listening, and thinking, all in one coherent package. That is enough to justify its occasional use in a general English class, but there's much more to be said for this approach. It can be used with profit in almost any course—in English or in any other content area. Every subject, every unit of study, has its clusters of key words and concepts; this approach can help students learn those words and concepts more thoroughly. This approach takes more time than most teachers are accustomed to spending on vocabulary study, but because it will lead to a more complete understanding of essential concepts and to more advanced thinking skills, that time will be well spent.

3
A Brief History
of the English Vocabulary

To do some of the activities in this book, students will have to know something about the history of the English language; they'll also have to know how to get certain kinds of historical information from a dictionary. When I was a beginning teacher, those words would have given me a sinking feeling in the pit of my stomach—the kind of feeling I have now when people start talking about the fine points of computer use. When I started my teaching career, I knew almost nothing about the history of English. I had never taken a course in the subject, and I had never paid attention to the historical information in my dictionary (i.e., to the material in brackets at the end of word entries). I did know, from the notes in my Shakespeare text, that word meanings change over time, but that vague, general fact was just about all I knew. This chapter is written for the sort of teacher I was when I started, someone who would have panicked if asked to guide students through an activity involving some knowledge of the history of English words.

Before I begin, I need to state one fact: To do these activities, you and your students will need a good dictionary, one that clearly indicates word origins and root meanings. The dictionary I use, and recommend, is the third or fourth edition of the *American Heritage Dictionary*, henceforth referred to as the *AHD*. I urge interested teachers to get a personal copy of this remarkable resource and to get as many class copies as the budget allows. When I did dictionary activities in high school, I borrowed class dictionaries from my fellow English teachers, so that I'd have at least one dictionary for every three students. There are, of course, other good dictionaries available, but I use the *AHD*, third or fourth edition, for all of the examples presented in this chapter.

I begin this chapter by describing how to determine whether a word is native or borrowed. This information is arranged in handout form, so that

FIGURE 3.1
Native Word or Loan Word?

Languages have family trees. We can trace English back to an ancient language called *Indo-European* (5000–3000 B.C.). Indo-European was the common ancestor of a large family with several major branches. One branch is called the Italic branch. In this branch, the language evolved from Indo-European to Latin and, finally, to the modern Romance languages: French, Italian, Portuguese, and Spanish. English is part of the *Germanic branch.* In this branch, too, the language went through major changes over the centuries. It evolved from Indo-European into a form called *common Germanic.* From that point, it divided into two smaller branches: North Germanic, the ancestor of most modern Scandinavian languages, and *West Germanic,* the ancestor of modern German and of English. When tribes speaking West Germanic migrated to England, they developed a common language, *English,* named after the Angles, the dominant tribe. The earliest form of the English language, *Old English* (or *Anglo-Saxon),* dated from 449 to 1100 A.D. The next stage was *Middle English,* which dated from 1100 to 1500. Finally, there is *Modern English,* which dates from 1500 to the present day.

A *native word* is a word that originated at some time within the internal development of English, without the influence of any outside language. Some native words were present in Indo-European itself and have gone through all of the historical stages, changing form a little but still keeping their identities. Other native words originated at later stages, in Germanic, West Germanic, or in some stage of English itself. Languages are always creating new words. They also like to borrow words from other languages. Here's an example of how borrowing works: During the Old English period, the Latin word *candela* was taken directly into English and given an English form, *candel,* later spelled *candle* in Modern English. This process of making an English word out of a word from another language is what is called *borrowing.* The new English word that results is called a *loan word* or a *borrowed word. Candle* is a loan word because it was borrowed into English from Latin, a language outside the historical development of English. Sometimes a word is a *hybrid,* part native and part borrowed: *candlestick* is an example because *stick* is a native word. Because a hybrid has a borrowed part, it is considered a loan word.

To determine whether a word is native or borrowed, we have to look it up in a dictionary and consult the bracketed information at the end, or beginning, of the entry. This information is the word's origin and history, also called its *etymology*. There's one simple rule to follow: *If an outside language is mentioned within the brackets, the word is a loan word; if no outside language is mentioned, the word is native.* Here are some examples of how to read the information within brackets. The examples are from the *American Heritage Dictionary*, Third Edition.

1. *seek.* (Middle English *sechen, seken,* from Old English *secan.* See **sag-** in Appendix.) This is a native word because no outside language is mentioned. The Middle English form was *sechen, seken;* the Old English form was *secan.* This word can be traced all the way back to Indo-European; the form in bold type, **sag-,** is its Indo-European root.

2. *cheese.* (Middle English *chese,* from Old English *cyse,* from Germanic **kasjus,* from Latin *ceasus.*) This is a loan word from an outside language, Latin. It was borrowed into common Germanic and has been part of English since the Old English period.

3. *classroom.* The two parts must be looked up separately: (French *classe,* from Latin *classis,* class of citizens. See **kele-2** in Appendix.) and (Middle English *roum,* from Old English *rum.* See **reue-** in Appendix.) This word is a hybrid; it is half-native and half-borrowed. Because it has a borrowed element, it is considered a loan word.

---

you can distribute it to your students. The information on this sheet is all you will need to guide a class through the activities presented in Chapters 4 through 9. In the remainder of this chapter, I go through the history of the English language in greater detail and offer some other teaching activities you might want to try. My aim is to try to entice you to introduce more history of English into your secondary classroom. But first, in Figure 3.1 you will find a basic handout that describes the differences between native words and loan words.

Now I'll go over these matters in greater depth. I begin with a thumbnail history of the English vocabulary. This history is a composite from many textbooks and from the *AHD*, with some of my own ideas and examples mixed in. Then, I illustrate how to interpret somewhat more complicated etymological information. I doubt that you will have occasion to use all this material in your classroom, but it should help you anticipate any possible questions and problems that your students may have. Finally, in the Applications section at the end of this chapter, I suggest some ways to make this material accessible and interesting to students.

Where English Words Come From

The ultimate source of English was an ancient language called *Indo-European*, dated by scholars in 5000 to 3000 B.C. Indo-European was the ancestor of a whole family of related languages. English developed within the Germanic branch of the family. Its immediate ancestors were *Germanic* and then a form of Germanic called *West Germanic*. Tribes speaking various forms of West Germanic migrated from northwest Europe to the British Isles in the fifth century of the modern era. They established a common language named *English* (in modern spelling), after the Angles, the dominant tribe. Th earliest stage of English was *Old English*, also called *Anglo-Saxon* by some scholars; this stage is traditionally dated from 449 to 1100 A.D. The epic poem *Beowulf* was composed in Old English. The second stage of the language was *Middle English*, traditionally dated from 1100 to 1500 A.D. Chaucer wrote in Middle English. The third stage of the English language, dated from 1500 to the present, is commonly known as *Modern English*. Because there were considerable differences between earlier and later forms of the language within this third period, scholars often speak of Early Modern English, the language of Shakespeare and the sixteenth and seventeenth centuries, and Late Modern English. However, for the purposes of this discussion, most of the time I just use the term *Modern English*.

The Ancestors of English

English is part of a large group of languages that derive from an ancient common language called Proto-Indo-European, or simply *Indo-European*. The whole group of related languages, the Indo-European language family, is called Indo-European because it includes languages from an area extending from the Indian peninsula throughout most of Europe. This family includes English and many other languages spoken by people who have immigrated from this broad geographic area to America throughout its history. (A diagram of all of the Indo-European languages is given on the inside back cover of the *AHD*.) As mentioned, most scholars agree that the common language, Indo-European, must have been spoken during the period 5000 to 3000 B.C. They have not agreed on where the original homeland must have been, although current theories favor a location in eastern Europe, in the steppe region north of the Black Sea. In any case, it is commonly agreed that, sometime after 3000 B.C., the original tribe of Indo-Europeans began a series of migrations throughout Europe and western Asia. As different groups of people became separated from one another, they inevitably began to modify their original common language; each isolated group began to develop the original language in its own way. For a while, these groups would still have been able to understand each other: They would have been speaking different dialects of the original language, rather than different languages. Over the centuries, however, these regional dialects grew so far apart that the speakers could no longer understand one another; that is, the dialects evolved into different languages.

Sometime after 3000 B.C., members of the original Indo-European tribe began their migrations. Eventually, a significant group called Germans settled in the northwest of Europe, in northern Germany and southern Denmark. For a time, this group spoke a common language, called Proto-Germanic or simply *Germanic*, but as the Germans themselves began to migrate further, Germanic broke down into separate dialects, which eventually evolved into a number of separate languages. Linguists have identified three distinct branches deriving from Germanic: North Germanic, the ancestor of Danish, Swedish, Norwegian, and Icelandic; *West Germanic*, the ancestor of German, Dutch, and English; and East Germanic, which produced a variety of dialects, all of which are now extinct. It is impossible to establish a firm timetable for these changes, which evolved gradually over many centuries. There are no extant texts in common Germanic, which, like Indo-European, has been reconstructed by scholars from its surviving descendants. The early stages of the three later branches, including West Germanic, have been largely reconstructed as well. The earliest extant text in any Germanic language, Bishop Wulfila's translation of the Bible into the East Germanic dialect called *Gothic*, dates only from around 370 A.D., near the tail end of this long transition period.

Most of the vocabulary of Germanic was inherited from Indo-European. There is a large common core of words that appear in Germanic and in other branches of the Indo-European family: words for body parts, kin members, common plants and animals, numerals, and basic actions. In addition to this inherited word stock, Germanic had a smattering of borrowed words from other languages, mainly Latin and Celtic. Finally, Germanic had a stock of words unique to it: the early forms of Modern English *back*, *bath*, *blood, boat, bone, child, dear, game, ground, oar, rat, sea, soul, theft*, and many others. We don't know where these words came from. They may have been borrowed, while the cognate form in the source language was later lost; they may have been invented during the Germanic period. In any case, because there is no evidence of borrowing, these words and their Modern English descendants should be considered native English words. The same is true for the smaller group of words that are found only in West Germanic, not in the other branches of Germanic, and not in any other known language: the earlier forms of *brook, crave, idle, knight, prick, sheep, soon*, and *weed*.

The Three Stages of English

Old English. In the first centuries of the Christian era, the dominant languages in England were Celtic and Latin. The first inhabitants of England we know anything about were the Celts, or Britons, as they were called (hence, of course, the name *Britain*). The Britons were conquered by the Romans in 43 to 46 A.D., and for the next three and a half centuries, England (more properly, Britain [the Romans called it *Britannia*]) was a part of the Roman Empire. With the decline of the Empire, the Romans gradually withdrew from the island, leaving for good around 410. The Britons were still there, but, without the protection of the Roman legions, they were easy prey for aggressive neighbors. Around the year 449, they were overwhelmed entirely by Germanic invaders from the European mainland. According to the traditional account, as given by Bede in his *Ecclesiastical History of the English People* (731), three Germanic tribes—the Angles, the Saxons, and the Jutes—came over the sea and took control of the land from the Britons, who were eventually driven out of central Britain entirely, retreating to Wales, Cornwall, Scotland, Ireland, and, across the channel, to Brittainy. These three powerful Germanic tribes were the founders of the English nation and the source of the English language.

It's impossible to know exactly which languages the invading tribes must have spoken. Although they came from somewhat different areas on the continent, they all came from the northwest of Europe, and they all must have spoken some form of West Germanic. In all likelihood, they spoke mutually intelligible dialects of West Germanic. In any case, they developed a common language relatively quickly, and this language came to be called English (Old English [OE] *Englisc*), after the name of the Angles. No texts in this early form of English appeared until the latter part of the seventh century, but we can assume that its basic elements were developed from 449 onward, as people sought a common language to communicate with each other. Hence, the traditional dating of Old English as beginning in 449 does make sense.

The vocabulary of Old English is overwhelmingly native. Many of the words in the core vocabulary can be traced all the way back to Indo-European. Others, as mentioned, can be traced back to Germanic or West Germanic. Many others were composed out of inherited words or parts of words during the Old English period itself. The users of Old English were extraordinarily creative linguistically; they created thousands of new words through two processes of word formation: compounding and derivation. These processes were, and are, thoroughly native; they were present in Indo-European and in Germanic, and they are still used in English today.

Compounding involves combining two independent words to form one new word, called a *compound*. Modern English examples are easy enough to find—*homework, classroom, football, basketball*, and so on—and students can have a good time finding, or inventing, colorful examples of their own. A fair number of Old English compounds are still in use today: *holiday* (OE *halidaeg*, from *halig* ["holy"] plus *daeg*, ["day"]); *handiwork* (OE *handgeweorc*, from *hand* ["hand"] plus *geweorc* ["work," "product"]); *bridegroom* (OE *brydguma*, from *bryd* ["bride"] plus *guma* ["man"]), and so on. A great many other compounds have been lost or replaced over time, including many that were both colorful and ingenious: *daegred*, meaning "dawn" (from *daeg* ["day"] plus *red* ["red"]); *run-wita*, meaning "councillor" (from *run* ["secret"] plus *wita* ["knower"]); *wyrdwritere*, meaning "historian" (from *wyrd* ["event," "fate"] plus *writere* ["writer"]), and so on. In Old English, the process of derivation was just as prolific as that of compounding. Derivation involves adding an affix, a word part that cannot stand alone, to a fully independent base word; the result is called a *derived word*, a new word derived from the base. In Modern English, as in Old English, affixes are of two kinds: Prefixes are added at the beginning of a word, as in *misdeed* (OE *misdaed*, from *mis-* plus *daed*); suffixes are added at the end of a word, as in *bloody* (OE *blodig* from *blod* plus *-ig*).

Because the users of Old English relied so much on native words and word processes, borrowing was not as common during the Old English period as it was later on. There were still a fair number of loan words in Old English, however, most of them borrowed from Latin. While still on the Continent, the Germanic tribes had substantial contact with the far-flung Roman Empire, and a number of Latin words were borrowed into Germanic and West Germanic. Most of these words are the names of items used in trade or domestic life; the source-words for these Modern English words were borrowed from Latin into Germanic or West Germanic during this early period: *butter, chalk, cheese, copper, dish, kettle, linen, pepper, pound, sack, tile,* and *wine*. The Germanic ancestors of the English brought these words with them when they first came to England. These Germanic invaders, whom we might as well call the English, were not Christians when they arrived in England. They were converted to Christianity gradually during the seventh century, after Pope Gregory sent Augustine to England in 597. The language of the Church was, of course, Latin, and the introduction of Christianity meant that the English had to assimilate a whole host of new concepts, embodied in Latin words, into their vocabulary. They did borrow a number of words, especially words of a more technical nature: the early forms of Modern English *abbot, altar, angel, apostle, canon, disciple, martyr, mass, monk, priest, psalm,* and many other ecclesiastical terms were borrowed directly from Latin. The interesting part of the story, however, is the way the English avoided excessive borrowing by relying on their native linguistic resources.

One thing the English did was simply translate Latin words. Latin *Salvator* became Old English *Neriend* ("Saver") or OE *Haelend* ("Healer"); Lat. *Creator* became OE *Scippend* ("Shaper"); Lat. *omnipotens* ("all-powerful,") became OE *eallmihtig* ("allmighty"); Lat. *evangelium,* which meant "good news," became OE *godspell,* which meant exactly the same thing. In some cases, the English borrowed a Latin word and added a native word or affix to it, producing a hybrid: *preosthad* (*preost* plus OE *-had*), meaning "priesthood"; *martyrdom* (*martyr* plus OE *-dom*); *sealmscop* (*sealm,* ["psalm"] plus OE *scop* ["singer"]); *munuclif* (*munuc* plus OE *lif*), meaning "monk-life," "monastic life." The most interesting words are ones in which the English capture the essential meaning of a Latin term with a kind of common-sense paraphrase: The OE word for penance or repentance was *daed-bot,* which meant "deed-remedy," "deed-compensation"; for a sermon or homily, the OE word was *lar-spell,* meaning "lore-speech"; the sin of wrath was *hatheortness* ("hot-heart-ness" in Old English), and a heretic was a *gedwol-man,* or "error-man." These are just a few examples of the widespread practice of using native words and processes to express the new concepts of Christianity. I see this practice as part of the effort of conversion: Christian clerics and missionaries must have used these new but familiar words to make the concepts of the new religion accessible to the common people, who did not know Latin and could neither read nor write. It's interesting to note that only a few of these ingenious native words survive. Most have been replaced by loan words borrowed later, after the new religion was firmly established and the practice of literacy was more widespread.

Still, although most of the Old English compounds have been lost, the types of compounds established in Old English have served as models for later users of English. Compounds based on these patterns are still being created today. See Figure 3.2 for the types of Old English compounds that are still in active use. The Old English examples have been literally translated into Modern English.

The topic of compounding is intriguing to students. Compounds are fun to create and interesting to discuss. The modern world is full of compounds; new ones are created every day, in advertising, in the world of technology, and in contemporary slang. Because Old English relied heavily on compounds, too, exploring the process of compounding is a good way for students to appreciate the earliest stage of English and its lasting effects on the English language. See the Applications section at the end of this chapter for several activities involving compounds.

Middle English. During the Middle English period (1100–1500), the size of the English vocabulary was enormously increased by borrowing. The first source of borrowing was *Old Norse*, the language spoken by the Viking raiders of the ninth and tenth centuries and by the Danish settlers who followed after them. From the tenth century on, substantial numbers of Danes were living permanently in England, and a large section of the northeastern part of the country was even called the Danelaw (the region subject to Danish law). These Danish settlers were farmers and tradesfolk, and they mixed in easily with the native English inhabitants, intermarrying and gradually coming to think of themselves as English. The languages of the two groups mixed easily as well. Both Old Norse and Old English were descendants of common Germanic, but they descended by different routes: Old Norse derived immediately from *North Germanic*, while Old English derived from *West Germanic*. Thus, the two languages had somewhat different forms. For example, common Germanic must have had a form like **skurtaz*, which meant something like "cut" (an asterisk indicates that a form is a scholarly reconstruction, that it is not found in any extant text). In Old English, this reconstructed form became *scyrte*, the old form of Modern English *shirt*; in Old Norse, however, it became *skyrta*, which was later borrowed into English as *skirt*. Despite such differences, the two languages were similar enough to make communication between the two groups relatively easy. Borrowing of Old Norse words into English must have begun in the tenth century, but, because the written record always lags behind actual speech, only a few Old Norse loan words are found in Old English texts. In

FIGURE 3.2
Old English Compounds: Then and Now

---

1. *Noun + Noun = Noun.* This compound is the most common Old English type. The first noun limits or narrows the second noun. Old English examples: *spear-death, wife-love, whale-road* (*whale-road* is a riddling circumlocution for the ocean; such words, called *kennings*, were common in Old English poetry). Modern examples: *fleabag, lamppost, conehead.*

2. *Object Noun + Acting Noun = Noun.* The first noun is the object acted upon by the second noun, which names a person who performs an action. Old English examples: *ring-giver* (a kenning for *king*), *ale-drinker, spear-bearer.* Modern examples: *tear-jerker, blockbuster, bench-warmer.*

3. *Adjective + Noun = Noun.* Old English examples: *holiday* (*holy* + *day*), *high-father, old-friend.* Modern examples: *oddball, wisecrack, blackbird.*

4. *Adverb + Noun = Noun.* Old English examples: *back-journey, after-comer, outlaw.* Modern examples: *downfall, output, back talk.*

5. *Adjective + Noun = Adjective.* These are very common in Old English. In translating this type into Modern English, one usually has to add an *-ed* which was not present in the original word. Old English examples: *mild-heart(ed), gladmind(ed), bright-edge(d).* Modern examples are very easy to find: *big-time, small-town, world-class.*

6. *Noun + Adjective = Adjective.* Old English examples: *battle-brave, morning-cold, life-sick.* Modern examples: *knee-deep, stone-cold, sky-high.*

7. *Adjective + Adjective = Adjective.* Old English examples: *powerful-strong, wise-firm, bright-adorned.* Modern examples: *flat broke, filthy-rich, squeaky-clean.*

8. *Adverb + Verb = Verb.* One might call this type a form of derivation, but, because most prefixes in Old English can stand alone as independent adverbs, one can also consider it a form of compounding. Old English examples: *overcome, withstand, through-break.* Modern English examples: *undermine, outperform, overeat.* New examples in Modern English are hard to find because of the popularity of a new type called a phrasal verb; in this type, the adverb is attached after the verb, as in "We *cooked out* on the new grill." The old type seems to have taken on new life, though, in computer language, in which one can *input* and *download* information.

---

the early Middle English period, however, large numbers of Old Norse loan words began to appear in written texts. Many of these loan words have remained in the English language right to the present day.

Old Norse loan words are not confined to special areas of activity or to a distinct level of society. The Danish settlers mixed with the English natives freely, with the result that Old Norse loan words became part of the vocabulary of everyday life. Some of these words name such basic concepts or objects that one would never suspect them of being loan words; *birth, call, crooked, dirt, egg, get, give, leg, lift, loose, rotten, sister, skin, take, weak, window*, and many other common, everyday words were borrowed from Old Norse. In fact, English even borrowed from Old Norse such basic items as the verb *are* and the pronouns *they, their*, and *them*. Not all Old Norse loan words, however, are so ordinary. English owes a debt to Old Norse for a group of especially vivid and precise verbs: *droop, gnash, nag, ransack, scowl, scream, skulk, slam, slaughter, snub*, and *stagger*, to name only a few. Nor are all Old Norse loan words confined to the physical or external world; some express complex internal or intellectual concepts: *anger, awe, awkward, law, meek, odd, sly, trust, ugly, want*.

Old Norse loan words look and feel like purely native words. Old Norse was, after all, derived from Germanic, just as Old English was; Old Norse might be described as a northern cousin of Old English. The addition of Old Norse loan words enriched the English language considerably, but they did not alter the basic nature of the English vocabulary.

The next infusion of borrowed words into Middle English had more far-reaching effects; it added a whole new dimension to the English vocabulary. This radical change was a direct result of the Norman Conquest (1066), when French-speaking Normans defeated the English army, and their leader, Duke William the Conqueror, became king of England. As a result of the Conquest, French became the language of the ruling class in England, while English was the language of the peasants and the lower classes. An amusing illustration of the difference in status between the two languages involves the names for domestic animals used for food. When the animals were alive, and under the control of English servants, they kept their English names: *calf, cow, sheep, deer*, or *swine*. When they were served as food to the French-speaking nobles, they were called by their French names, which were eventually borrowed into English and which survive to this day: *veal, beef, mutton, venison, pork*, and *bacon*. This example appears in Sir Walter Scott's novel *Ivanhoe*, although it was first pointed out in 1653 by John Wallis in his *Grammatica Linguae Anglicanae*.

For some two hundred years after the Conquest, the French nobles who controlled English social and political institutions spoke French and made relatively little effort to learn English. In time, however, they began to feel more affinity for England than for France, and they began to use English as well. When they did so, they brought thousands of their French words into English. These words still dominate in the areas where the French ruling classes held sway: in government, the military, education, religion, recreation, social and political structure, the judicial system, literature, and the arts—in fact, in just about every activity and institution of English society and culture. As a result of this massive infusion of French words, many native words were simply lost for good. In the Middle English period, those ingenious native compounds mentioned earlier were replaced by the French terms that survive to this day: *penance, sermon, homily, heretic*. In cases in which French loan words were added on top of surviving native words, the English vocabulary acquired a whole new dimension, that is, a second, more formal register. In many instances, speakers of English now can choose between a basic, native way of saying something and a more formal, French equivalent. Do we *play games* or *participate in sports* ? Do we *like to eat food*, or do we *prefer fine dining*? Since the relation of native words to French or Latin loan words is explored extensively later in this book (Chapters 5 through 9) the matter won't be discussed in any depth here.

Because Middle English borrowed so extensively from French, and from Latin (which was the language of the Church, scholarship, and the universities), the language relied much less on its native resources of compounding and derivation. Compounding did go on, and an important new type was borrowed into English from French: *Verb + Object Noun = Noun*, as in *pastime*, from French *passe tiemps*. Still, compounding was not a major source of new words in Middle English. What happened with derivation was somewhat more complicated. A number of Old English affixes ceased to be productive. In Old English, *for-* ("entirely") and *with-* ("against") were actively used to form new words. While some of those words are still in the language today—*forlorn, forsake, withhold, withstand*—the prefixes *for-* and *with-* are simply historical fossils; they were not used to make new words after the Old English period. Many OE affixes did remain productive, however, and they were combined with newly borrowed words to form hybrids in Middle English. In a typical example, the borrowed word *faith* was combined with native affixes to form five Middle English hybrids: *faithful, faithfulness, faithless, unfaithful,* and *unfaithfulness*. In Middle English, people also began to make hybrids the other way, by combining native roots with borrowed affixes. Many of the French and Latin words borrowed in Middle English were derived words, and, in time, some of the French–Latin affixes were detached and used to form new English words. Among the first affixes used in this way were *re-* and *-able*, which were joined with native words to produce *believable*, *renew*, and *unthinkable*. This latter process was just getting started in Middle English, but, from the sixteenth century on, it became a highly prolific means of extending the English vocabulary.

Modern English. The next great infusion of borrowed words occurred in the sixteenth and early seventeenth centuries (1500–1640). This was the time of the English Renaissance, when English scholars had a revived interest in classical languages and texts. In attempting to translate these texts into English, scholars often found their native language inadequate to convey the complex thoughts of the originals. Hence, they made a conscious effort to enhance the English vocabulary by extensive borrowing of Latin and Greek words. They went way too far, and critics mocked their proposed loan words as "inkhorn terms," words that came from the scholar's ink bottle rather than from actual experiences or needs. Nevertheless, thousands of loan words introduced into English at this time are still in use today. These words, like their sponsors, tend to be learned and scholarly, but many of them have become widely familiar. In the final analysis, the Renaissance contributed even more words to the English vocabulary than did the Norman Conquest.

To get a sense of the number and kind of words borrowed directly into English between 1500 and 1640, I did a little experiment: I started with the letter A and went through a few pages of my *AHD* (Third Edition), looking for words that didn't have Middle English or French in their etymologies. Then, I checked them in the *Oxford English Dictionary* (OED) to find out whether they did enter English during this time period. Here are the words that definitely did: *abdicate, abdomen, aberration, abnegation, abort, abrupt, abrogate, abscess, abscond, abstemious, abstruse, accelerate, acclamation, accommodate, accretion, accumulate, accurate, acute, addict, adequate, adulterate*, and *adumbrate*. I'm certain there were more; many other words were listed as either from French or Latin, but I chose not to include them. This list seems typical of the kinds of words borrowed at this time. Most of them are long and learned; they represent various fields of specialized learning, and they express complex thoughts and mental processes. Some of these words are in common usage today, but most of them are more likely found in the intellectual discourse of the educated.

In fact, it would be difficult to engage in serious intellectual discourse without these types of words. In Chapter 7, I offer a list of twelve synonyms for the native word *think*: *analyze, concentrate, consider, contemplate, deliberate, examine, investigate, ponder, reason, reflect, speculate,* and *study*. Of these twelve words, all are derived from Latin or Greek, and four were introduced into English between 1500 and 1640: *contemplate, deliberate, investigate,* and *speculate*. Because there are so many of these long, Latinate words in the language, some scholars see the English vocabulary as having three tiers or levels: an ordinary level (native words); a formal level (loan words from French); and a learned level (loan words from Latin or Greek). There's clearly some truth in this view, and it's easy enough to find examples to illustrate it: *think/reflect/deliberate*; *ask/question/interrogate*; and *rise/mount/ascend*. Still, in many cases, French and Latin loan words are indistinguishable; in my list of thinking words, for instance, *concentrate* and *consider* are French loan words, but they are as learned in meaning and tone as the four Latin loan words. For my purposes in this book, I consider French and Latin loan words as a single group, and I stick with just two levels or registers—the ordinary and the formal.

Many of the learned classical words borrowed during the Renaissance had to do with natural science and technology, which were rapidly becoming major forces in the world. The association of Latin and, especially, Greek words with science and technology became common at this time, and has been ever since. Many of these early scientific terms were loan words in the traditional sense: *Anthropology* and *geography*, which first appeared in English in the sixteenth century, were based on preexisting Latin words. As time went on, however, the names for later fields and discoveries were rarely based on actual words, but were put together, in English, from classical roots and affixes that had been borrowed earlier. Words like *photography* and *antibiotics*, for instance, were not based on actual Latin or Greek words; quite obviously, these words name modern inventions. The Greek-derived forms *photo-* ("light"), *-graphy* ("writing"), *anti-* ("against"), *bio-* ("life") were already part of the English language, and they were simply put together when the need arose. The word *photography* was introduced into English by Sir John Herschel in 1839, the year that the process of photography first became widely known. Likewise, the word *antibiotics* entered English in the twentieth century, when the properties of these drugs were first discovered. These words are typical of most modern scientific words, in English or in other modern languages; they're new creations made from borrowed classical parts. They can be called loan words because they're made up of borrowed parts, but only the parts are borrowed, not the word as a whole.

Throughout the Modern English period, English has borrowed from living languages as well. It has been borrowing continuously from French, and, to a lesser extent, from Italian and Spanish. In recent years, words from the Near and Far East have begun to be borrowed in increasing numbers, and that trend will surely continue. Here, for instance, are some familiar loan words of Arabic or Japanese origin: from Arabic, *alcohol, algebra, assassin, candy, cotton, harem, magazine, mattress, sugar,* and *syrup*; from Japanese, *bonsai, geisha, hibachi, judo, jujitsu, karate, kareoke, origami, samurai, soy, tsunami,* and *tycoon.*

If you have recent immigrants in your classroom, you could explore the loan words from the native languages of these students. In many American classrooms today, that native language is likely to be Spanish. English has had long-standing contact with Spanish: first, when Elizabethan explorers encountered the New World; then, in the American West; and today, with the large influx of Hispanic people into the United States. As a result, Modern English, and American English in particular, has acquired many Spanish loan words that a class can collect and explore. Here's an extensive, but not inclusive, list: *barbecue, bonanza, cafeteria, cargo, chocolate, cigar, cockroach, Colorado, creole, embargo, fiesta, filibuster, Florida, loco, marina, mosquito, mustang, Negro, Nevada, plaza, patio, ranch, savvy, silo, stevedore,* and *vigilante.* Prominent recent borrowings include *barrio, junta, salsa* and the now-indispensable *macho* and *machismo.* If Hispanic students can see all of these Spanish words included in English, they may feel more motivated to learn English. English is a highly inclusive language, and you can demonstrate that fact convincingly to your students. English has borrowed words and concepts from throughout the world, and it will continue to do so in the future.

Although Modern English has relied heavily on borrowing, it has also added a great many words through derivation and compounding. In fact, in Late Modern English, derivation has become the major source of new words. Modern English today has an extensive stem of active affixes, affixes that are used to form new words. Some of these affixes are native, but the majority have been borrowed from French, Latin, or Greek. Some of the foreign affixes were borrowed into Middle English as parts of borrowed words and didn't become independent prefixes until the sixteenth or seventeenth century. Others were borrowed directly into Modern English and were used to form new English words almost at once. See Figure 3.3 for the current system of active English affixes.

Because many of the affixes in Figure 3.3 are used freely in Modern English without regard to their origins, the language now has enormous resources for making new hybrid words. The practice of joining native affixes to borrowed roots, begun in Old English, has become even more productive in Modern English; modern examples include *airy, beautiful, outclass, partnership, pointless, sainthood, saintly, stylish, stylishness,* and *underestimate*. The reverse process, joining a borrowed affix to a native root, has become almost as common; modern examples include *bakery, betterment, breakage, dishearten, forbearance, lovable, murderous, re-read,* and *starvation*. Sometimes, in Modern English, two synonymous affixes, one native and one borrowed, are attached to the same root, as in *misplace* and *displace*. This situation can produce confusion, as with *disinterested* and *uninterested,* but it can also produce subtle differences in meaning and tone. The French–Latin *humanity* tends to refer to the human race in the abstract; *humanness* refers more to the personal qualities of being human.

Some of the most prolific affixes in Modern English are those of Greek origin. Greek suffixes entered the language from French or Latin during the Middle English period. The prefixes were borrowed directly from Greek during and after the Renaissance, when English scholars acquired the ability to read the Greek language. Greek affixes are widely used in the areas of science and technology: *biology, biologist, biological, geology, geologist, geological, physicist, scientist, sociology, technology,* and so on. Greek affixes are also widely used in politics: *capitalism, communism, fascism, socialism, communist, socialist, ideology, ideological,* and so on. The suffix *-ist* can attach to anybody who specializes in anything: *columnist, manicurist, medievalist,* and, of course, *specialist*. Likewise, the prefix *-ize* can make a verb out of just about any word: *editorialize, homogenize, pasteurize,* and, of course, *specialize*. Although some columnists like to editorialize against recent coinages, such as *finalize* and *prioritize,* the fact remains that *-ize* and the other Greek affixes are enormously prolific and extremely useful.

Like derivation, compounding has also made a comeback in Modern English after being eclipsed by the massive borrowing in Middle English. The Early Modern period was a time of great linguistic creativity. The Old English compound types continued to thrive, with the *Adjective + Adjective = Adjective* type becoming more common, as in words such *sudden-bold, crafty-sick,* and *deep-contemplative*. Also prolific at that time was the *Verb + Object Noun = Noun* type, which was first introduced in Middle English. In Shakespeare's plays, a busybody is called a *carry-tale,* a *find-fault,* or a *please-man*. The old favorites *busybody, pickpocket,* and *rotgut* were coined in Early

FIGURE 3.3
Common Prefixes and Suffixes

---

1. **Prefixes**
   Native: *after-, fore-, mis-, over-, out-, un-, under-, up-*
   French–Latin: *circum-, counter-, de-, dis-, ex-, extra-, in-, inter-, intra-,*
       non-, mini-, pre-, pro-, post-, re-, sub-, super-, trans-
   Greek: *anti-, auto-, hyper-, hypo-, micro-, mono-, neo-, pseudo-*

2. **Suffixes for Adjectives**
   Native: *-ed, -en, -ful, -ish, -less, -ly, -some, -ward, -y*
   French–Latin: *-able, -al, -ant, -ent, -eous, -ian, -ible, -ive, -ous*
   Greek: *-ic, -istic*

3. **Suffixes for Nouns**
   Native: *-dom, -er, -hood, -ing, -ness, -ship, -ster*
   French–Latin: *-age, -ance, -ary, -ation, -ence, -ery, -ity, -ment*
   Greek: *-ism, -ist, -ite, -(o)cracy, -(o)logy*

4. **Suffixes for Verbs**
   French–Latin: *-ate, -fy, -ify*
   Greek: *-ize*

Modern English. American English has been a rich source of colorful compounds. Some American compounds conform to the established types: *cloudburst, moonshine, punchdrunk,* and *roughneck.* One modern type that is common in America, *Verb + Adverb = Noun,* is easy enough to explain; it is a noun formed from a phrasal verb: One cooks out at a *cookout,* and one gives away things at a *giveaway.* Other American compounds are a lot harder to classify, but they clearly show the creative power of compounding in Modern English: *bellhop, crybaby, daydream, freeze-dried, hand-pick, know-how, make-believe, paydirt, popcorn, practice-teach, slam dunk, sleepwalk, stir-fry, striptease,* and *zip-lock.*

Slang is an area in which compounding and all types of linguistic creativity thrive. I went looking for colorful compounds in Robert Chapman's *Thesaurus of American Slang* (Harper & Row, 1989), and I was not disappointed. I wanted to see whether the eight types of compounds that were operative in Old English (see Figure 3.2) are still active today. I found examples of all types, with some types more prolific than others. For the nouns, types one, two, and three were all common, while type four was hard to find. Here are some samples: for type one, *bonehead, breadbasket, fish-eye*, and *nest egg*; for type two, *cliff-hanger, crowd-pleaser, nit-picker*, and *party-pooper*; for type three, *bigmouth, greenback, oddball*, and *sourpuss*; for type four, *backtalk*, and perhaps *backside*. Of the adjective types, type five was the most common, just as it was in Old English, with type six fairly common and type seven quite hard to find. Here are some samples: for type five, *bush-league, cut-rate, highbrow, low-rent*, and *strong-arm*; for type six, *dog-tired, king-size*, and *stone-dead*; for type seven, *dead broke, filthy-rich*, and *squeaky clean*. Type eight, the old verb type, was quite rare, with only three examples: *back-track, outclass*, and *outpoint*. Type eight has been largely replaced by the modern phrasal verb, for which I found plenty of examples: *freak out, goof off, put down*, and *screw up*, to name a few. While I could have found many more colorful words if I had explored the areas of excretion and sex, I hope what I did find illustrates the value of exploring slang as a source of interesting words.

At the start of the twenty-first century, the English vocabulary is in excellent shape. It has an enormous word hoard. It has enlarged its native Germanic stock with massive borrowings from French, Latin, and Greek, and with substantial recent borrowings from other languages. Its power to create new derived words is stronger than ever, because it has developed an extensive system of affixes upon which to draw. Its power to create new compounds is also strong; it has retained its older types of compounds and also developed new ones. English has a formidable vocabulary now and the means to keep on increasing it in the future.

A Closer Look at Etymologies

(*Note to the reader:* The next section of this chapter offers some guided practice in reading the etymological information in dictionary entries. This practice will give you a chance to see how all of these broad historical trends are illustrated in the histories of individual words. If you've had enough information thrown at you, you might want to skip this section and go directly to the Applications at the end of the chapter. These applications are specific teaching activities that you can use to bring some of these historical developments home to your students.)

A good way to become more comfortable with all this historical information is to practice figuring out the etymologies of selected words. I've developed an exercise that provides such practice. I use it in a full course in the History of English, and I offer it here as a guide for interested secondary teachers. It should help you get a better handle on this material, so that you can answer any questions your students might have when looking up etymologies. You certainly wouldn't need to use this whole exercise to prepare your students for the activities set forth in this book. You might want to use it, though, in a special unit on the history of English or in a unit on how to use a dictionary.

The exercise involves working through a list of selected words, figuring out their etymologies from the information given in the *AHD*. In choosing the words, I tried to do three things: illustrate the typical historical patterns followed by common types of English words, anticipate common problems and confusions that students are likely to have when using the dictionary, and show students how rich and flexible the English vocabulary actually is. The list starts with words that have descended all the way from Indo-European and ends with words that have been coined in recent American English. When I present this activity to a class, I have the students look up the words and report on the etymologies, and I'm there to clear up any confusions that may arise.

Before asking the students to move through the list, I do two things. First, I review certain key terms. A *native word* originated within the internal historical development of the English language; a *loan word* or *borrowed word* came into that development from a language source outside it. A *hybrid* is a word that has a native part and a borrowed part; because it does have a borrowed part, it is technically a loan word. A *compound* is a word composed of two parts that can each function as independent words. A *derived word* is composed of an independent part and an *affix*, a part that can't stand alone.

Next, I go over the form of bracketed etymologies and explain why some entries in the *AHD* don't have them. If the students have enough copies of the *AHD*, I direct their attention to the discussion of etymologies in the Guide to the Dictionary section; I also explain the material myself. The students need to know two key points. They need to know that, as explained in the Guide section, the brackets are arranged to allow the user to move backward in time: "The most recent stage before Modern English is given first, with each earlier stage following in sequence." If a word has no bracketed etymology at the end of its entry, it is most likely a compound or derived word "formed in English from words or word elements that are entries in the Dictionary." Thus, while the entry for the compound *footstep* has no etymology, a reader can find the etymologies of its components in the entries for *foot* and *step*. After the students are aware of these technical points, the class is ready to move on to the actual list. I usually divide up the list and assign a few words to separate student groups, which then report to the whole class. Following is the list, and a detailed etymology of each word as derived from the *AHD*. I've also added some personal commentaries from time to time, the kind of things I'm likely to say in the course of class discussion.

> **1. foot.** [Middle English *fot*, from Old English *fot*. See **ped-** in Appendix I.]

Modern English *foot* appeared as *fot* in Middle English, with the Modern English form coming directly from the Old English form *fot*. Because there is no reference to any other language in its historical development, *foot* is clearly a native word, with a root, *ped-*, that can be traced back to Indo-European. This is a typical entry for a native word.

> **2. sea.** [Middle English *see*, from Old English *sae*.]

Modern English *sea* is another native word; its earlier forms appeared in Middle and Old English. The fact that it cannot be traced back to Indo-European makes no difference as to its native status; native words can enter the language at every stage of its development. We know, in fact, that this word was inherited into Old English from common Germanic, but all students need to know is that the word did not come from a language outside of English.

> **3. cook.** [Middle English *coken*, from *coke*, cook, from Old English *coc*, from Vulgar Latin **cocus*, from Latin *cocus*, *coquus*, from *coquere*, to cook. See **pek-w-** in Appendix I.]

Modern English *cook* is a loan word borrowed from Latin, probably when the Germanic tribes were still on the continent. The immediate source of the word was a hypothetical form, **cocus* (remember that an asterisk indicates that a form is a reconstruction, that it is not found in any extant text) in Vulgar Latin. There's nothing wrong with the students having a few laughs over the word *vulgar*, but they should then be asked to look up its etymology in the *AHD*. They will find that it originally meant "common" or "ordinary," not "crude" or "obscene." The *AHD* has a helpful entry for each stage of Latin mentioned in the various etymologies: *Latin* refers to classical, literary Latin, "the Latin language and literature from the end of the third century B.C. to the end of the second century A.D."; *Vulgar Latin* refers to "The common speech of the ancient Romans, which is distinguished from standard literary Latin and is the ancestor of the Romance languages"; *Late Latin* refers to the Latin language as used from the third to the seventh century A.D.; *Medieval Latin* refers to the language as used from 700 to 1500; and *New Latin* refers to the language as used since 1500.

4. port. (1) [Middle English, from Old English, from Latin *portus*. See **per-2** in Appendix I.]

Port, too, is a loan word. It has had the same form and meaning since Old English; hence, no older forms are given in the bracket. The fact that the word has an Indo-European root, **per-2,** might confuse some students; they might see the Indo-European root as a sign that the word must be native. They need to be reminded that many other languages, such as Latin here, also derive from Indo-European, that English has borrowed most of its loan words from other languages within the Indo-European family. Modern English *port* is Indo-European in origin, but it did not descend directly into English from Indo-European; it entered the history of English from an outside source.

5. sky. [Middle English, from Old Norse *sky*, cloud. See **(s)keu-** in Appendix I.]

Sky is a typical loan word from Old Norse. It looks and feels like a native word, the name for a basic natural fact, but it turns out be a loan word after all. The word was probably used in Old English, but, like most Old Norse loan words, it was not recorded in written form until Middle English. Students should note that the word has an Indo-European root, **(s)keu-,** because Old Norse, like English, is derived from Indo-European.

6. print. [Middle English *preinte*, from Old French, from feminine past participle of *preindre*, to press, alteration of *prembre*, from Latin *premere*. See **per-4** in Appendix I.]

Print is typical of thousands of loan words during the Middle English period. It descended from Indo-European to Latin to Old French (the French language from the ninth to the early sixteenth century), and it was borrowed from Old French into Middle English.

7. abrupt. [Latin *abruptus*, past participle of *abrumpere*, to break off: *ab-*, away; see *AB-1* + *rumpere*, to break; see **reup-** in Appendix I.]

Because no earlier forms are given, we know that *abrupt* was borrowed from Latin during the Modern English period, and in the form it still has. This is the typical pattern for thousands of loan words in the Early Modern period.

8. antibiotic. No etymology is given in the *AHD*, which, as the Guide section indicates, does not provide etymologies for compounds or derived words formed in English from components that are listed as separate entries. Because this is clearly a derived word (actually, it's a special case, since neither part can stand alone), we can get at its origins by looking up the entries for each part: For *anti-*, we find [Greek, from *anti*, opposite. See **ant-** in Appendix I.]; for *biotic*, we find [Probably Greek *biotikis*, from *biotos*, life, from *bioun*, to live, from *bios*, life. See **gwei-** in Appendix I.]. Both parts of the word appear to be of Greek origin, but, because there are no Greek forms given for the full word, we can assume that the full word did not exist in the Greek language. *Antibiotic* is typical of many scientific or technical terms that have entered Modern English. It was not borrowed from Greek; it was formed, in English, from Greek or Latin roots that have been part of the special, "scientific" vocabulary of English since the Renaissance. How should we classify *antibiotic*? It was not borrowed from any other language; it was formed in English in the twentieth century, when antibiotics were first discovered. Still, because it was formed from borrowed parts, such a word would still be considered a loan word in the eyes of most linguists.

9. footstep. Because the entry has no brackets, we must assume this is another word formed from parts already in the language. As shown previously, we know that *foot* is a native word, which existed in Old English. The same is true for *step*, which has the following etymology: [Middle English, from Old English *staepe, stepe*.]. Because both parts are native and can stand alone, *footstep* is clearly a native compound.

10. footprint. Another word with no bracketed information. As shown, *foot* is a native word, while *print* is a loan word from French. Thus, the full word is a hybrid compound.

11. footage. Nothing in brackets. As shown, we know that *foot* is native. The suffix *-age*, however, was borrowed from French; it has the following etymology: [Middle English, from Old French, from Vulgar Latin **-aticum*, abstract n. suff., from Latin *-aticum*, n. and adj. suff.]. Because *-age* is just a word part, which cannot stand alone, *footage* is not a compound. It is a derived word, a hybrid of a native root and a borrowed suffix.

12. skinhead. Another Modern English word, with no etymology given. *Skin* is a loan word from Old Norse; it has the following etymology: [Middle English, from Old Norse *skinn*. See **sek-** in Appendix I.]. *Head* is a native word that can be traced back to Indo-European: [Middle English, from Old English *heafod*. See **kaput-** in Appendix I.]. Thus, we have a very contemporary compound word, which is a hybrid of two words with very long histories.

13. soul food. A Modern English compound, invented by American Blacks, from two ancient native English words. *Soul* can be traced back to Old English, to Germanic actually, although the *AHD* etymology doesn't go back that far: [Middle English, from Old English *sawol*.]. *Food* can be traced back to Indo-European: [Middle English *fode*, from Old English *foda*. See **pa-** in Appendix I.]. From an example such as this, students can realize that all of the inherited wealth of the English vocabulary is at their disposal today.

14. roadkill. This is a very recent American compound. It didn't appear in the first three editions of the *AHD*; it appears for the first time in the fourth edition, which was published in 2000. When students look up the two parts of *roadkill* in the *AHD*, they'll find that both are native English words with Indo-European roots. *Road* has this etymology: [Middle English *rode*, *rade*, a riding, road, from Old English *rad*. See **reidh-** in Appendix I.]. *Kill* has this one: [Middle English *killen*, perhaps from Old English **cyllan*. See **gwele-** in Appendix I.]. Again, from an example such as this, students can see that the ancient words and word processes are still very much alive in our current language.

Applications

1. Because science and technology have such prestige today, new inventions tend to be given impressive Greek or Latin names that sound "scientific." Here are a few common names that come to mind: *audiotape, automobile, calculator, computer, microwave, photography, radio, telephone, television,* and *videotape*. Everybody seems to know what these things are and what they can do, but, in most cases, the names don't tell us much about how these items really work. Confronted with the need to name these new things, an Old English speaker would have been more likely to take words already in existence and combine them into self-explaining compounds: thus, an automobile might have been called a *self-mover* or a *motor wagon*. Without worrying about word origins, see if you can come up with compound names for these ten modern inventions, names that really describe how these things work. A *hint:* The root meanings of these modern names might give you some ideas; *telephone*, for instance, derives from Greek *tele-* "far, far off" and Greek *phone* "sound, voice."

2. These eight words are examples of eight types of compounds used in Old English. See if you can find modern examples of each type: *Windbag*, for instance, is a compound of two nouns, *wind* and *bag*; if you combine *house* and *cat* to make *housecat*, you'll be making an

example of this type of compound. Analyze the two parts of each type; then, try to find or make an example of each type. Look anywhere you like for examples, and feel free to use modern slang terms.

1. windbag
2. crowd-pleaser
3. sorehead
4. back talk
5. first-rate
6. dog-tired
7. dead wrong
8. overcome

3. Old English speakers and writers often came up with vivid, highly descriptive compound names. They called anger *hot-heart-ness* and dawn *day-red*; they spoke of *summer-long* days and *morning-cold* spears. The ability to create powerful compounds is still alive today. Look at *skyscraper* for a tall building or *boom box* for a loud portable radio. Look around you and see how many powerful compounds you can find. Feel free to create your own, too.

4. The word *ugly* was borrowed from Old Norse; it derives from the Old Norse noun *uggr*, meaning "fear." What does the word *ugly* mean in the following three sketches? Does it have the same meaning in each one? Does it have any trace of the original Old Norse meaning in any of the three sketches?

   a. Let's face it, dear old Uncle Joe isn't just homely; he's downright ugly. His mouth is way too large for the rest of his face, but his teeth still won't fit inside it. When he smiles, all you can see is those big buck teeth pointed right at you. And when he talks, he can spray saliva a good five feet away.

   b. The knife had cut deeply into his leg. There was an open gash on his inner thigh, at least five inches long and more than an inch deep. The bleeding had ceased flowing, but blood was still oozing at the jagged edges. It was a very ugly wound.

   c. In the third period, the game turned ugly. Behind 6–1 and totally frustrated, the Bears became more interested in hitting people than in scoring goals. The Lions kept their poise, but when Lion forward Luc Godette was checked viciously into the boards, the game turned into a full-scale brawl. Both benches emptied, and players were punching and wrestling all over the ice.

5. Words borrowed from Old Norse often have very complex and subtle meanings. Write a verbal charade for each of these three Old Norse loan words: *awe*, *skulk*, and *sly*.

6. In the sixteenth and seventeenth centuries, many words were borrowed into English directly from Latin. These Latin loan words tend to be very learned and formal in tone, even more formal than the French–Latin words borrowed during the Middle English period. Hence, in some cases, the English vocabulary has triplets, three synonyms with three different degrees of formality: *ask/question/interrogate*; *rise/mount/ascend*; *think/reflect/deliberate*. In each of these triplets, the first word is native, the second a French–Latin loan word, and the third a loan word directly from Latin. See if you can find some more triplets like these. Try starting with simple native verbs: *eat*, *lie*, *see*, *speak*, and so on.

7. The suffix *-ize* is very popular in Modern English. It can be used to make a verb out of just about any word. Although it is certainly useful, critics claim that it is used too much, and that many new *-ize* forms are either ugly or unnecessary. Write your reactions to the *-ize* words in the following examples: "Our billing system has been *computerized*;" "Please have your requests *prioritized* before submitting them;" "I've had all my sweaters *personalized*;" "The plans will be *finalized* this week." Are these *-ize* words necessary, or could the same idea be expressed in other words? What tone do these words have? You might want to consult the entries for these words in the fourth edition of the *American Heritage Dictionary* before writing your responses.

8. The suffix *-ist* is also very popular in Modern English. It, too, can be added to just about any word. As a result, some critics claim that it, too, is overused, that it is often used in trivial ways. Analyze what meaning and/or tone *-ist* has in the following words: *scientist*, *manicurist*, *capitalist*, *racist*, *sexist*, *receptionist*, *specialist*, and *generalist*. You might want to start by consulting the *AHD* entry for *-ist*.

9. The borrowed prefix *dis-* and the native prefixes *mis-* and *un-* have similar meanings and often are attached to the same words. As a result, the meanings of the derived words are sometimes hard to distinguish. Distinguish clearly between the following paired words by using each word in a sentence that clearly illustrates its meaning: *disable/unable*; *displace/misplace*; *disbelief/misbelief*; *misinformed/uninformed*; *disinformation/misinformation*; and *disinterested/uninterested*.

10. Write a brief essay explaining the different meanings and uses of the following terms: *Chicana, Chicano, Hispanic, Latina,* and *Latino.* Be sure to discuss how *you* feel about these words and whether you find some more acceptable than others. Consult the usage notes for these words in the fourth edition of the *AHD*, but draw on your own opinions as well.

11. Loan words from Yiddish are very popular in some regions of America. Because they often have very distinctive meanings that are hard to translate into other words, writing a verbal charade can be the best way to illustrate what they mean. Write a verbal charade for one or more of the following Yiddish loan words: *chutzpah, kibitz, kvetch, schlep, schlock, schmaltz,* and *schmooze.*

4
Etymology
Root Meanings and Current Meanings

E*tymology*, the study of the origin and historical development of words, is so interesting and helpful to students that I urge you to look into it. I'm sure most teachers of English and of other subjects do use etymological knowledge on occasion. I still remember my tenth-grade biology teacher writing *bio-* ("life") and *-ology* ("study of") on the board at the first class: When I learned the root meaning of this strange and forbidding word, I understood, for the first time, what the course would be about. In this chapter, I lay out various ways in which etymology can be used in the English classroom. The focus is on helping students acquire and understand words and on developing their thinking and writing skills in the process.

In introducing etymology to students, I point them toward finding the original, or first, meaning of a word or word part—what I like to call the *root meaning*. Of course, a word's root meaning may no longer be its primary meaning in current use: The word *fast* originally meant "fixed" or "firm," as in *fasten* or *steadfast*; now, it's more likely to mean the exact opposite, "quickly moving." This kind of historical change is not the focus here. In this chapter, the focus is on finding root meanings that are still in operation, still alive.

Knowledge of root meanings can be extremely useful to students and to teachers. Often, awareness of a word's root meaning can help students understand its current meaning better, especially if the word expresses a highly abstract idea and is long and unfamiliar in its form. Much of the problem in teaching and learning grammar comes from the long, Latinate terms. You can usually avoid terms like *predicate nominative*, but basic terms like *preposition* and *transitive* can be demystified through exploring their root meanings. The roots of *preposition* are Lat. *pre-* ("before") and Lat. *pos/posit* ("place"): A preposition is a word "placed before" a noun. The roots of *transitive* are Lat. *trans* ("across," "over to") and Lat. *itus*, a form of *ire* ("go," "pass.") With a transitive verb, the action "passes" from the subject "over to" an object, as in "Sammy Sosa hit the ball" (the action of Sosa, the hitter, is passed onto the ball, which probably flies out of the park). With an *intransitive* (from Lat. *in-* ["not"]) verb, the action does not pass on to an object; it stops with the verb, as in "He yawned." When intimidating terms are explained in this way, with root meanings and concrete examples, students get a clearer understanding of the concepts involved.

If you focus on root meanings, you can help your students in a variety of ways. Doing so can certainly help them enlarge their general vocabularies, and thus increase their reading and writing skills. A focus on root meanings can help your students understand key concepts in a single subject area and find conceptual links between all of the subjects they study. It can help them better understand what you are really asking for with common "school words," such as *analyze*, *imply*, or *infer*. Finally, if your students pursue root meanings actively, in the ways suggested and illustrated in this chapter, they can improve their writing and thinking skills during the very process of inquiry.

Indo-European Roots

Now that the third and fourth editions of the *AHD* have reinstated the Appendix of Indo-European Roots, you and your students have an invaluable etymological resource right at your fingertips. This appendix is not hard to use. Secondary students can use it with very little guidance; and when they do use it, they'll discover a whole hidden network of common concepts behind words that appear totally unrelated.

If you are already familiar with the *AHD* and its amazing appendix, you will understand my enthusiasm. Let me illustrate, though, what it can do. I like to explore connections between words, and it occurred to me one day that the words *infant* and *infantry* might be related. They certainly look related, but appearances can be deceiving. What common meaning, if any, could the two words share? What does a baby have to do with a group of foot soldiers? To pursue that question, I checked the etymologies of both words in the *AHD* and found that they do derive from the same root: Latin *infans*, meaning "unable to speak" (*in-* ["not"] and *fans* ["speaking"]). *Infant*, of course, retains the root meaning exactly. In *infantry*, the root meaning must have been extended from "baby" to "young person"; apparently, at some point, the practice developed of having the younger soldiers, the *infantry*, go on foot, while the older soldiers, the officers, rode on horses.

Having established this connection, I couldn't resist going farther. The

AHD entry for *infant* refers the reader to the root *bha-2* in the Appendix of Indo-European Roots. When I looked up *bha-2*, I found that the core meaning of this root is "speak," and that it underlies a whole collection of familiar words I'd never suspected of being related. Here's a partial selection, adapted from the Appendix entry:

> affable, ban, banality, banish, blasphemy, confess, defame, euphemism, fable, fame, fate, infant, infantry, phone, preface, prophet

How is each of these words related to the root meaning? What does each of these words have to do with speaking? I decided that I'd try to answer that question by writing a definition for each word in terms of its root meaning; I'd try to use the word *speak*, or a close synonym, such as *talk* or *say*, in each definition I wrote. Writing definitions using a common root meaning proved to be an interesting challenge.

Some of the derived words could be connected to speaking quite easily. A *phone* is "a machine people use to speak with each other." A *prophet* "says things before they happen." To *confess* is to "tell people what you've done." A *ban* is "a statement that prohibits something." Romeo is *banished* from Verona by an "official declaration" from the Prince. *Blasphemy* is "speaking badly of God or religion." A *preface* is a "statement that introduces a book." Others were a bit more of a stretch. An *affable* person is "easy to talk to." To *defame* someone is "to speak badly about someone, to spread rumors." *Euphemism* is "using pleasant words to say something unpleasant." I had the most trouble defining *banal*, *fable*, *fame*, and *fate*, but the struggle was well worth it. I saw these words in a new and fresher way after defining them in terms of their common root meaning. Here's what I eventually came up with. A *banality* is an "over-used expression, a cliche." A *fable* is "an old story passed on by speaking." *Fame* is "people talking about you, what people say about you." Your *fate* is "what has been said or decreed by some controlling power." Until I wrote this definition, I'd never thought to connect *fate* to the idea of speaking; I'd just thought of *fate* as an abstract power. Defining *fate* as the specific statement of an actual intelligence brings the ancient power to life. I found working with Indo-European roots like this so interesting that I've gone on to try it often in the classroom. I give the class a cluster of related words and ask them to guess the root meaning. When they do, I then ask them to write a definition for each word, using the root meaning in their definitions. Finally, I ask them to read and discuss their definitions as a whole class. Writing the definitions is the heart of the activity, the time when the students really begin to take ownership of the words.

Including the root meaning in the definition makes the task more difficult, but it leads to greater understanding in the end.

Bha-2 is one of many prolific Indo-European roots. Starting with any one of them yields the same result: surprising connections between seemingly unrelated words. I've explored many other roots listed in the *AHD* Appendix. Here are some others I've found especially promising for classroom study, followed by some of their important derivatives:

1. *bher-1* ("carry," "bear children"): bear, bier, birth, bring, burden, differ, euphoria, fertile, metaphor, paraphernalia, transfer, wheelbarrow

2. *deik-* ("show," "pronounce"): dictate, digit, edict, index, indicate, judge, policy, preach, predicate, predict, teach, token

3. *gen-* ("birth," "family," "origin"): gender, gene, genealogy, generate, generic, generous, genial, genius, genocide, germ, germinate, heterogeneous, homogeneous, ingenious, innate, kin, kind, king, naive, nation, native, nature, pregnant, progeny

4. *kel-1* ("cover," "conceal"): cellar, clandestine, color, conceal, hall, hell, helmet, hole, hollow, holster, occult

5. *man-2* ("hand"): command, commend, demand, emancipate, manacle, maintain, maneuver, manicure, manipulate, manufacture, manure, manuscript

6. *weid-* ("see"): advise, evident, guide, history, idea, providence, supervise, survey, view, vista, television, wise, wit

While I do recommend these particular roots for use in a secondary classroom, I want to issue some general advice to any interested teachers. Before I use a given root or given word with a class, I always experiment with it, just as I've done earlier. I define each derived word, using the root meaning, and I assess each definition I write. Using the root meaning simply won't work well in defining certain words: If I find that I can't produce a clear and accurate definition of a given word, I drop that word from the group of derivatives. With some words, using the root meaning yields a sense that is clear enough but no longer current or complete. For instance, the large group derived from *gen-* contains *gender* and *nation*. Defining *gender* as "an identity acquired at birth" would not be acceptable to many people today; defining a *nation* as "a group of people related by birth" makes sense only if it refers to place of birth, not family relationship, but it still leaves out immigrants. The writing of definitions should not be the end of the activity; the sharing and discussion of definitions can lead to important refinements of meaning.

Latin Roots

I would like to see every secondary student familiar with the *AHD* Appendix and able to use it, but I realize that working with Indo-European roots in this detailed way is not for every secondary class. It's a difficult challenge, and, while it can foster better understanding of individual words and better conceptual thinking, it doesn't yield major dividends in vocabulary development. Some teachers may well decide that working with Latin roots is more practical, more immediately useful. There are great clusters of English words that derive from the same Latin root. The members of these clusters resemble one another; they are similar in both meaning and form. If students can learn the root meaning and recognize some of the words in the cluster, they are well on the way to learning them all.

I've spent a good deal of time introducing the study of Latin roots to secondary classes. I try to do it in an active way, which requires writing and thinking, not just memorizing. Let me illustrate my approach by describing a week I spent in Elaine Burnham's ninth-grade Honors English class.

I began by offering the class a choice: a short story or Latin roots? To my amazement, they chose Latin roots. Once I was sure they knew what a root is—the semantic core of a word, the part to which affixes are added—I started with a root I've found accessible and fruitful: *vert/vers*. (Please note that the technical form of a root should have hyphens fore and aft (for example, like *-vert-*), because a root can take both affixes and suffixes. In this book, I dropped the hyphens for convenience.) I wrote *vert* and *vers* on the board, along with the Latin forms *vertere* and *versus*. I told the class that many English words with *vert* or *vers* in them come from the Latin verb *vertere*, which means "turn" or "change." I explained that this verb, like many Latin verbs, had different forms for its present system (*vert*) and its past system (*vers*), and that words were formed from both of those forms. After getting these basic facts out of the way, I asked the class for some English words with *vert* or *vers* in them. Suggestions flew out, and the board filled up quickly: *vertebra, vertebrate, versatile, vertical, version, verse, vertigo, vertex, versus*. I monitored the suggested words, making sure that they derived from *vertere*. If I wasn't sure of a word's origin, I checked it in a dictionary.

My next move was to talk a little about affixes. Again, the class seemed perfectly clear about how affixes work: Prefixes are added to the front of a root and usually change the meaning; suffixes are added to the back of the root and usually change the word's "part of speech" function. We did a few examples on the board: *re-* plus *vers* produces *reverse*, meaning "to turn

FIGURE 4.1
Latin Prefixes (with Examples)

Forms	Examples
ab- (a-, abs-) "away from"	abnormal, abduct, absent, abound
ad- (ac-, af-, ag-, al-, ap-, ar-, as-, at-) "towards," "to," "near"	adhesive, accept, affix, aggravate, ally, apply, arrive, assign, attract
circum- "around," "about"	circumference, circumspect
com- (co-, col-, con-, cor-) "with," "together," "fully"	compare, co-exist, collide, congress, correspond
contra- (contro-) "against," "opposite"	contrast, controversy
de- "down," "down from," "away from," "apart"; "to make opposite," "reverse"	decline, depend, depart, deregulate, deodorant
dis- (di-) "apart," "aside"; "to reverse," "remove," "undo"	disperse, disclose, discount, divide, dilute
e- (ex-) "out of," "out," "from"	exclude, explode, erupt, exit
extra- (extro-) "outside," "beyond"	extraordinary, extrovert
in- (il-, im-, ir-) "not" [in- #1]	incredible, illegal, impossible, irregular
in- (il-, im-, ir-) "in," "into," "within" [in-#2]	inspect, intrude, import, illusion, irrigate
inter- "between," "among"	intercept, interfere
intra- (intro-) "within," "inward"	intramural, introduce
ob- "against," "opposite," "to"	object, obstruct, obey
per- "thoroughly," "intensely," "through"	perfect, persistent, permit
pre- "before," "earlier"	precede, prepare
pro- "for," "forward," "in place of"	progress, process, pronoun
post- "after," "behind"	postpone, postwar
re- "again," "back"	reverse, rewrite
sub- (sup-, sus-) "below," "under," "from below"	submerge, support, suspend
super- "above," "upon," "over"	supervise, superfluous
trans- "across"	translate, transmission

© 2001 by Thomas Carnicelli from *Words Work*. Portsmouth, NH: Heinemann.

back" or "to change to the opposite direction"; *reverse* plus *-al* produces *reversal*, a noun meaning "a change back to a previous course." Then, I went over two prefix sheets I had passed out to the students. One contained common prefixes, their common meanings, the different forms a prefix can take when it is assimilated to different consonants, and current examples of every form of every prefix. I'd developed this form (Figure 4.1) after perusing countless word books and testing hundreds of words, and I think it's a useful tool for any student to keep for reference.

I know that this form in Figure 4.1 is long, and that some teachers may want to pare it down. It is long because not every prefix attaches to every root; I've tried to make the list long enough to generate a good number of derivatives from almost any Latin root. As for the meanings of the prefixes, I've labored to come up with the meanings listed, but I still know full well that they won't always work. The main thing I wanted Elaine's class to get from this sheet was the variant forms that a given prefix can take, because the next thing I wanted them to do was combine these prefixes with *vert* and *vers*.

The other prefix sheet I gave them (Figure 4.2) is the same on the left, but the right column is left blank. I call it the Latin Prefix Work Sheet. This is the basic sheet I use when working with Latin roots. It's designed so that students working with a given root can write each derived form next to the prefix attached to it. The simple forms for that same root can be written on the back of the sheet. In Elaine's class, the students became accustomed to the prefix list by generating a few derived forms with *vert/vers*: *avert, extrovert, pervert*. Then, I asked them to try to define each word, using the root meaning "turn" or "change" in their definition. With a little prompting, they defined *avert* as "to turn away from," *extrovert* as "a person turned outward," and *pervert* as "to change completely." Because the students were clearly ready to begin, Elaine and I broke the class into small groups, asking them to fill up their prefix sheets (combined forms in the right column, simple forms on the back) with as many words as they could find. We also asked them to define each word they found, using the word *turn* or *change* in each definition. We left them with one final warning: Check each word's etymology to be sure that it really did come from Latin *vertere*.

All of this takes a lot longer to explain here than it did in Elaine's class. Half-way through the first forty-five minute period, the students were in small groups busily working. They finished their word lists and definitions by the middle of the next period, leaving us the rest of that period for sharing definitions and discussing them. In Figure 4.3, you will find a composite prefix work sheet with all of the words the various groups generated. The

FIGURE 4.2
Latin Prefix Work Sheet

Forms	Combined with _____
ab- (**a-**, **abs-**) "away from"	
ad- (**ac-**, **af-**, **ag-**, **al-**, **ap-**, **ar-**, **as-**, **at-**) "towards," "to," "near"	
circum- "around," "about"	
com- (**co-**, **col-**, **con-**, **cor-**) "with," "together," "fully"	
contra- (**contro-**) "against," "opposite"	
de- "down," "down from," "away from," "apart"; "to make opposite," "reverse"	
dis- (**di-**) "apart," "aside"; "to reverse," "remove," "undo"	
e- (**ex-**) "out of," "out," "from"	
extra- (**extro-**) "outside," "beyond"	
in- (**il-**, **im-**, **ir-**) "not" [in- #1]	
in- (**il-**, **im-**, **ir-**) "in," "into," "within" [in- #2]	
inter- "between," "among"	
intra- (**intro-**) "within," "inward"	
ob- "against," "opposite," "to"	
per- "thoroughly," "intensely," "through"	
pre- "before," "earlier"	
pro- "for," "forward," "in place of"	
post- "after," "behind"	
re- "again," "back"	
sub- (**sup-**, **sus-**) "below," "under," "from below"	
super- "above," "upon," "over"	
trans- "across"	

students wrote the original list of simple forms on the backs of their work sheets: *vertebra*, *vertebrate*, *versatile*, *vertical*, *version*, *verse*, *vertigo*, *vertex*, and *versus*. Some students wrote all their definitions on the backs of their work sheets as well, but most used a different paper.

The definitions were quite good, especially considering the fact that the class had never done this activity before. Using a dictionary, and without relying on help from either Elaine or me, the groups came up with clear, concrete definitions for most of the words. Here are some of their better ones: An *adversary* is "a person who turns on someone and becomes their enemy"; to *advertise* is "to turn attention towards an idea or message"; a *controversy* or *controversial* issue "turns people against each other"; a *conversation* is "a dialogue in which two or more people take turns speaking"; to *diversify* is "to make a change to the makeup of something" or "to give variety/change to something"; something *irreversible* is "unable to be changed"; to *subvert* or be *subversive* is "to change things from below, from within"; to be *versatile* is "to be able to change"; a *vertical* line is "turned 90 degrees from horizontal"; *vertigo* is "when you feel like the world is turning."

Not all the written definitions were so successful. Many students struggled with mathematical and scientific terms like *transverse*, *vertebra*, and *vertex*, but confusion was cleared up through class discussion. I was no help with such terms, but several students were. They explained that the *vertex* is the top angle of a triangle, the high point from which the sides turn downward. One student carefully explained how a *transverse* line is "turned across" a series of parallel lines. There was discussion as to whether a *vertebra* should be defined as "a part of the spinal chord that turns" or as "a part of the spinal chord that allows a person to turn." Both definitions sounded good to me! I was able to contribute my bit by explaining *verse*: A line of poetry is called a verse because it "turns before it reaches the right margin." I even drew a little diagram. Carried away, I then explained that *prose*, too, has the root *vers* hidden in it. The word *prose* derives from *vers* plus the prefix *pro-*, and means "turned forward." After the words with common prefixes had been discussed, I told the class that *anniversary*, *universe*, *universal*, and *university* are all *vert/vers* words, too. The students were able to figure out the connections easily: An *anniversary* marks the turning of a year, or the yearly return of a day; *uni-* ("one") and *vers* mean "turned into one, whole." Although writing the definitions is, to my mind, the most important part of this whole activity, sharing and refining definitions in class discussion is a vital part as well.

Introducing the activity and then working with *vert/vers* took two full

FIGURE 4.3

Words Derived from *Vert, Vers*.

Forms	Combined with *vert, vers*
ab- (a-, abs-) "away from"	avert, aversion
ad- (ac-, af-, ag-, al-, ap-, ar-, as-, at-) "towards," "to," "near"	adverse, adversity, adversary, advertise
circum- "around," "about"	
com- (co-, col-, con-, cor-) "with," "together," "fully"	convert, conversion, converse, conversation
contra- (contro-) "against," "opposite"	controversy, controversial
de- "down," "down from," "away from," "apart"; "to make opposite," "reverse"	
dis- (di-) "apart," "aside"; "to reverse," "remove," "undo"	diversity, diversify, diverse, divert
e- (ex-) "out of," "out," "from"	
extra- (extro-) "outside," "beyond"	extrovert
in- (il-, im-, ir-) "not" [in- #1]	irreversible
in- (il-, im-, ir-) "in," "into," "within" [in- #2]	inverse, inverted
inter- "between," "among"	
intra- (intro-) "within," "inward"	introvert
ob- "against," "opposite," "to"	obverse
per- "thoroughly," "intensely," "through"	perverted, perversion, pervert, perverse
pre- "before," "earlier"	
pro- "for," "forward," "in place of"	
post- "after," "behind"	
re- "again," "back"	reverse, revert, reversion, reversal
sub- (sup-, sus-) "below," "under," "from below"	subvert, subversive
super- "above," "upon," "over"	
trans- "across"	transverse

forty-five-minute periods. The third meeting of the week for Elaine's class was a double period. For that meeting, we gave the class another Latin root to work on: *spec/spic/spect*, from the Latin verbs *specere* and *spectare*, which mean "see" or "watch." The students quickly formed into working groups, and we made it a competition to see which group could identify and define the most derived words.

This root yields an impressive array of widely used and significant English words; I was amazed at the connections I found when I first examined it. Using their dictionaries and the prefix sheet, Elaine's students found a wealth of important words, with the winning group coming up with forty-one. Here are the significant simple words they found: *special, specific, specify, specimen, specious, spectacle, spectacular, spectator, specter, spectrum*, and *speculate*. Here are the derived words, arranged according to the prefix list: *aspect, circumspect, despicable, despise, despite, disrespect, expect, inconspicuous, inspect, introspection, perspective, prospect, respect, retrospect* (an addition to the prefix list), *suspect* and *suspicious*. The list doesn't add up to forty-one because I have omitted suffixed forms like *inspector, introspective*, and so on.

Students found most of these relatively easy to define with the root meaning "see" or "watch" or with some word that clearly involves seeing. In addition to clear and basic definitions, they produced several that show a high degree of personal understanding: to be *circumspect* is "to view from all sides"; something *conspicuous* is "easily noticeable"; to *inspect* is "to look into something thoroughly"; to be *introspective* is "to look into one's mind"; something *special* is "something that's not seen every day" because there's "nothing that looks like it"; something *specious* "looks good, but isn't."

These last two words bring up a significant issue. Some of these words, especially the ones without prefixes, have undergone semantic development so that their connection to their original root meaning is no longer clearly apparent. Their meanings have become general and abstract and are no longer limited to concrete, physical actions. The *AHD* defines *special, species, specific, specimen*, and *specious* without reference to actual, physical seeing, and one could argue that definitions of these words in terms of their root meaning are too limited in scope. I concede that such definitions can be too limited, but I don't think they distort the meanings of the words. As just indicated, Elaine's students defined *special* and *specious* in ways that demonstrate a clear understanding of the basic concepts, even though one can judge something as *special* or *specious* without looking at it physically. Their definitions of the other three words are also accurate, if somewhat limited: They defined *species* as something that "looks the same as its close relations"; *specific* as "having a definite appearance"; and *specimen* as "something closely observed." These could be sharpened and refined—that's why sharing and class discussion are important—but they're pretty accurate already. In their scientific uses, at least, both *species* and *specimen* do involve physical forms and meticulous physical viewing.

Although I want to alert you to this problem, I still strongly advocate the practice of asking students to use root meanings in their definitions. This practice can help students better understand abstract intellectual terms by showing them the concrete, physical meanings those words originally had. In discussing such words with a class, a teacher can point out how most of the words for mental operations have their origins in the physical world. In Elaine's class, for instance, we brought up the words *see* and *grasp* for discussion. The class could readily see that these words, which can be used literally to express concrete and physical actions, are used as metaphors for the intellectual process of *comprehension* (a word that also happens to be a physical metaphor for a mental action). Hence, in comparing root meanings with current meanings, the students became aware of the semantic process called "metaphorical extension of meaning." This process goes on all around us: Tables have *legs*; rivers have *mouths*; computer language depends on physical metaphors to make complex technical and mental processes understandable. Elaine's class found other good examples of the process in discussing the words *perspective* and *spectrum*. These words had given most of them trouble. During the class discussion, students familiar with art were able to define *perspective* in concrete, physical terms as "seeing and showing something in three dimensions, seeing all the way through it." The class was then able to understand more generalized and abstract uses of the word *perspective*: *To put something in perspective* is "to see it in all its dimensions, to see the full picture." Students familiar with physics had defined a *spectrum* as "the band of colors visible to the human eye." In the class discussion, students could see how that physical image has been extended metaphorically in such common phrases as *broad spectrum of opinion*.

Because there were still a few minutes left in the double period, I thought I would challenge Elaine's class by seeing if they could find the common Indo-European root behind a group of words that look totally unrelated. I gave them the cluster of words derived from the Indo-European root *bha-2*, the cluster I worked through earlier in this chapter. They guessed the root meaning, "say" or "speak," in, quite literally, one minute, and they were busily whipping through the list, defining the words in terms of this root meaning, when the period came to an end. Any feeling I had that working with Indo-European roots might be too difficult for high school students was effectively shattered.

I felt Elaine's class did a terrific job, especially since they'd never done this activity before. Now that I've had a chance to analyze what they wrote, I can identify several things I'd want to stress in follow-up lessons. First of all, I'd want to give students more practice in combining the meanings of both parts of a word: the prefix and the root. Students tend to apply the root meaning rather creatively, and to ignore the way that meaning is limited and directed by the prefix. For example, several students defined *advertise* as "to change people's minds about what they will buy." That sounds plausible enough and has the root meaning right in it, but it's not an accurate definition. It ignores the meaning of the prefix *ad-* ("to"). What an *advertisement* does is "*turn* attention *to* a product."

A second common problem involves not checking on the word's actual derivation. Creative students can work a root meaning into the definition of any word, whether it has any historical reason for being there. Elaine's students were especially creative in working with words from *spec/spic/spect*. They defined *speck* as "barely visible"—a good definition, but a lucky accident, because *speck* comes from an Old English word and is not derived from Latin *spec*. *Speck* is a classic example of a "false cognate," a word that looks as if it derives from a certain root but actually doesn't. Elaine's students were even more creative when they defined *aspic* as "a garnish to make salads look good." I really enjoy this one, but it's just a clever guess. If the students had looked up the word's real origin, they would have discovered that it derives from *aspis*, the Latin word for an asp.

These are problems that all groups experience when learning this activity. These rough spots can be ironed out in time, as students get more practice. As students become more proficient at this activity, I also recommend nudging them to write more extended definitions, full-sentence definitions that clearly illustrate what a word means. At first, classes tend to stop at basic, minimal definitions. In Elaine's class, for instance, most students defined an *extrovert* as "a person turned outward" and left it at that. I'd push students to extend this kind of definition and illustrate it like this: "An extrovert is a person turned outward, towards other people; an extrovert is usually the life of the party." This is the form I'd work toward: a general statement, followed by a specific example. Several of Elaine's students were clearly trying to make their definitions more specific but got stuck between a general statement and a specific example, as in this definition of *conversion:* "a change in which one adopts a new religion." In a subsequent lesson,

I'd try to help a student who wrote such a definition to separate it into two parts: "A *conversion* involves a full or complete change from one thing to another, as when a person converts to a new religion." Writing a definition in terms of the root meaning is really only a first step toward mastering a word. The next step is using the definition in a meaningful sentence. A student who can do that has gone a long way toward owning the word.

Studying a single root in such detail takes a good deal of class time—Elaine's class needed most of two forty-five-minute periods. Hence, after investigating many Latin roots in this way, I assembled a list of Fifteen Common Latin Roots which I recommend for detailed study. I've rejected some common roots because they proved too confusing to explore; if I had difficulty with them, I assumed that students would as well. Others I rejected because studying them yields insight into only a few significant English words. The roots I chose give students access to large groups of significant words, and shouldn't present an average secondary English class with overwhelming problems. These roots are challenging, but reasonably so. The list (Figure 4.4) is ranked in order of how many significant words the study of the root can involve.

I have provided a lot of variant forms so that students will have better luck finding derivatives. I've also listed infinitives (which end in *-re* or *-i*) and, when relevant, past participles (which end in *-us*) to answer the question students most often ask: Why does the same root have more than one form, as with *vert* and *vers*? The most common answer is that the present and past systems of Latin verbs often had different consonant stems, and words could be derived from either stem: *vert* is from the present system, and *vers* is from the past. Other variant spellings of a root usually reflect the fact that some Latin words entered English via French. Latin words with *ten* or *tin* kept their Latin spellings when they were borrowed directly into English, but they were spelled *tein* (later *tain*) in French; thus, English words spelled with *-tain* must have been borrowed from French, not directly from Latin. These are fairly abstruse matters, and there's no real need to bring them up until or unless students ask about them.

There are, of course, other Latin roots that a class can explore with profit, but working with any one of these fifteen in Figure 4.4 should provide students with a productive experience. It will increase their store of significant words, although that is not my sole aim. I believe students learn the most from this activity when they write definitions using the root meaning. As they struggle to write their definitions, they learn much more than the meanings of individual words; they learn how to write and think with increased precision.

FIGURE 4.4
Fifteen Common Latin Roots

Forms	Sources	Meanings
1. spec, spic, spect	*specere* or *spectāre*	"look at," "see"
2. vers, vert	*vertere, versus*	"turn," "change"
3. mov, mot, mob	*movēre, mōtus*	"move"
4. pon, pos, poun	*pōnere, positus*	"place," "put"
5. ced, cess, ceas	*cēdere, cessus*	"go," "yield"
6. cap, capt, cept, cip, ceive	*capere, captus, -cipere, -ceptus*	"take," "seize"
7. mitt, mit, mis, miss	*mittere, missus*	"send," "let," "go"
8. duc, duct	*dūcere, ductus*	"lead," "draw out"
9. tract	*trahere, tractus*	"pull," "drag"
10. vis, vist, vid, view	*vidēre, vīsus,* or *vīsitāre*	"see"
11. ten, tain, tin	*tenēre*	"hold," "hold on to"
12. scrib, script	*scrībere, scrīptus*	"write"
13. voc, vocat	*vocāre, vocātus*	"call," name"
14. plic, pli, ply, play, ploy	*plicāre*	"weave," "fold," "bend"
15. grad, gred, gress	*gradi, gressus*	"step," "walk"

© 2001 by Thomas Carnicelli from *Words Work*. Portsmouth, NH: Heinemann.

Latin Roots Across the Curriculum

When I was in high school, I studied a broad range of different subjects, which remained entirely separate in my mind. I never thought to make connections between them. Each subject had its own key terms, and I duly memorized a definition particular to that subject. I never noticed that these terms might be related to terms in other fields. In biology, I memorized the definition of *organism* as "a living thing," but I had no idea why that strange and foreign term was used, and I never noticed how similar it was to *organ* or *organize* or even *organic*. I know that my secondary experience is still the

FIGURE 4.5
Key Words from Common Roots

spec/spic/spect "see," "look at"	aspect, introspection, perspective, species, specimen, specious, spectrum
vert/vers "turn," "change"	controversial, diversion, extrovert, introvert, universal, verse, vertebra, vertebrate, vertex, vertical
mov/mot/mob "move"	emotion, mob, mobility, mobilize, momentum, motivate, motive, motor, promotion, remote
pon/pos/pound "put," "place"	appositive, component, composition, compound, deposit, exponent, positive, preposition, proposition, transpose
ced/cess/ceas "go," "yield"	access, cede, concede, concession, excessive, incessant, precedent, predecessor, procedure, process, processor, recession, succession
cap/cip/capt/cept/ceive "take," "seize"	capacity, capability, caption, concept, conception, contraceptive, inception, incipient, perceive, perception, precept, preconception
mitt/mit/miss/mis "send," "let," "go"	commission, commitment, emission, intermittent, missile, mission, premise, remission, submissive, submit, surmise
duc/duct "lead," "draw out"	conducive, deduce, deduction, duct, ductile, duke, educate, inductive, product, reduce

norm, and now that I've seen what the study of etymology can do, I can only say, "What a wasted opportunity!"

The study of root meanings can help students better understand unfamiliar terms, but it can do much more: It can help students make conceptual connections between disparate fields of knowledge. In studying the root *vert/vers*, Elaine's class discovered connections between literature (*verse*), geometry (*vertex, vertical*), political history (*controversy, subversive*), psychology (*extrovert, introvert*), and biology (*vertebra, vertebrate*). Their study of *spec/spic/spect* led them to connections between art (*perspective*), biology

tract "pull," "draw"	abstract, attract, contract, distract, extract, intractable, protractor, subtraction, traction
vis/vist/vid/view "see"	providence, provision, review, revise, television, video, visa, visible, visual
ten/tain/tin "hold," "hold on to"	abstinence, content, continent, continual, continue, detention, entertain, maintain, pertinent, sustain, tenable, tenacious, tenant, tenet, tenor, tenure
scrib/script "write"	conscription, describe, inscription, manuscript, postscript, prescription, scribe, script, scripture, subscribe, transcript
voc/vocat "call," "name"	advocate, evoke, invocation, provocation, revoke, vocabulary, vocal, vocation, voice, vowel
plec/plic/pli/play/ploy "weave," "fold," "bend"	apply, complicated, duplicate, employ, explicit, implication, implicit, imply, inexplicable, multiple, multiply, pleat, pliable, pliers, plywood, replica
grad/gred/gress "step," "walk"	aggression, congress, digression, grade, gradient, gradual, graduate, ingredient, progress, progression, regression, transgression

(*species*, *specimen*), psychology (*introspection*), and physics (*spectrum*). In choosing my fifteen most useful Latin roots, I was constantly surprised by the unsuspected connections I found between terms in widely separated fields. All of the fifteen yield large numbers of common and useful words, but I focus here on what I call Key Words, words that students would be likely to encounter in studying a specific school subject and/or in their reading of intellectually challenging discourse (Figure 4.5). In listing these so-called Key Words, I make no claim to inclusiveness; I merely want to demonstrate the wide range of connections the study of a common root can reveal. For the sake of providing a complete and usable list, I repeat the words derived from *vert-/vers-* and *spec-/spic-/spec*.

Although I think of this list as a guide to help teachers decide what roots they want their classes to study in depth, I can also imagine times when a teacher might want to use just these clusters of related words. If, for instance, I were teaching literature to a class dominated by scientific and technical types, I might want to give the class the cluster derived from *mov/mot/mob*. We could then explore the connections between *motors* and *motives*, between *emotion* and *momentum*. The advantage of giving students clusters of related words to explore is that it encourages them to move from the known to the new. They will surely know some of the words in a given cluster, and they can use those familiar words to make sense out of words they don't yet know. If, for instance, a student happens to be familiar with the word *detention*, that student may easily see how the root meaning "hold" applies to it: A student in detention is "held away" from other activities. With this concrete example of how the root meaning applies to a familiar word, the student can then be led to apply the root meaning to other words in the cluster—first to familiar ones, such as *continue* or *tenant*, then to less common ones, such as *tenacious* or *pertinent*.

There's no limit to what you can do in using these clusters of common roots to bring different worlds together. If a student doesn't understand what an *implication* is, surely that student will know some word from the *plec/plic/pli/ply* cluster. How about *plywood* or *pleats* (or even *two-ply* toilet paper)? All of these words derive from the same root, which means "weave," "fold," "bend." The basic idea is folding something so that it has a layer hidden inside. In a pleat, a single piece of cloth is doubled over, and then sewn shut. Plywood is not literally folded, but it is made up of hidden, inside layers. An implication is like a pleat or a piece of plywood in that it, too, involves a hidden layer. An implication is a meaning hidden beneath the surface meaning of a statement. The implicit meaning, the meaning "folded inside," is on the second or hidden layer. If someone wants to identify and talk about that meaning, they make it *explicit* or "unfolded." Two-ply toilet paper has a hidden layer, too, just like plywood, but, as a teacher, I think I'd try the pleats and plywood first and save the toilet paper analogy for emergencies.

I first became aware of the power of a common root to connect disparate fields of study when I was in a full faculty workshop at a local high school. The topic was how to teach specialized vocabulary words in the various subjects. Somehow, the word *integer* came up, and a math teacher duly defined it as "a whole number." Then, someone asked why a whole number was called an *integer*. Nobody could answer until, lo and behold, a Latin teacher spoke up and provided the root meaning of the term: *integer* derives from Latin *in-*, meaning "not," and a form of *tangere*, meaning "to touch"; thus, an integer is "untouched, intact, whole." What followed then was quite remarkable. A social studies teacher made a connection to the process of *integration* in American society. Then, an English teacher made a connection to *integrity* as an ideal of human behavior. Finally, somebody mentioned "The Untouchables," a popular television program starring incorruptible federal revenue officers during the Prohibition era. From math to Latin to social studies to English to popular culture—all in a single bound! We all learned from this experience, and we vowed to be more alert to the common root meanings that terms in disparate fields may share.

That habit of alertness is, of course, precisely what I want to advocate. Teachers who notice the similar forms of words and have the curiosity to look up their root meanings will be able to help their students make the exciting connections between subjects that I never even thought to make as a secondary student. Such connections can be made whenever an opportunity arises: When a term with a common root comes up, an alert teacher can pounce on it and get the students to make connections to other terms in other fields. Systematic study of roots and related words is fine and good, but so is taking advantage of "teachable moments."

Getting to the Root of Problem Words

I conclude this chapter on etymology by discussing a few common school words that usually cause students a great deal of trouble: *affect/effect*, *analyze*, and *imply/infer*. A little etymological knowledge may help students get a better grasp (note the physical metaphor!) of these troublesome terms. The most common problem with *affect/effect* is using *effect* for *affect* as a verb, as in, "The experience effected me greatly." A way to combat this mistake is to stress the root meanings of the prefixes in each case: *ad-*, *af-* means "to" while *ex-*, *ef-* means "from" or "out of." Both *affect* and *effect* come from Latin *facere*, meaning "do" and "make." Thus, using the root meanings of both prefixes and root, we can define *affect* as "do something to" and *effect* as "make something from" or "cause." With these etymological definitions in mind, students should be able to correct the sample sentence to either "The experience affected me greatly" or "The experience effected a big change in my attitude." I'm not saying this problem will disappear overnight, but an etymological approach is certain to help.

Students often seem a little intimidated by the words *analyze* and *analysis*. These words can sound foreign, technical, and difficult. Their root meaning, however, is concrete and familiar: Both words derive from the Greek verb *analuein*, which means "unloosen" or "untie." Thinking of *analysis* as untying or untwisting a knot or cord is a good way to visualize the process. I like to explain it further by asking students to examine a piece of twine. A piece of ordinary twine looks like a single strand of fiber, but when it is examined and untwisted, it is found to be two or more strands twisted together. This process of untwisting is the process of analysis: We break something into its component parts to better understand it. In practice, the terms *analyze* and *analysis* are often used rather loosely in school assignments. "Analyze the major causes of the Civil War" is somewhat illogical: It's the Civil War that is being analyzed; the causes are to be identified through analysis. Thus, "Identify the major causes" would be better, but best of all, I think, would be a simple, direct question: "What were the major causes of the Civil War?" I always opt for the direct question over the abstract description of the intellectual process. The student who writes a careful answer to "What's the best way to re-paint a car?" is writing a *process analysis* without even knowing it.

As just mentioned, the words *explicit*, *implicit*, and *imply* all have the common root *plec/plic/pli/ply*, which means "fold" or "weave." To *imply* something is to "fold" or "weave" it into a statement, to suggest it rather than state it directly. An *implicit* meaning is "folded into" a statement. If that meaning is made *explicit*, it is "unfolded" and stated directly. These words and concepts can be made clear to most students. The problem arises when describing the process of making implicit meanings explicit. The adjectives *implicit* and *explicit* are a perfect pair of opposites: One means "folded in" and the other means "unfolded." There is, however, no perfect opposite for the verb *imply*. If I *imply* something, or "fold it in" to my statement, you can't *exply* it, or "unfold it," because there is no such verb as *exply* in English. We do have *explicate*, which is close but not the logical opposite of *imply*. The logical opposite of *imply* is the verb *infer:* I imply something, and you infer it; I fold it in, and you draw it out.

The words *imply* and *infer* are exact opposites in meaning, yet no two words are more frequently confused. People are always using *infer* when they mean *imply*. And why wouldn't they? *Infer* starts with the prefix *in-*; it looks as if it should mean "put in." How can a word beginning with *in-* come to mean "draw out?" The etymology of the word provides a likely answer. In the Latin verb *inferre*, which means "bring in" or "carry in," the underlying image seems to be that of bringing something into the mind or, perhaps, of bringing something into the open, where it can be subject to the mind's scrutiny. So, it's a matter of bringing something hidden *into the open* rather than bringing something *out of hiding*. I know full well that *infer* will continue to be confused with *imply*, but sorting out their very different root meanings may help students use them more accurately.

Although I've focused on learning a few specific words here at the end, ones that produce endless problems for students and teachers, I hope I've made it clear that my approach to teaching etymology is not simply a way for students to learn more words. I want students to increase their vocabularies, but I also want them to increase their writing and thinking skills at the same time.

5
Native Words and French–Latin Loan Words
Seeing the Differences

The English vocabulary is made up of *native words*, words that have been part of English since its Indo-European beginnings, and *loan words*, words borrowed into English from some other language. The most common sources of loan words into English have been French and Latin. Because it's often difficult to know whether a word was borrowed directly from Latin or from Latin by means of French, scholars tend to classify all loan words from these sources as simply *French–Latin loan words*, and this is the term I use throughout this book.

These two main types of words tend to have different qualities. Native words tend to be short, concrete, and familiar to all users of English, regardless of social or educational status. They tend to name physical things that are actually perceptible by the senses. If they do name internal, nonphysical things, they name the most basic of human emotions and attitudes. Native words are the bedrock of the English vocabulary; they name the basic elements of our common human experience:

Parts of the body: *head, hand, foot, eye, mouth*
Family members: *mother, father, son, daughter, wife*
Basic activities: *eat, drink, sleep, speak, think, laugh*
Basic qualities: *hot, cold, light, dark, good, evil*
Basic emotions: *love, hate, sorrow, hope, fear*
The natural world: *earth, land, sea, sun, wind, rain*

French–Latin loan words in English come in all shapes and sizes. Some of them look and act just like native words. With a little effort, I've been able to find a short, familiar French–Latin loan word for each of the previous categories:

Parts of the body: *face, stomach*
Family members: *aunt, uncle, cousin, niece, nephew*

84

Basic activities: *move, turn, touch, cry, try*
Basic qualities: *large, brief, fresh, clear, plain, simple*
Basic emotions: *pain, pleasure, joy, grief*
The natural world: *air, plant, flower, branch*

The fact that French–Latin loan words are used for such basic things shows how thoroughly they have been integrated into the English vocabulary. Still, this list is a bit of an aberration. The most important French–Latin loan words in English are not short, basic, and familiar; they tend to be just the opposite. They tend to be longer, usually two or more syllables in length. They tend to refer to nonphysical things, to mental operations and complex emotions, to abstract ideas, to things created by the human mind, rather than to natural facts. If native words tend to name basic things, French–Latin words name special things, for example *banquets* (French–Latin), not just *meals* (nat.). Many French–Latin words are not commonly used in ordinary speech, and are not generally familiar to people with little formal education. Here's a much more typical list of French–Latin loan words, classified in terms of the things they name:

Mental operations: *analyze, communicate, compare, contrast, decision, define, express, imagination, intelligence, introspection, interpret, logic, reason, rational*
Emotions and attitudes: *affection, anxiety, belligerent, charity, compassion, conservative, curiosity, envious, excitement, gracious, jealousy, sympathetic*
Social and political institutions: *administration, citizen, congress, democracy, economy, executive, government, judicial, nation, organization, public, society, state*
Cultural forms and activities: *art, college, culture, curriculum, discipline, education, history, language, literature, mathematics, music, painting, poetry, science, university*
Abstract ideas: *beauty, class, complexity, diversity, equality, essential, honor, ideal, integrity, justice, maturity, moderation, patriotism, sophistication, style, unity*

This list could be extended indefinitely. Obviously, we couldn't say very much about our thoughts and feelings or about the complex modern world in which we live if we didn't have access to French–Latin loan words.

Native and French–Latin words tend to be used in different areas of experience, but there's still a good deal of overlap between them. Often, a native and a French–Latin word are very similar in meaning, and the language offers us a choice between them: Do we choose native *ask* or French–Latin *inquire*, native *find* or French–Latin *discover*, native *wish* or French–Latin *desire*? In such cases, an experienced writer or speaker chooses on the basis of tone. In general, one can say that native words tend to be down to earth and ordinary in tone, while French–Latin words have a more special, more formal tone. If you are talking or writing casually to a known audience, you tend to use an ordinary style or register. (Remember, a *register* is a style appropriate to a specific audience and occasion.) An ordinary style has a larger percentage of native words. If you are making a speech on a special occasion, or writing about a serious subject for an educated audience, you will choose to use a more formal style or register. A formal style of English has a larger percentage of French–Latin words.

In the next four chapters, I offer a variety of activities designed to make students aware of the importance and distinctive features of native and French–Latin words. In the next three chapters, the focus is on writing style. The activities in Chapters 6 and 7 ask students to explore the properties of native words; those in Chapter 8 focus on the value of a balanced style, a style that combines the best features of both native words and French–Latin loan words. Finally, in Chapter 9, the two types of words are discussed in a larger context; I set forth a series of inquiries that will help students explore how native and French–Latin words are used to express important cultural values in American society.

These four chapters are essentially independent of each other; any one of them can be taught by itself. I have, in fact, taught each of them separately. To do so, however, I needed to provide some kind of basic introduction to what native and French–Latin words are. Here are some things I recently tried with both Elaine Burnham's and Donna Bakke's senior English classes. I began with the handout shown in Figure 5.1.

I started with the translation of the Pledge of Allegiance into French to startle the students into realizing how deeply French–Latin words are interwoven into the English language. It's quite easy to translate the Pledge into French, because all of the French–Latin words in the Pledge still exist in modern French, with the sole exception of *plege*, which existed in Old French but is apparently no longer used. When the students compared the French and English versions of the Pledge, they were surprised to see that they could actually read the French almost as well as the English version. They lost the feeling that French is a totally "foreign" language. When the

FIGURE 5.1
Native Words and French–Latin Loan Words: A First Look

Je plege allegeance au drapeau des Etats-Unis de l'Amerique, et a la republique qu'il represente, une nation, sous Dieu, indivisible, avec liberte et justice pour tous.

I pledge allegiance to the flag of the United States of America, and to the republic for which it stands, one nation, under God, indivisible, with liberty and justice for all.

Substitutions. Try to find native substitutes for the French–Latin words.

I _____ to the flag of the _____ of America, and to the _____ for which it stands, one _____, under God, _____, with _____ and _____ for all.

Translations.

I. Translate these sentences into something more clear and concrete.

    1. Johnny exhibits aggressive behavior in interactions with his peers.
    Trans.: Johnny bites and spits on the other children.

    2. James needs to improve his proficiency in the area of language arts.
    Trans.:

    3. John has difficulty recognizing the property rights of other individuals.
    Trans.:

    4. Although not always appreciated by the students, the cafeteria food is nutritionally sound.
    Trans.:

    5. Where volition exists, a mode of operation will be discovered.
    Trans.:

II. Translate these sentences into more formal language.

    6. The bride wore good clothes.
    Trans.: The bride was dressed in an elegant white gown.

    7. On an application for college or a job: I like to play games.
    Trans.:

    8. The North beat the South in the big fight at Gettysburg.
    Trans.:

    9. Sarah was always good at school, and she got a prize when she got done.
    Trans.:

    10. Women, rub this cream on your armpits, and you won't sweat so much.
    Trans.:

---

students tried to find native substitutes for the French–Latin words, they really struggled. This was the best effort:

> I give my heart to the flag of the land of America, and to the _____ for which it stands, one homeland, under God, unbreakable, with freedom and rights for all.

In their first efforts, the students tended to use other French–Latin words, such as *pay homage, joined sections, authority,* and *realm,* but we made them check word origins in the class dictionaries. The students liked some of their translations, and so do I: "give my heart" instead of "pledge allegiance" is forceful and dignified; "freedom" and "liberty" are certainly comparable; the original "justice" is a noble abstraction, but the more specific "rights" is powerful, too. The students saw "unbreakable" as less successful; it's a bit too homely and concrete, and it doesn't capture the idea of division in "indivisible." The students admitted defeat when it came to "United States," "republic," and "nation." These words are particularly difficult to translate because they name institutions, not people or natural objects. I told the students that French–Latin words are commonly used to name social, political, and educational institutions and that those institutions in turn tend to rely on French–Latin words in their formal, or "official," statements. I wanted the students to begin to connect French–Latin words with public, not personal, language.

I wanted to continue to stress that connection in the first set of translation sentences. The first four of these "flowery" sentences are the kind of palliatives that often appear on school report cards. They are official school jargon—"educationese." The students had fun cutting through them to hidden facts. Here's a sampling of their efforts: for Item 2: "James can't read and write," "James needs to learn to read and write better," and, of course, "James sucks at English;" For Item 3, translations were "John steals things," "John takes things without asking," and "John steals from other kids" (*kids,* from Old Norse, is not strictly native, but I let it pass). For Item 4, responses were "The food stinks, but it's healthy," "The kids hate the cafeteria food even though it's good for them," and "The cafeteria food is good for you, but kids hate it." Sentence 5 is a French–Latin version of the all-native proverb, "Where there's a will, there's a way." Students figured this one out, but it did take a bit of prodding. I like to use proverbs as examples of the clear, concise writing that a use of native words can produce. Because I use some proverbs in Chapter 6, I thought I'd introduce one here.

After letting the students have some fun with inept or dishonest uses of French–Latin words, I tried to turn the tables with the second set of translation sentences. In these, the original, all-native sentences are crude and inept, and the students needed to use French–Latin words to improve them. In Item 7, I specify a situation in which a certain amount of formality is definitely called for. Here are two of the better translations: "I enjoy participating in several sports," and "I participate in many extracurricular activities, particularly sports." In Item 8, I wanted to introduce an issue that I develop further in Chapter 9, the rhetoric of war, that is, the heavy use of French–Latin words to give dignity and stature to warfare. Obviously, the native words *beat* and *big fight* make the Civil War sound like a schoolyard rumble. Here are two of the more interesting translations: "The Union conquered the Confederacy in the battle of Gettysburg," and "The North defeated the South in a tremendous battle at Gettysburg." As written, sentence 9 shows little respect for or understanding of what Sarah achieved. A more serious and dignified statement would be more appropriate. The translations rely heavily on French–Latin words, sometimes a little too heavily: "Sarah was rewarded for her scholastic achievements," "Sarah was an excellent student, and she received an award when she graduated," and "Sarah was an exceptional student, and she received an honorable award for her triumphant success." Sentence 10 would get someone fired very quickly from an advertising agency. A little euphemism is clearly in order to disguise the gross physical facts. Here are some of the more interesting translations: "Ladies, apply this underarm deodorant, and it will prevent perspiration," "Ladies, this sensual deodorizing cream absorbs your perspiration and leaves you feeling fresh and clean," and "Apply this cream gently to your underarms to eliminate excessive perspiration." All of these translations rely heavily on French–Latin words: *absorb, apply, deodorant, deodorizing, eliminate, excessive, fresh, gently, perspiration, prevent,* and *sensual*. It's interesting to note that *underarm* is a native softening of the crude native term *armpit*, and that the second translation chooses to omit mention of the offending body part entirely.

Working with this handout took each of the two classes a full fifty-minute class period. They spent the time writing and then sharing and discussing what they had written. I felt this handout worked quite well as an introduction to the two main types of English words. It gave students a chance to explore language alternatives actively by doing some register-shifting on the ten sample sentences. As they worked on the sentences, they got a good sense of the tonal differences between the two types of words, and they were introduced to various areas in which the choice between the two is a significant issue. Finally, the classes enjoyed working with the sample sentences and were ready to explore native and French–Latin words further.

After this introduction, Donna's class moved directly to the activity described in Chapter 6. Because I had more time available in Elaine's class, I decided to try one more introductory activity before moving on. I wrote up three different versions of a job application letter, one using all-native words (Item 1); one using all French–Latin words, except for grammatical fillers (Item 2); and one using a balanced mixture of the two types (Item 3) (see Figure 5.2). I tried to say exactly the same thing in each letter. The only differences between them are in style or register, in the kinds of words used.

The students' reactions to these three letters were extremely interesting. The great majority chose the writer of the third letter as the person they would hire. A few chose the writer of the second letter, and none chose the writer of the first letter. The reasons the students gave were quite revealing.

Students felt that the writer of the first letter, the all-native letter, was "a kind, good person" who would be a "good worker," but they didn't care for the letter; they called it "too abrupt," "plain," "brief," "very short, simple," "weak," and "vague." I find the term *vague* particularly intriguing because the content of this letter is just the same as that of the other two; none of them is more specific than the other.

Two students said they would hire the writer of the second, all French–Latin letter. One said that the writer is "very good with words" but is "conceited"; rather than being turned off by the writer's tone, this student was impressed by the writer's self-confidence: "He/she thinks that he/she is the best, and I would like to see it." The other student who chose the writer of the second letter felt that "this person said all they wanted to, and got it across professionally." On the other hand, the great majority of the students felt the style of the second letter was simply "too formal." While they acknowledged that the writer has "an education" and "a good vocabulary," they felt that the writer uses "too many big words." One student said that the style makes the writer "almost snooty." Another felt that the letter sounds as if the writer "was using a thesaurus for every other word," while a third said that the writer "could be a little friendlier and sound more like a real person than a robot."

In responding to the first letter, most students liked the person, but found the style too informal for the occasion. In responding to the second letter, most students found the style too formal and not personal enough. The majority found the third letter "just right," "not too plain and not too

FIGURE 5.2
Which of These Candidates Would You Hire, and Why?

---

1. I'm a good worker. I come in on time every day, and I'm almost never out sick. I do my work carefully and well, never taking short cuts. I want things done right. I will be leaving here with good will on both sides. My boss understands why I have to leave, and she thanked me for telling her ahead of time. She also said she'll be sorry to see me go, and that she'll have a hard time finding someone else. I know you'll be glad if you hire me. I'm a good worker, and I won't let you down.

2. I have an excellent record as an employee. I am extremely reliable; I'm always punctual and rarely absent. I am meticulous in completing assigned tasks, never resorting to expedients. I insist on perfection. I'll be departing from my present position on amicable terms. My supervisor respects my reasons for pursuing a change, and she appreciates the fact that I gave her ample advance notice. She informed me that she is accepting my resignation with regret, and that she expects to have difficulty replacing me. If you decide to offer me a position, I'm sure you won't regret it. I'm an effective employee, and I won't disappoint you.

3. I have an excellent work record. I'm reliable; I come in on time every day, and I'm rarely out sick. I do my work meticulously, never taking short-cuts. I'm a perfectionist. I'm leaving my present position with good will on both sides. My supervisor understands my reasons for leaving, and she appreciates the fact that I gave her plenty of advance notice. She told me that she'll be sorry to see me go, and that she expects to have a hard time replacing me. If you decide to offer me a position, I'm sure you won't regret it. I'm a good employee, and I won't disappoint you.

©2001 by Thomas Carnicelli from *Words Work*. Portsmouth, NH: Heinemann.

formal." They described the writer of the third letter as a real person, but one with something in addition to mere sincerity: "A real down-to-earth person who seems educated"; "The third one was down to earth, got the point across, but wasn't pushy or stuck-up. The person also had a professional approach." One student summed up the three letters with considerable flair: "I would hire the third applicant. The first seems a good candidate for McDonalds, and the second would expect too much salary. The third would be fairly productive and not over-exaggerate."

Reading, responding to, and discussing these three letters took about half of a normal class period. I thought this activity worked quite well as a further introduction to a study of the two main types of English words. It gave students something of a real context in which to judge the effectiveness of different writing styles. It also gave them a good example of the advantages of a balanced style.

These three warm-up activities serve to introduce any one of the following four chapters. Donna's class did the first two warm-ups and moved on to writing an all-native paragraph (Chapter 6). Elaine's class did all three warm-ups and then moved on to comparing words for relationships (Chapter 9), and then to an attempt to rewrite a Frost poem (Chapter 8). The key point is that a class needs some kind of introductory warm-up before exploring any one of the activities described in the next four chapters.

6
An All-Native Style?

T*rying* to write a good descriptive paragraph entirely in native words is an interesting challenge for any writer or class. To create even more of a challenge, one can use the narrow definition of a native word, excluding loans from Old Norse and the early Latin loan words into Old English. I enjoy this challenge, as a writer and as a teacher. I learn something useful from it every time I try it. Students can learn a good deal from it, too, both about the vocabulary of English and about the process of writing.

The best way to find out what this task involves is to try it for one's self, and that's what I intend to do right now. I'll provide a kind of "movie of my mind" as I proceed. I urge you to do the same—record your thinking as you compose an all-native paragraph. You can stop reading right now and start composing, or you can read this account of my composing process first. Either way, I do urge you to try this activity on your own before you try some version of it with a class.

The task is to write a descriptive paragraph, a *good* descriptive paragraph, using only native words. First, I'll need to find a likely subject. As I write, I'm sitting in my study—maybe I can describe it. I make a list of the objects surrounding me and start looking up a few. I know that modern technology is dominated by Greek and Latin derivatives; hence, I fully expected *computer* and *telephone* to be the loan words they are. I am surprised, though, by how many common indoor items have loan words for their names: *chair, desk, lamp, paper, pen, pencil, table*. I think I'll try something that is less modern, less dependent on human inventions. I happen to be looking out the window on a cold March day in Maine. Why don't I just describe what I see? The natural world is not a human creation, and it hasn't changed too much over time. Most of the words we use to describe it *should* be native. I think I'll just describe the scene outside my window, trying to use the words that naturally come to mind. I'll leave out *automobile*.

I'll start by making a list of physical objects and sensations. Here's what I can see and what I would feel if I were outside right now: the sky; the sun, pale and weak; pine trees, shaking in the strong wind; cold air; brown grass; bare ground; dead leaves; one small bird on a branch. This is, obviously, a pretty spare list, but it's a pretty spare scene. If I were to characterize it in a word, I'd call it *bleak*, At this point, I could play it safe and make a paragraph by just stringing this list together with a few fillers and connectors:

> It's a windy day in late March. There's a pale sun in the sky, but the air is still cold and a strong wind is shaking the trees. The grass is brown, and there are dead leaves on the bare ground. There's one small bird on a branch.

My goal, though, is to write a respectable paragraph, not just a shopping list in sentence form. My paragraph is like the first draft of a reluctant student writer. It needs some sentence variety and some verbs other than *is* and *are*. It could also use a few personal touches to give it a human voice. I'll make some changes and additions, nothing fancy. I want to keep the spareness, the bleakness of the actual scene. Here's my first effort at a decent all-native paragraph:

> It's a windy day in late March. There's a pale sun in the sky, but the air is still cold. The wind is blowing strongly, bending and shaking the trees. Now that the snow has gone, I can see the bare ground, the brown grass, and the dead leaves I forgot to rake up last fall. The only living thing out there is one small bird on a branch.

This sounds pretty good to me, but I doubt that it's one hundred percent native. When I get out my dictionary and check, I confirm that most of the words do turn out to be native ones, but not all of them. Four of the words are loan words from Old French: *March, pale, air,* and *branch*. A fifth word, *sky*, was borrowed from Old Norse. Here's the paragraph again, with the loan words in bold type:

> It's a windy day in late **March**. There's a **pale** sun in the **sky**, but the **air** is still cold. The wind is blowing strongly, bending and shaking the trees. Now that the snow has gone, I can see the bare ground, the brown grass, and the dead leaves I forgot to rake up last fall. The only living thing out there is one small bird on a **branch**. (Version 1)

I call this paragraph "version 1" because I'll be working with it from now on. My job now is to keep revising this paragraph until it's all-native and it conveys the impression or mood I want to convey: I feel that this scene is spare and bleak, and I want to convey those qualities to the reader. I'll go sentence by sentence. You learn some interesting things when you look up word origins: *March* comes ultimately from Latin *Mars*, the name of the Roman god of war—an appropriate name for a blustery month. To replace *March*, I'll try *winter*, which I confirm as a native word. I'm not satisfied with *late winter*, though; it's not quite accurate. To me, sitting here in Maine, late March is not quite part of winter; it's a bit closer to early spring. When I confirm that *early* and *spring* are both native words, I decide to try them, at least for a while. They make me uneasy, though; they're not quite bleak enough, and they might raise false hopes. *Early spring* in Maine means cold, occasional snow, and lots and lots of mud. Readers in warmer climes might think of flowers and flocks of chirping birds. Here's the revised paragraph:

> It's a windy day in early spring. There's a **pale** sun in the **sky**, but the **air** is still cold. The wind is blowing strongly, bending and shaking the trees. Now that the snow has gone, I can see the bare ground, the brown grass, and the dead leaves I forgot to rake up last fall. The only living thing out there is one small bird on a **branch**. (Version 2)

The second sentence poses many problems. Several possible substitutes for *pale* turn out to be loan words: *faint* and *feeble* are from Old French; *weak* is from Old Norse. The closest native synonyms are *dim* and *dull*. Both *a dim sun* and *a dull sun* sound a little off to me. I don't really know why—I do know that *dim sun* reminds me of Chinese food, but I doubt that's the whole reason. To me, both *dim* and *dull* focus on lack of light, but I realize that I want to focus more on lack of warmth, on the sun's lack of power to dispel the cold. I think I'll hold off and move on to *the sky*. The only native synonym I can find is *the heavens*, but that sounds ridiculously old-fashioned. I think I'll just drop *sky* entirely—no great loss when I think of it: Where else could the sun be? I'm not making much progress, am I? So far, I've got "There's a ___ sun." Maybe working with the rest of the sentence will help. How frustrating it is not to be able to use *air*! All the other elements, *earth*, *fire*, and *water*, have native names. Why did we need to borrow *air* from French? In any case, we did borrow it, and it is, to be truthful, a richly expressive word. The closest native substitute I can come up with is *weather*, which is obviously a much broader, more general term. *Cold weather* sounds like a weather report; *cold air* we can actually feel. At this point, I'm going to stop dithering and make some decisions. I'm not going to try to replace either *pale* or *sky*, and I'm going to focus more strongly on lack of warmth. Here's the revised sentence, now one hundred percent native, set in the revised paragraph:

> It's a windy day in early spring. The sun is shining, but the sunlight has no warmth to it. The wind is blowing strongly, bending and shaking the trees. Now that the snow has gone, I can see the bare ground, the brown grass, and the dead leaves I forgot to rake up last fall. The only living thing out there is one small bird on a **branch.** (Version 3)

The revised sentence 2 sounds a little stiff to me, but it does convey what I want to convey. On to the last loan word. I can come up with three native substitutes: *bough, limb,* and *twig.* None of these words is quite the right size. I'm looking at a rather small pine tree right outside my window. It has branches that are larger than twigs but smaller than limbs or boughs. I could try to avoid the whole issue and say " in the pine tree by the window," but the dictionary won't let me: *Pine* is from Latin, and *window* is from Old Norse. I could just say "in a tree," but I'd like to be a little more specific. Because the tree is by the house, and *house* happens to be a native word, I guess I'll go with *in the tree by the house.* It's a little wordy, but I like the contrast between the sheltering house and the frigid bird outside it. With this revision added, here, finally, is an all-native revision of the original paragraph:

> It's a windy day in early spring. The sun is shining, but the sunlight has no warmth to it. The wind is blowing strongly, bending and shaking the trees. Now that the snow has gone, I can see the bare ground, the brown grass, and the dead leaves I forgot to rake up last fall. The only living thing out there is one small bird in the tree by the house. (Version 4)

As I step back and look at this paragraph as a whole, I find that I'm still not very happy with it. For the first time, I notice the repetition of *windy* and *wind,* and I don't like it. It doesn't add anything to the description; it just looks careless, and it is. Also, I'm still troubled by the prominent position of *early spring.* It doesn't strike the harsh note I want to start with. I'm not talking about signs of spring; I want to show how bleak and cold the scene really is. As I look over the paragraph, I realize that the key word *cold* has gotten lost in the revision process. To get it back in, and to give it strong emphasis, I'm going to put it in place of *windy* in the first sentence. Then, to give it even more emphasis, I'm going to reinforce it with another short, harsh native word, *raw.* That ought to keep *early spring* from raising any false hopes. With these changes included, here's my final all-native paragraph:

It's a cold, raw day in early spring. The sun is shining, but the sunlight has no warmth to it. The wind is blowing strongly, bending and shaking the trees. Now that the snow has gone, I can see the bare ground, the brown grass, and the dead leaves I forgot to rake up last fall. The only living thing out there is one small bird in the tree by the house. (Version 5)

It's hardly a literary masterpiece, but it's a decent descriptive paragraph. The challenge is over, and I've enjoyed trying to meet it, but trying to write an all-native paragraph is just an exercise; it doesn't necessarily make for better prose. Hence, I think it's important to take this exercise one step farther and try to rewrite the final all-native paragraph *without* the all-native restriction. Here, for instance, is my "best" version of the paragraph, the version I'd choose to write without the restriction.

It's a raw day in late **March**. The sun is shining, but the **air** is still cold. The wind is blowing strongly, bending and shaking the trees. Now that the snow has gone, I can see the bare ground, the brown grass, and the dead leaves I forgot to rake up last fall. The only living thing out there is one small bird in the tree by the **window**. (Version 6)

The paragraph is still heavily native—the subject more or less assures that—but I've put in a few loan words (in bold type) that I want to use. I never really wanted to get rid of *March*, anyway; March is March, not *late winter* or *early spring*, but both at once. In the first sentence of version 5, I used the double adjectives in *cold, raw day* to counteract any positive impressions created by *early spring*. Now that *late March* is back, I feel I can get by with one harsh adjective, *raw*, to set the tone. I can then take *cold* and use it again to describe *the air* that I want to reintroduce in the second half of the second sentence. "The air is still cold" captures the concrete, physical sensation of coldness that I wanted to convey right along; it seems to me much stronger, much more physical, than my rather stilted and abstract "the sunlight has no warmth to it." Finally, I prefer *window* over the native *house* because *window* sharpens the contrast between the two living things: the observer, warm inside, and the small bird, cold outside.

Every time I try this activity, I become excited about its educational value. Both parts of it can have great value for students—both the challenge of trying to write an all-native paragraph and the challenge of trying to explain the choices one makes. The challenge of writing an all-native paragraph can make students aware of the range and "feel" of native words. They can learn that native words tend to be concrete and physical, describing basic elements of the natural world (*sun, wind, trees, snow, ground, grass, leaves*), basic qualities (*cold, raw, strong, small*), basic actions (*see, bend, shake*), the basic conditions of all existence (*dead, living*). Student writers need to discover the strengths of native words, lest they become overly enamored of the academic and abstract. At the same time, the challenge of writing an all-native paragraph will show students the practical impossibility of an all-native style. If the *sky* we live under and the very *air* we breathe are named in loan words, then it's obvious that loan words are part of the very marrow of the English language. Trying to write all-native paragraphs will ultimately lead student writers to increased appreciation for both the native and borrowed elements of the English vocabulary.

The challenge of writing an all-native paragraph can make any writer more thoughtful in choosing words. In doing this exercise, the writer can't merely stick with the first word that comes to mind. If the first word happens to be a loan word, the writer must search for alternatives and choose from them. In pondering alternatives, the writer may decide to reject them, as I rejected *dim* and *dull*, or come up with something better—I came up with the powerful adjective *raw* because the demands of the exercise led me to it.

The second part of the exercise—the attempt to write explanations for one's decisions—reinforces the need for thoughtfulness. Experienced writers tend to make their choices intuitively, but it's a good idea to urge beginning writers to pay more conscious attention to the meanings and tones of words. To do this exercise, a writer must refer to a dictionary all the time, anyway. After checking a word's origin, it's only natural to check out the word's meaning: When I looked up *bough* and *limb*, I realized that they name bigger branches than the one I had in mind. Explaining one's choices leads the writer to think both about each individual word and about the larger context that word is in: My worry that "early spring" could strike too positive a note led me to realize how much I wanted to convey a dominant impression of coldness and bleakness. That realization led me to add two harsh adjectives, *cold* and *raw*, in the first sentence and to recast the second half of sentence 2 entirely. Even though I'm an experienced writer, I felt that I understood my purpose better, and revised my paragraph more effectively, because I was forced to analyze and explain my various choices.

I've analyzed my own experience with this exercise at some length, but, as I said earlier, I do hope that you will try this challenge on your own. By doing so, you can experience the value of this activity for yourself, not just take my word for it.

The ultimate issue is, of course, to get your students to try this activity and learn from it. I have several suggestions for how to do that. You could, of course, simply explain the whole exercise briefly and assign it, but it will work better with a practice activity first. Here's a practice activity that worked quite well with Donna Bakke's senior writing class.

The class had already done several of the general warm-up activities described in Chapter 5; hence, the students had some idea of what native and borrowed words are. I began by giving every student a copy of version 1 of my March scene paragraph, the one with five loan words in it:

> It's a windy day in late **March**. There's a **pale** sun in the **sky**, but the **air** is still cold. The wind is blowing strongly, bending and shaking the trees. Now that the snow has gone, I can see the bare ground, the brown grass, and the dead leaves I forgot to rake up last fall. The only living thing out there is one small bird on a **branch**.

I told them why I'd chosen a natural scene rather than something involving lots of man-made objects, and then I asked them to characterize the scene as I had described it. The general consensus was to call it "dreary." After this brief opening, I asked them to revise the paragraph to make it one hundred percent native. They worked individually, in pairs, or in small groups, using dictionaries to look up word origins or asking me to do it. Meanwhile, I wrote version 1 on the board, with wide spaces between the lines. After about twenty minutes, they had finished their individual revisions, and we were ready to work as a class to produce the best all-native paragraph we could. They made suggestions to replace each loan word, and I wrote these on the board over the loan word in question. The class discussed each possibility, argued for and against it, and eventually reached a consensus.

I'll summarize the discussion by going loan word by loan word. For "March," the class debated between *late winter* and *early spring*. Some said *spring* gives a hopeful or positive impression and that *late winter* is drearier. Others said that early spring is dreary enough in Maine, anyway. For *pale*, either *dim* or *dull* was considered acceptable in both meaning and tone. For *sky, in the heights, over us,* and *overhead* were suggested, with *overhead* getting the nod, because there is no mention of *us* anywhere else in the passage. It was the second part of the second sentence that caused the most problems. Many alternatives were suggested and discussed. One person gave up trying to find a replacement for *sky* and suggested *it's still cold out*. Others offered *the world outside is still cold, the earth is still cold,* and *the breath of mother earth is cold* (later revised to *the earth's breath is cold*). We spent quite a bit of time discussing the image of the earth's breath, but the class finally rejected it on the basis of tone, arguing that this "romantic" and "poetic" metaphor is inconsistent with the concrete and earthy language of the rest of the passage. *The world outside is still cold* was chosen over the simple *it's still cold out*, probably because of its greater concreteness. *Twig, tree,* and *limb* were suggested for *branch,* and the compound *tree-limb* got the most support.

After a long and lively discussion (this was a ninety-minute class period), the students reached a rough consensus on this paragraph:

> It's a windy day in early spring. There's a dull sun overhead, but the world outside is still cold. The wind is blowing strongly, bending and shaking the trees. Now that the snow is gone, I can see the bare ground, the brown grass, and the dead leaves I forgot to rake up last fall. The only living thing out there is one small bird on a tree-limb.

After this version was written on the board, I asked the class to look at it and make any further changes. One student noticed the repetition of *windy* and *wind* and didn't like it. I had to agree. Then the class discussed whether to change one or the other, or both. They decided to keep *wind* because it's the subject of the third sentence. In looking for substitutes for *windy,* they discussed the importance of setting the desired tone right in the first sentence. The first sentence without *windy* is simply, "It's a day in early spring." If that has any tone, it's a positive rather pleasant one. They realized that the paragraph needs a strong adjective right at the start to set the tone of dreariness. After further discussion, a student suggested *raw,* and the class agreed it did the job. So, their final consensus paragraph looked like this:

> It's a raw day in early spring. There's a dull sun overhead, but the world outside is still cold. The wind is blowing strongly, bending and shaking the trees. Now that the snow is gone, I can see the bare ground, the brown grass, and the dead leaves I forgot to rake up last fall. The only living thing out there is one small bird on a tree-limb.

A darn good paragraph, I'd say! To tell the truth, I prefer it to my own: It seems to handle the problems of sentence 2 with much less fuss. I also thought the class discussion went well. The students looked carefully at individual words, but they also stayed focused on the mood and tone of the paragraph as a whole. The reasons for and against individual words were sometimes lost in the give-and-take of the rapid discussion, but the students did get lots of practice comparing alternatives and justifying choices. After this warm-up, I felt that the students were ready to write all-native paragraphs, with accompanying commentary, on their own.

Of course, I had the overwhelming urge to read them the commentary I wrote when I worked through this exercise. I always wish I could take my students inside my own mind as I'm writing, take them right inside the

FIGURE 6.1
Writing an All-Native Paragraph

Objectives: To write a unified, effective descriptive paragraph, using only native words.

To write down your thoughts as you are working through this task, explaining the choices you make and assessing the results. (Directions for this part will be given in parentheses.)

1. Choose something to describe—a scene, an action, a situation. (Why did you choose this topic? Was it a good one to write about?)

2. Make a list of significant details.

3. Think about the general impression you get from what you see. Keep that impression in mind as you write your description.

4. Write a full paragraph, using the words that come naturally to mind.

5. Check the origins of the words and underline any words that are not native. (Write down the origins of all the loan words.)

6. Rewrite the paragraph, sentence by sentence, until it's 100 percent native. (Write down every native word you consider using. Explain why you chose the native words you used in your final paragraph. Explain why you didn't choose the other native words you considered.)

7. After you've written the best all-native paragraph you can, revise it without limiting yourself to native words. Just make it the best paragraph you can. (Compare your "best" paragraph to the all-native paragraph you wrote. Is it better than your all-native one? Why?)

---

writing process and show them how much thought needs to be involved in choosing every single word. I would have read them some of my commentary, but the bell rang—just as well, I suppose. I'm sure they wouldn't have found listening to it as exciting as I found writing it. Students learn a lot more from writing their own paragraphs and commentaries.

To help them in that activity, I developed a detailed set of directions (Figure 6.1). These are rather elaborate, but they can, of course, be simplified as needed.

After the student paragraphs and commentaries are written, they should be shared in some way—read aloud, displayed, maybe even published in some form. However interesting these final products turn out to be, the greatest value of this activity lies in what the students learn about English words and about the process of careful writing.

Applications

1. After you've written an all-native paragraph, try this exercise in reverse. Take your paragraph and try to write it entirely in French–Latin loan words. (Don't count little filler words such as *the, of, in, you,* or *it*—you'll never be able to replace those.) You can try to write a serious paragraph or an outrageous one. You will probably sound ridiculous at times, no matter what you do. Here, for example, is a semi-serious rewrite of version 5 of the paragraph discussed in this chapter:

   > It's a frigid, unpleasant nonnocturnal period at the commencement of the vernal season. The solar rays are evident, but they cannot increase the temperature of the atmosphere. The moving air is gusting vigorously, inclining and agitating the pines. Now that the season of hibernation has passed, I can perceive the exposed soil, the barren lawn, and the faded foliage I neglected to remove the previous autumn. The sole animal in view is an avian creature in the pine by the domicile.

   After you've rewritten your all-native paragraph, answer this question: Which native words were the hardest to replace, and why?

2. In the story "Backward Boy," by Gene Coghlan, a slightly retarded, semi-literate boy named Auber shows a real gift for descriptive writing, even though his grammar and spelling are very rough. Auber's teacher is pleased with his writing and encourages him. Then, one day, Auber's mother, who went to college, tries to "help" her son by writing a paper for him. Auber's teacher is appalled by this paper. Here's the paper: The words are Auber's mother's, and the spelling is Auber's. Why do you think Auber's teacher hated it? What's wrong with it as a description? Try to rewrite it to make it better. Then, discuss your changes in terms of the kinds of words, native or borrowed, you used and omitted.

   Our ranch lies out in the beautiful woods ajacent to the flowery right side of the pitcheresk highway leading west from Wasilla, passing through Bulldozer, and trailing to an end in gorjes Goose Creek Canyon. Our home is a sturdy log structure with quaint dormer windows which overlook the snowy caps of the incomprabel Chucach Mountains. Queenly birches and stately spruce trees form a heavenly hallo around the flower strewn clearing surrounding our modist home. Our life is a marvlously kalidoscoopic bowl of fun and we live every inch of it to the uttermost hilt. We children play in the sparkling waters of our haply gurgling creek among the brilliant-hued rainbow trouts and the shy ferns fringing the sylvan banks . . .

3. **Translating proverbs.** It's interesting to discover how many proverbs, or traditional "words of wisdom," are expressed in an all-native vocabulary. Clearly, the concise, down-to-earth, words have helped to keep these sayings alive for centuries. Here's a handful of all-native proverbs:

Better late than never.
Finders keepers, losers weepers.
Where there's a will, there's a way.
Here today, gone tomorrow.
While there's life, there's hope.
Live and learn.
Many hands make light work.
Out of sight, out of mind.
Still waters run deep.
Where there's smoke, there's fire.

Try translating some of these into French–Latin loan words. Here are sample translations of the first four:

Tardiness is preferable to nonattendance.
Discoverers retainers, misplacers complainers.
Where there's a desire, there's a solution.
Present the current moment, departed the subsequent.

Translate the first four proverbs yourself. Then, go on to translate the entire list, working alone, with a partner, or in a small group. If all of the class members make translations, the final products can be read aloud, compared, and discussed. In the discussion, the class can comment on how well each translation captures the meaning of the original proverb.

4. Writing proverbs. It's always an interesting challenge to create your own all-native proverbs. Although most proverbs are anonymous, some do have recognized authors. Benjamin Franklin (1706–1790) composed or popularized a number of proverb-like sayings that are still familiar today. Not all of them are all-native, but some of the most familiar ones are the following:

> Early to bed and early to rise, makes a man healthy, wealthy, and wise.
> Never leave that till tomorrow, which you can do today.
> God helps them that help themselves.
> A word to the wise is enough.

In writing your own all-native proverbs, you might try some cynical variations of familiar ones:

> Never do today what you might get out of doing tomorrow.
> Early to bed and early to rise, makes a man healthy, wealthy, and dull.
> The early bird gets less sleep.

These are fun to do, but, ultimately, you should try to write something entirely original. If you look carefully at lots of other proverbs, and reflect on your own experience, you should be able to come up with your own "words of wisdom."

7
What Native Words Can Do

The attempt to write an all-native paragraph is just an exercise, an exploration of what native words can and cannot do. Nobody with a real purpose for writing sets out to write an all-native paragraph, or an all-borrowed paragraph. In real writing situations, writers choose their words to suit their subject and their audience; they don't worry about word origins.

Still, although they may not even be aware of word origins, good writers have developed a strong, intuitive sense of the value of native words. Writers with an interest in a simple and direct style are bound to rely heavily on native words. In this chapter, I focus on the two twentieth-century writers who are most commonly associated with such a style; Ernest Hemingway and George Orwell. I look at how these two writers use native words in their own writing, and I illustrate some ways that students can become involved in the study of writing style.

Ernest Hemingway

Although Hemingway's works are no longer as popular as they once were, Hemingway is still an important American author whose books are widely read in American schools. He's also accessible and appealing to secondary students. They're interested in what he has to say about love and courage— two issues of some importance in their own lives—and they're intrigued by the famous "Hemingway style." Looking closely at Hemingway's writing is a good way to introduce students to the study of style in writing.

A good Hemingway story to begin with is "In Another Country." This is a short, appealing story that appears in many popular anthologies. After the students have read the whole story and discussed it, they could take a close look at Hemingway's style. They could start with the wonderful opening paragraph, but I particularly recommend the following passage:

The boys at first were very polite about my medals and asked me what I had done to get them. I showed them the papers, which were written in very beautiful language and full of *fratellanza* [brotherhood] and *abnegazione* [self-denial], but which really said, with the adjective removed, that I had been given the medals because I was an American. After that their manner changed a little toward me, although I was their friend against outsiders. I was a friend, but I was never really one of them after they had read the citations, because it had been different with them and they had done very different things to get their medals. I had been wounded, it was true; but we all knew that being wounded, after all, was really an accident. I was never ashamed of the ribbons, though, and sometimes after cocktail hour, I would imagine myself having done all the things they had done to get their medals; but walking home at night through the empty streets with the cold wind and all the shops closed, trying to keep near the street lights, I knew that I would never have done such things, and I was very much afraid to die, and often lay in bed at night by myself, afraid to die and wondering how I would be when I went back to the front again.

This is vintage Hemingway, but it's a mistake to think of "the Hemingway style" in the abstract. That style is used to reflect the attitudes of literary characters. Many of those characters are similar to one another, and perhaps similar to their creator, but the style of any Hemingway story or novel should be viewed in terms of its function within that specific work. Why is the passage written in this way? What does the style *do* in the story? These are the key questions for this passage, and for any Hemingway passage.

Here's a plausible answer for the extracted passage. Basically, in this passage, native words are used to express truths, while French–Latin words often—not always—are used to express falsehoods. The style relies more heavily on native words as the narrator moves closer to the full truth about himself. At first, the emphasis is on his public honors, which are described in French–Latin loan words: *medals, papers, beautiful language, citations, ribbons*—I'd also include the two Italian words, which I think Hemingway uses to underscore the meaninglessness of all these fancy words. The narrator knows that this "very beautiful language" is really empty rhetoric, because it is not based on real deeds. Throughout the passage, deeds or facts are described in predominately native words: "what I had done to get them" (*done* appears five times, *get* three times); "I had been wounded, it was true." In the middle of the passage, the narrator acknowledges the truth of his relationship to the other soldiers, and he does so largely in native words: "I was their friend against outsiders. I was a friend but I was never really one of them . . ."—a statement that contains only one French–Latin loan word (really). Though he admits that he sometimes likes to *imagine* (French–Latin, appropriately) himself acting like them, he finally acknowledges, in the long last sentence, the truth of his own nonheroic nature: "I knew that I would never have done such things. . . ." This statement is expressed entirely in native words. In fact, the passage from "but walking home at night" to the end has a very high percentage (91%) of native words. The final tone of simple human honesty is created by an almost exclusive reliance on native words.

In mulling over this passage, I was struck by the narrator's comment about the other soldiers. He uses French–Latin loan words to describe them, but in simple, nonjudgmental loan words: ". . . it was *different* with them and they did *very different* things. . . ." There is none of the "very beautiful language" found in the "citations": The narrator does not use high-sounding loan words such as *heroism*, *bravery*, or *courage*. Why not? Because he distrusts all official praise-words? Because he's not sure that it's even possible to make such judgments? To begin to answer these questions, one has to look at the characterization of the narrator in the story as a whole. In any case, this extreme wariness about using the grand French–Latin abstractions is an attitude shared by many of Hemingway's narrators and characters, and quite probably by Hemingway himself.

If students have read and discussed the story carefully, they should have little trouble understanding the narrator's state of mind here—his feelings about the medals, the other soldiers, and himself. I'd expect class discussion to lead quite naturally to issues of style and word choice. If necessary, a few general questions might help things along: How does the narrator feel about "the very beautiful language" of the citations? Does he ever use such language himself? If not, why not? Does his language change at all during the course of the passage? Most students should pick up the contrast between the fancy language of the citations and the simple language used to express facts and truths. The style of the passage can be explored very fruitfully just in terms of fancy versus simple words, with no reference at all to word origins. If, however, a class has some interest in word origins, they might want to do a little dictionary work. They wouldn't need to look up the origins of all the words. A focus on the second sentence and on the last sentence from "but walking home at night" to the end, would show them how the contrast between French–Latin and native words reflects the contrast between the false and the true in the narrator's mind.

Following are two other examples of the use of a simple, heavily native style in Hemingway's short fiction. They're both descriptions of natural scenes, and they're both from the two-part story entitled "Big Two-Hearted River." French–Latin loan words, defined as borrowings from French or Latin after the Old English period, are in italic. (This definition excludes only those few basic loan words from Latin, words such as *cheese*, *dish*, or *sack*, which appeared in Old English. These early loans lack the more elevated tone of most French–Latin loan words; see the discussion of Old English in Chapter 3). The first passage is from mid-way in "Part One;" the second is the opening of "Part Two."

> 1. Nick slipped off his pack and lay down in the shade. He lay on his back and looked up into the pine trees. His neck and back and the small of his back rested as he stretched. The earth felt good against his back. He looked up at the sky, through the *branches*, and then shut his eyes. He opened them and looked up again. There was a wind high up in the *branches*. He shut his eyes again and went to sleep.

> 2. In the morning the sun was up and the *tent* was starting to get hot. Nick crawled out under the *mosquito* netting stretched *across* the mouth of the *tent*, to look at the morning. The grass was wet on his hands when he came out. He held his trousers and his shoes in his hands. The sun was *just* over the hill. There was the meadow, the *river*, and the swamp. There were birch trees in the green of the swamp on the other side of the *river*.
>
> The *river* was *clear* and smoothly fast in the early morning. Down about two hundred yards were three logs all the way *across* the stream. They made the water smooth and deep above them. As Nick watched, a mink *crossed* the *river* on the logs and went into the swamp. Nick was *excited*. He was *excited* by the early morning and by the *river*. He was *really* too hurried to eat breakfast, but he knew he must. He built a little fire and put on the *coffee* pot.

Both of these passages are dominated by native words, and both illustrate how essential native words are to concrete description of natural facts. In the first passage, Hemingway comes very close to writing an all-native paragraph. The passage has eighty-two words in it, and seventy-five of them are native words in the strict sense—91 percent in all. If the definition of *native* is broadened to include early borrowings from Latin ("pine") and Old Norse ("down," "sky"), the percentage rises to 95 percent. There is only one French–Latin loan word in the entire paragraph, *branch*, a word that, along with *pine* and *sky*, frustrated my efforts to write an all-native paragraph, as described in Chapter 6. In terms of content, the native words are used to name or describe external facts: parts of the body (*neck*, *back*, *small*, *eyes*); natural objects (*shade*, *trees*, *earth*, *wind*); and physical actions (*lay*, *looked*, *rested*, *stretched*, *shut*, *opened*, *sleep*). The first passage is entirely concrete and physical; there are no abstract words and no descriptions of internal feelings—the only possible exception, "felt good," clearly describes a physical sensation, not an inner state.

In the second passage, French–Latin loan words are a bit more prominent, making up roughly 10 percent of the total words. They have very little effect, however, on the simple style of the passage: Some describe physical facts or objects (*tent, mosquito, river, clear, crossed, coffee*); several are merely functional (*across, just, really*); only one of them, *excited*, describes an internal feeling. The other words are mostly native (including one early loan from Latin, *pot*, and two from Old Norse, *crawled* and *get*). These words constitute roughly 86 percent of the total. There are also three words of uncertain origin—*log, mink,* and *swamp*, which are entirely concrete and could easily pass for native. If these three words are grouped with the native words, native words constitute 90 percent of the total. However they are defined, native words still dominate the passage. They are used to describe concrete, physical facts: objects (*sun, grass, hill, birch trees, fire*); actions (*held, watched, built*); sensations (*hot, wet*), and sense perceptions (*smoothly fast, smooth,* and *Down about two hundred yards*). They keep the focus on the external facts of the scene, not on any internal reactions of the observer. Only in the last two sentences do we get any sense of what that observer, Nick Adams, may be feeling.

Classes studying techniques of description might look at these passages out of context. They could talk about the high proportion of concrete, physical words and the general absence of words expressing value judgments or emotional reactions. Both passages are classic examples of the common credo: "Show—Don't Tell." Classes with an interest in word origins could go somewhat farther. They could be asked to look up the origins of each word, or they could be given the two passages as they are printed here, with the loan words underlined or in italic. Then, they could calculate the percentage of native words, and classify the kinds of things to which the native words refer. In this way, they'd clearly see how essential native words are in helping a writer create a good, concrete description of a natural scene.

Finally, though, I would want a class to go still farther, to relate these passages to the story in which they appear. I'd want a class to have read and discussed "Big Two-Hearted River" thoroughly before asking them to discuss the function of the style. Because the story is told through the perspective of Nick Adams, the only character, the question I'd ask is this: "What does the style reveal about Nick's state of mind?"

Following are some things I'd expect the students to say. If they've read the story carefully, they'll know that Nick is making this trip to get away from something, presumably his war experiences. As he walks into the country, he begins to get away from his problems: "Nick was happy. He felt he had left everything behind, the need for thinking, the need to write, other needs. It was all back of him" (from Part One). He wants to escape from his own past, from his own feelings and thoughts, to lose himself in the natural scene. In the first passage, that's exactly what he does. There are no human thoughts or emotions expressed. The very basic, virtually all-native style makes no distinction between human and nonhuman objects: the trees, the shade, Nick's neck and back are all physical objects, natural facts. When he falls asleep listening to the wind, Nick's human consciousness is momentarily stilled. In the second passage, Nick is very much awake, and the effort to lose himself becomes more difficult. Nick is clearly seeking to concentrate on what he can see and feel physically, but he has to struggle to keep his human emotions under control. This passage contains more French–Latin loan words, and I'd hope students would see these words as expressing obstacles that Nick is trying to avoid. Words such as *tent* and *coffee* emphasize Nick's inescapable connection to the human, industrial world, and one word, *excited*, describes the human, nonphysical nature he is seeking to suppress. Hemingway repeats *excited* and gives it special emphasis. I can't help wondering whether he chose *excited* because, as a loan word, it's different from the native words surrounding it, just as Nick, as a human being, is a foreign element in the natural world. That supposition might be pushing this native/loan word business a bit too far, but I'd be pleased to see students suggest this possibility. After all, if they read Hemingway with care, they'll learn that his "simple style" is not as simple as it first appears.

Hemingway is, of course, something of a special case. Such a heavily native style is rare in English or American literature. The only other good writer, to my knowledge, who has such a style is the late Raymond Carver. Still, Hemingway's general attitude toward language—his distrust of fancy foreign words and his preference for ordinary native ones—has been shared by many writers and writing teachers during the past half-century.

George Orwell

George Orwell makes a powerful case for this attitude in his classic essay, "Politics and the English Language" (1946). This essay has had an enormous influence on the teaching of writing in America. For many years, no

Freshman English anthology was without it. It hasn't been used as widely in secondary schools (although it certainly could be), but secondary writing teachers certainly know of it and use its ideas and methods. There's no need to reiterate all those ideas here, but I do emphasize Orwell's methods of illustration.

What struck me most when I first read Orwell's essay were his "translations" of long French–Latin abstract words into specific, and ugly, facts:

> Defenceless villages are bombarded from the air, the inhabitants driven out into the countryside, the cattle machine-gunned, the huts set on fire with incendiary bullets: this is called *pacification*. Millions of peasants are robbed of their farms and sent trudging along the roads with no more than they can carry: this is called *transfer of population* or *rectification of frontiers*.

I was also impressed with Orwell's famous reverse translation of *Ecclesiastes* from the vigorous, predominately native style of the King James version to a Latinate monstrosity:

> I returned and saw under the sun, that the race is not to the swift, nor the battle to the strong, neither yet bread to the wise, nor yet riches to men of understanding, nor yet favour to men of skill; but time and chance happeneth to them all. (*Ecclesiastes* 9:11)

> Objective consideration of contemporary phenomena compels the conclusion that success or failure in competitive activities exhibits no tendency to be commensurate with innate capacity, but that a considerable element of the unpredictable must invariably be taken into account.

These examples really brought Orwell's points home to me, just as they have to the many classes who have read this essay with me. I've used this technique of translation, or register-shifting, often in my own teaching of style. Sometimes, I translate a passage into a different register and present the two versions to a class for analysis and discussion. Sometimes, I ask the students to do the translating, individually or in small groups. Composing and/or comparing versions in different registers involves students actively in issues of meaning and style. It's one of the best methods of teaching writing and reading, and I've included a number of specific examples of it in this book.

Orwell was the spiritual founder of the Doublespeak movement in America. The Committee on Public Doublespeak was formed by the NCTE in 1972 to combat dishonest uses of language in the public sphere, primarily in politics and advertising. This committee has done some valuable work. Its book, *Teaching about Doublespeak* (Dieterich, 1976), is a goldmine of practical ideas for teaching at every level, from elementary school through college. The Committee also publishes the periodical *Quarterly Review of Doublespeak*. Because I can add little to the strong work of others in this area, I simply refer you to these valuable sources.

Also, I think the English profession has gone a little overboard in its relentless attack on fancy words and its almost universal advocacy of the Plain Style in writing. I'd like to offer a mild corrective to this overemphasis on plainness. I'll use Orwell's famous essay here in a somewhat unusual way, to argue for a more balanced view of good style than many of Orwell's followers would advocate. I happen to think Orwell himself would agree with me. Near the end of his essay, Orwell makes a long and interesting statement that has received less attention than it deserves. If students examine this statement closely, both for its ideas and for its style, they can learn a great deal about the English vocabulary and about the act of writing. I present the passage here with the French–Latin loan words in italic. A few words of uncertain origin are so simple and familiar that they sound just like native words: *fake, fit, job, blur,* and *switch.* I'll consider them to be native words in my analysis. Here's the passage:

> [1] On the other hand it [the defence of the English language] is not *concerned* with fake *simplicity* and the *attempt* to make written English *colloquial.* [2] Nor does it even *imply* in every *case preferring* the Saxon word to the Latin one, though it does *imply using* the fewest and shortest words that will *cover* one's meaning. [3] What is above all needed is to let the meaning choose the word, and not the other way about. [4] In *prose,* the worst thing one can do with words is to *surrender* to them. [5] When you think of a *concrete object,* you think wordlessly, and then, if you want to *describe* the thing you have been *visualizing* you *probably* hunt about till you find the *exact* words that seem to fit it. [6] When you think of something *abstract* you are more *inclined* to *use* words from the start, and unless you make a *conscious effort* to *prevent* it, the *existing dialect* will come *rushing* in and do the job for you, at the *expense* of blurring and even *changing* your meaning. [7] *Probably* it is better to put off *using* words as long as *possible* and get one's meaning as *clear* as one can through *pictures* and *sensations.* [8] Afterwards one can choose—not simply **accept** [bold emphasis is Orwell's, italic emphasis is mine]—the *phrases* that will best *cover* the meaning, and then switch round and *decide* what *impression* one's words are likely to make on another *person.*

Before asking students to analyze Orwell's word choice, I first urge them to take in all the excellent advice about writing he has to offer. I'm not at all sure that anyone can really think "wordlessly," but I like the advice about "visualizing" one's subject and trying "to put off using words as long as possible." Anyone who writes much knows how quickly the current buzzwords can "come rushing in and do the job for you." Orwell wants the writer to be in control of language, rather than being controlled by it. He sums it all up in sentence 3: ". . . let the meaning choose the word, and not the other way about."

Orwell is writing here about ideas, about abstract concepts and mental operations. This is an area in which native words are few and far between. The Anglo-Saxons were not intellectually backward; they could, and did, discuss abstract concepts in their own native vocabulary. Over time, though, those native words have been largely replaced by loan words, mostly from French or Latin. A few native words do survive, but the loan words are much more plentiful and precise. For the one basic native verb *think*, one can quickly come up with at least a dozen French–Latin loan words to express specific kinds of thinking: *analyze, concentrate, consider, contemplate, deliberate, examine, investigate, ponder, reason, reflect, speculate, study*. The list could easily be extended.

Thus, when Orwell wants to discuss abstract concepts in English, he has to lean heavily on French–Latin loan words. The language gives him no real choice. There is, for instance, no native synonym for *simplicity* in sentence 1. It's an ironic situation: Native words are *simple, direct, clear,* and *natural,* but the names for those qualities are all French–Latin loan words. In fact, this entire passage is extremely difficult to translate into native words; I know, because I've tried it—I simply couldn't come up with close native equivalents for many of the key words: *imply, prose, concrete, describe, visualize, abstract, conscious, dialect, change, clear, picture, sensation, phrase, impression, person.* Clearly, even George Orwell, a leading advocate for a plain and honest style, has to rely heavily on loan words to make his case.

Despite the restrictions imposed by his subject, Orwell still manages to keep his style accessible and down to earth. He does so by carefully mixing in native words whenever he can. In sentence 2, the important final statement is dominated by native words: *the fewest and shortest words, one's meaning.* Sentence 3, probably the most important statement in the whole passage, is entirely native. Sentence 4 is clearly a balance of native and French–Latin loan words. While sentence 5 is dominated by loan words, Orwell does balance off the borrowed *concrete object* with the native *thing,* and he adds a concrete image with the native words *hunt about till you find.* In sentences 6 and 7, the key words are mostly borrowed ones, but Orwell does insert some native or homely phrases: "When you think of something," "from the start," "come rushing in to do the job for you" (not really native, but certainly down to earth), "It is better to put off," and "get one's meaning." In sentence 8, Orwell stresses the forceful native word *choose* over the loan word *accept*, thus reinforcing the main point of the entire passage.

If, after analyzing this passage, students aren't convinced that Orwell was choosing, consciously or intuitively, to balance loan words with native words, they could be asked to translate the whole passage into French–Latin words. Although it's impossible to translate many of Orwell's original loan words into native words, it's quite easy to omit or translate most of his native words (except, of course, for the grammatical fillers) and still have a coherent statement. Here, as an illustration, is what Orwell could have written if he hadn't used native words to balance his style:

> Conversely, it is not concerned with false simplicity and the attempt to render the style of printed texts colloquial. Nor does it even imply in all cases preferring the Saxon term to the Latin term, although it does imply using the most concise phrasing that will convey one's intention. What is ultimately necessary is to allow the sense to determine the phrasing, and not vice versa. When you consider a concrete object, you consider it nonverbally, and then, if you want to describe the object you have been visualizing, you probably deliberate until you discover the exact phrasing which seems to match it. When you consider an abstraction, you are more inclined to initiate the process verbally, and unless you make a conscious effort to prevent it, the existing dialect will surge in and complete the process for you, at the expense of obscuring or changing your sense. Probably it is preferable to avoid verbalizing for an extended period and attempt to clarify one's ideas through pictures and sensations. Finally, one can select—not simply *accept*—the phrases that will best cover one's intention, and then manipulate and decide what impression one's phrases might create in another person.

Terrible, isn't it? Or *ghastly*, to use a native term. Writing and/or reading this kind of thing should make anyone appreciate the deft way in which Orwell uses native words in his original passage. Those native words play a subordinate role in expressing the main ideas, but the passage would be pompous and pedantic without them.

Orwell's style in the original passage illustrates perhaps the most common and important use of native words in intellectual discourse. When an abstract subject requires a heavy reliance on French–Latin loan words, use of native words can provide a needed balance. They can keep the discussion from becoming too abstract, too difficult for any but the most specialized reader to follow. They can keep the writer down to earth and in touch with the audience. Native words can rarely carry an abstract discussion, but they can always give such a discussion a human voice.

Applications

1. Here are three versions of the opening sentence of George Orwell's essay, "Politics and the English Language." One is Orwell's original prose; the other two are imitations. Analyze each sentence in terms of its meaning and tone. Which of the three makes you most want to continue reading? Why?

   a. Most people who bother with the matter at all would admit that the English language is in a bad way, but it is generally assumed that we cannot by conscious action do anything about it.
   b. Most people who pay any attention to the matter would recognize that the English language is deteriorating, but it is generally assumed that we cannot by conscious action improve the situation.
   c. Most people who think about it at all can see that the English language is in a bad way, but they don't think we can do anything about it.

2. Here's an anonymous lyrical poem from the Middle Ages. No one knows anything about the speaker and situation, but this is one of the most famous short poems in the English language. Discuss the poem and try to explain its power and lasting appeal.

   WESTERN WIND
   O Western wind, when wilt thou blow,
   The small rain down can rain?
   Christ, if my love were in my arms,
   And I in my bed again!

3. When students apply to college, they are usually asked to write a brief essay explaining why they want to go to college. Following is the opening paragraph of such an essay. Do you think it would make a favorable impression? If not, how could you revise it to give the candidate a better chance? Please explain how you hope your revisions will change the reader's perception of the student writer.

   The pursuit of a higher education has long been a personal objective of mine. I formed this objective in junior high school, when I received an award in the annual Science Fair. That award changed my life by revealing to me that I might have some academic potential in the science area. My subsequent achievements in high school have revealed that potential to be a reality. I've done well in my advanced courses in chemistry and biology. I've also derived personal satisfaction from them. At this point, I am sure that I want to study chemistry or biology in college, and I am quite confident that I can do well.

8
Creating a Balanced Style

In Chapters 6 and 7, the primary focus is on native words. I've been more or less rooting for humble, feisty native words against their haughty and prestigious French–Latin adversaries. It's not really a contest, of course: Native and French–Latin words work with each other in an effective style, not against each other. Still, I haven't yet suggested ways to help students see the positive values of French–Latin words. In this chapter, I focus more on what French–Latin words can do, both in a highly formal style and in a balanced style, a style in which French–Latin and native words really do work together.

If native words can provide concreteness, directness, and sincerity, French–Latin words can provide complexity, subtlety, and eloquence. There are times when eloquence is needed. Formal occasions require a formal style: graduations, weddings, funerals, retirements. One can certainly speak simply on such occasions, but these are times when formality and eloquence are expected and appreciated. We also expect a formal style in the major speeches of our political leaders. Some of the finest examples of formal prose in America have been written for important political occasions: the Declaration of Independence, the Preamble to the Constitution, Lincoln's Second Inaugural Address, and the Gettysburg Address. Even in this modern, often cynical age, not every political speech is self-serving Doublespeak; an eloquent speech by a political leader can still inspire people to follow high ideals: John F. Kennedy's Inaugural Address and Martin Luther King, Jr.'s "I Have a Dream" speech are two more recent examples.

Any of these famous texts could be used to introduce students to the virtues of a formal style. My favorite text for that purpose, though, is the concluding paragraph of Lincoln's Gettysburg Address:

> But in a larger sense we cannot dedicate, we cannot consecrate, we can-

not hallow this ground. The brave men, living and dead, who struggled here, have consecrated it far above our power to add or detract. The world will little note nor long remember what we say here, but it can never forget what they did here. It is for us, the living, rather, to be dedicated here to the unfinished work which they who fought here have thus far nobly advanced. It is rather for us to be here dedicated to the great task remaining before us; that from these honored dead we take increased devotion to that cause for which they gave the last full measure of devotion; that we here highly resolve that these dead shall not have died in vain; that this nation, under God, shall have a new birth of freedom; and that government of the people, by the people, and for the people, shall not perish from the earth.

Obviously, syntax and rhythm contribute mightily to the power of this passage, as do the short stretches of native words ("it can never forget what they did here"). Still, it's the French–Latin words that express most of the central ideas and give the passage its elevated tone: *dedicate, consecrate, devotion, cause, resolve, nation, government, people.* When exploring this speech with a class, I'd first want the students to hear it read aloud—by me or a student volunteer. Then, I'd want to leave time for questions and general impressions. Only then would I have the class take up word origins. Depending on their prior experience, I might ask the class to look up the word origins, or I might provide them myself, with the French–Latin words in italic:

> But in a *larger sense* we cannot *dedicate*, we cannot *consecrate*, we cannot hallow this ground. The *brave* men, living and dead, who struggled here, have *consecrated* it far above our *power* to *add* or *detract*. The world will little *note* nor long *remember* what we say here, but it can never forget what they did here. It is for us, the living, rather, to be *dedicated* here to the *unfinished* work which they who fought here have thus far *nobly advanced*. It is rather for us to be here *dedicated* to the great *task remaining* before us; that from these *honored* dead we take *increased devotion* to that *cause* for which they gave the last full *measure* of *devotion*; that we here highly *resolve* that these dead shall not have died in *vain*; that this *nation*, under God, shall have a new birth of *freedom*; and that *government* of the *people*, by the *people*, and for the *people*, shall not *perish* from the earth.

Either way, the students would quickly discover how important French–Latin loan words are to the style. Next would come the real challenge: asking the class to translate the original passage entirely into native words. This is a tough challenge—an almost impossible one, really—and it would be somewhat easier if attempted in small working groups. Having seen it done, I'd expect the students to come up with some powerful individual phrases, but I'd be surprised if they actually preferred their full all-native versions to the original. In fact, I'd expect this activity to convince even the most cynical class that fancy words do have their uses.

French–Latin words are not, of course, to be used only for special occasions. They are indispensable to intellectual discourse in English. It's impossible to discuss abstract ideas in English without relying heavily on French–Latin loan words. That general fact could be established by picking almost any passage out of a secondary or college textbook. The focus here, though, is on style, on a writer's choice of French–Latin words to express precise nuances of meaning and tone. Good examples aren't hard to find. I offer a couple from two authors who are widely read in American schools—Henry David Thoreau and Robert Frost. Students can be fooled by the rustic, down-to-earth stances of these two writers. Thoreau and Frost do not, however, write in simple, native terms; their styles are, in fact, a subtle mixture of native and French–Latin words.

Henry David Thoreau

Students can learn a good deal about Thoreau, and about French–Latin words, by exploring the language of this famous passage from *Walden*, with the French–Latin words in italics:

> I went to the woods because I wished to live *deliberately*, to *front* only the *essential facts* of life, and see if I could not learn what it had to teach, and not, when I came to die, *discover* that I had not lived. I did not wish to live what was not life, living is so dear; nor did I wish to *practice resignation*, unless it was *quite necessary*. I wanted to live deep and suck out all the marrow of life, to live so *sturdily* and *Spartan*like as to put to *rout* all that was not life, to cut a broad swath and shave *close*, to drive life into a *corner*, and *reduce* it to its lowest *terms*, and, if it *proved* mean, why then to get the whole and *genuine* meanness of it, and *publish* its meanness to the world; or if it were *sublime*, to know it by *experience*, and be *able* to give a true *account* of it in my next *excursion*.

I've used this passage in college classes many times. I present it as it's printed here, except that the French–Latin loan words are underlined instead of italicized. Then, I ask each student to translate all the loan words into native equivalents and to write an analytical paper comparing their new versions with the original passage. Finally, as a whole class, we read the revised versions aloud and discuss them. I read one, too, since I've translated the passage myself.

Here's a revised version of Thoreau's passage. It contains some of the best suggestions my college students and I have come up with over the years.

> I went to the woods because I wished to live thoughtfully, to meet only the needed truths of life, and see if I could not learn what it had to teach, and not, when I came to die, find out that I had not lived. I did not wish to live what was not life, living is so dear, nor did I wish to hold back, unless I had to. I wanted to live deep and suck out all the marrow of life, to live so roughly as to put to flight all that was not life, to cut a broad swath and shave near, to drive life back against the wall, and break it into its smallest bits, and, if it showed itself mean, why then to get the whole and true meanness of it, and tell its meanness to the world; or if it were wonderful, to know it first-hand, and be ready to give a true reckoning of it in my next life.

Let me point out what one can learn from trying to translate Thoreau's passage by comparing it to this revised version. I'll draw on my own discoveries and on those my classes have come up with. In general, it's not too difficult to capture some of the directness and energy of Thoreau's voice and some of his physical imagery. The problems come in trying to capture the subtleties of Thoreau's thinking, in trying to translate French–Latin words that express complex mental concepts.

The most difficult terms to replace are *deliberately, essential facts, practice resignation, reduce it to its lowest terms, genuine,* and *experience*—all French–Latin words. Thoreau's *deliberately* suggests a conscious effort to make decisions about how to live; *thoughtfully* in the revised version suggests paying careful attention to what happens, but not necessarily making careful prior decisions. Thoreau is setting out to control his life, not simply to reflect upon it. The phrase "essential facts" is simply impossible to translate into native words. The best effort I've seen is "core truths," but the origin of *core* is not known, and the word can't really be counted as native. "Facts" are not the same as "truths;" *truths* are generalizations drawn from specific *facts.* Thoreau wants to examine the facts in order to ascertain the truth about life, or the true nature of life. "Practice resignation" suggests a conscious, deliberate effort to accept and live with inevitable limitations; to "hold back" suggests that one could do something but chooses not to, while another possible substitute, "give up hope," suggests a passive surrender rather than an active, philosophical acceptance and a willingness to continue. "Reduce it to its lowest terms" is a mathematical metaphor. Because there are no native words to express the basic concepts of mathematics (*number, add, subtract, multiply,* and *divide* are all

French–Latin words), one is forced to shift to some other metaphor: "Break it into its smallest bits" captures Thoreau's sense of aggressive seeking, but it makes him sound more like a chain-saw operator than a philosopher. *Genuine* could be seen as just a fancy word for the native *true*, but *genuine* suggests that a rigorous process of inquiry has been conducted, and that spurious alternatives have been rejected. This is, of course, just the kind of deliberate inquiry that Thoreau set out to do. The word *true* describes only the product, not the intellectual process. Finally, to know something "first-hand" means to do something, to participate in it directly; Thoreau's "know it by experience" implies both active living and conscious reflection. *Experience* suggests the accumulation of knowledge and wisdom from doing things for one's self.

This is a challenging activity, but a valuable one. Students must really struggle to translate Thoreau's words, but they end up with increased respect for Thoreau as a writer and thinker, and with an increased awareness of how indispensable French–Latin loan words are to describe complex intellectual processes. Frankly, I've tried this activity only at the college level, so I don't know how well it would work with secondary students. If students are seriously studying Thoreau and *Walden*, they should be able to handle it. Perhaps they could simply do the second part of the activity: Compare Thoreau's original passage to a single revised version, such as the one presented here. In comparing the two versions, students would certainly learn a good deal about Thoreau's thinking and attitude toward living, and about the balance of native and French–Latin elements in his writing style.

Robert Frost

For a final example of the power of a balanced style, I offer a poem by Robert Frost. Frost is accessible to students because his style seems simple and speechlike much of the time. Frost, however, is the ultimate register-shifter. One moment, he sounds like a folksy New England farmer; then, he drops in a French–Latin word or phrase that such a farmer would never use. He balances native and French–Latin words in an infinitely subtle way. It's this balance that gives his poems their distinctive voice.

My favorite way to introduce students to the subtleties of Frost is to give a class his well-known little poem *Fire and Ice,* with the French–Latin loan words underlined (but italicized here):

FIRE AND ICE

Some say the world will end in fire,
Some say in ice.
From what I've *tasted* of *desire*
I hold with those who *favor* fire.
But if it had to *perish* twice,
I think I know enough of hate
To say that for *destruction* ice
Ice is also great
And would *suffice*.

I then ask students to try to find native substitutes for the emphasized words and compare them with Frost's original choices. I ask them to pay attention to the meanings of the words and to their tones. Finally, I ask them to characterize the speaker of the original poem: Is he a farmer? A philosopher? A hermit? Is he convincing, trustworthy? Does he know what he's talking about? What's his tone of voice? Is he dead-serious, playful, a mixture of the two? (Please permit me to use *he*, even though the speaker isn't identifiably male. Students equate the speaker with Frost, anyway. In this kind of situation, I let students use the gender of the poet to identify the speaker: Emily Dickinson's "I" speaker is a "she.")

I've used this activity many times, in both high school and college classes, and always with the same result: Students realize that the French–Latin words cannot be replaced without ruining the meaning and tone of the poem. I've used it as a paper assignment and on take-home exams. I've also used it as a basis for whole-class discussion. I used it most recently in Elaine Burnham's senior English class. The students were well prepared for it; they had spent the week exploring the differences between native and French–Latin words and had developed a good sense of tonal differences. We spent a full hour discussing the poem and possible changes to it. I'll go through the poem, describing what Elaine's students did with it, but occasionally adding in my own thoughts on it.

The first two lines of the poem are entirely native. Native words tend to express physical facts, and Elaine's students agreed that these two lines define the world's end in physical or geological terms: Will there be another Ice Age, or one final holocaust? They saw the speaker's voice as simple and casual, and his attitude as matter-of-fact, as if he is presenting a pointless argument he's heard many times before.

In the next line, the speaker makes a radical shift in focus, from physical to human causes of destruction. He then goes on to state that human emotions, "desire" and "hate," are capable of destroying the world, twice over. This is a rather strong indictment of the human race. Who is this guy, and why should we believe him? I asked Elaine's students that question and it provided a focus for much of our discussion. To get at it, they started with the word *tasted*. They came up with various native substitutes, which I dutifully wrote on the board: *eaten, seen, felt,* and *swallowed*. They compared each of these to *tasted* and rejected them all. They felt that *seen* and *felt* were too weak, and that *eaten* and *swallowed* were too strong. If the speaker has "seen" desire, they argued, he may not have had personal knowledge of it. If he has "felt" desire, he may have personal knowledge of the feeling, but he may not have acted on it or tried it. Frost's "tasted" implies that the speaker has had actual, physical experience with "desire"; he hasn't just stared longingly at something. At the same time, he has only "tasted" it, not "eaten" or "swallowed" it. Those two words seemed much too strong to Elaine's students: They argued that a speaker who has "eaten" or "swallowed" something destructive might be thoroughly corrupted by it, but that a speaker who has only "tasted" it has not given in wholly to it. Hence, they preferred Frost's original "tasted" and felt it portrays the speaker as less than perfect but fully capable of moral judgment. After they had finished this most interesting discussion, I felt free to add my own two cents' worth. I can't help picking up a hint of Eve and the Forbidden Fruit in the word *tasted*. After all, it was Eve's "desire to be wise" that led her to "taste" the apple and destroy the world as it was originally created. I asked the students if this thought had occurred to any of them, but I don't recall getting much response. That's OK; I still think it fits!

The class moved on to the word *desire*. They came up with various native substitutes: *wanting, wishing, lust,* and *greed*. None of these words quite satisfied them. *Wishing* and *wanting* seemed a bit too passive and ordinary; Frost's "desire" struck them as stronger and more serious: Little children *wish* and *want*, they argued, but only adults *desire*. They saw *lust* and *greed* as powerful enough, but more limited than the word *desire*, which, they felt, could refer to a deep, destructive desire for many things: power, wealth, an unsuitable or unavailable person. In terms of tone, the students felt that the French–Latin *desire* was not a word an ordinary farmer or working class person would use. They felt that the speaker's use of this word characterizes him as a person who has read a lot or acquired some form of advanced education. This word seemed to increase their respect for the speaker: They saw him as both experienced and unusually thoughtful.

If Frost gives his speaker a fancy word at the end of line 3, he brings the speaker back down to earth in line 4. The students agreed that the phrase "I hold with" is folksy and colloquial, something an old New England farmer might well say. They came up with several native substitutes for *favor: love, like, believe in, follow, go with*. They rejected *love, believe in,* and *follow* as too definite: The speakers says he "favors" fire in this contest, but he doesn't appear to be making a strong commitment. They felt that *like* and *go with* capture the tentative meaning of *favor* better, and I agree. In terms of tone, they felt that *favor* is a fairly ordinary word that anyone might say. While that's true enough, I asked them to see how "favor" works in the line as a whole. I wrote the line on the board in three different forms:

> I hold with those who like fire.
> I hold with those who go with fire.
> I hold with those who favor fire.

When they compared these three versions, they felt that the homely words *like* and *go with*, when combined with *hold with* make the entire line too folksy and the speaker a little too ordinary. They felt that, in its context, *favor* is a little more sophisticated, and more appropriate for a speaker who uses the elevated *desire* in the previous line. Again, I agree. We then explored the tone of *favor* a little further. I think it's playfully ironic. Frost's speaker sets up a contest or competition between *fire* and *ice* right in the first two lines. The word *favor* suggests picking a winner, a "favorite," in a sporting contest. In this contest, the speaker "favors" fire; he's putting his money on desire, so to speak. Speaking of the end of the world as if it were just a sporting contest is, of course, ironic understatement (saying something heavy in a light way). After some discussion, Elaine's class came to see the possible irony behind the word *favor*. I then asked them how seeing that irony affected their view of the speaker. They felt that it makes him more likeable, more clever and witty, but not necessarily more educated. As New Englanders, they knew all about ironic understatement; they knew it as the trademark of the traditional Old New England Farmer, but they also knew it as part of their ordinary lives.

While the idea of the world perishing twice is a kind of grim joke, the tone of line 5 is predominately serious, mostly because of the somber loan word *perish*. The students dutifully came up with several native substitutes, but they weren't happy with any of them: *dwindle, die, end, stop*.

They looked up *perish* and were impressed by its emphasis on violence and destruction: The *AHD* defines it as "to die or be destroyed, especially in a violent or untimely manner." The students had heard it used in news reports of terrible accidents: People "perish" in fires and plane crashes. They considered it a rare and special word, one not often found in ordinary speech. They also felt it has tragic overtones, that it's not strictly factual. In comparison to *perish*, the students found all of the native substitutes lacking. They pointed out that *stop* could be only temporary, that *end* and *die* are final enough, but that neither has any suggestion of violence or destruction. They liked the emotional quality of *dwindle*, but felt that it lacks the idea of violent destruction suggested by the image of "fire." In terms of tone, the students felt that line 5 is more educated than folksy, and that the speaker is now treating the serious subject with entire seriousness. They found that this same serious tone carried into all-native line 6, which they perceived as neither folksy nor educated, just ordinary, neutral human speech.

The loan word *destruction* in line 7 is a lot like *perish* in line 5. It's a strong, solemn, somewhat elevated word. As the longest word in the poem, it gets power and emphasis from its very size. We discussed this word for some time. We compared it to *construction:* One means "put together"; the other means to "tear down" some preexisting structure. They knew that *destruction* is usually applied to physical things, like buildings or cities or forests, and that it is rarely applied to people: A person's career or reputation can be destroyed, but the person dies or is killed, not destroyed. The students could see how well *destruction* works in Frost's poem: It refers to the tearing down of the "world," the entire physical universe. For this one, the students came up with some powerful native substitutes, which they discussed at some length. Here's the list: *ending, death, breaking up, slaughter, downfall, wreckage, wrecking.* Through a process of elimination, they settled on *breaking up, wreckage,* and *wrecking.* All three fit into the syntax of the line, and all three have the same basic meaning as *destruction.* I did have to tell them that *wreckage* and *wrecking* are loan words, too—from Old Norse, rather than from French or Latin—but these are still Germanic, rather than Romance, words, and one could stretch the definition of *native word* to include them. No one really wanted to choose one of these three over *destruction*, though. Their reasons weren't fully articulated, but I suspect that the associations of these three native words are just too limited and mundane: it's hard to hear them without thinking of broken machines, broken man-made objects. The word *destruction* refers to a physical process, but it is also general and abstract; it focuses more on the process, not the object.

In the last two lines, Frost has the speaker resort again to ironic understatement. "Would suffice" works like "favor" in line 4; it's a casual, matter-of-fact way to talk about a great catastrophe. The students came up with lots of good native substitutes for this final phrase: *be all right, be enough, would do, would work.* All of these would, indeed, work as well as "would suffice" in terms of meaning and in terms of their ironically understated tone. The only real difference is the rhyme. Frost ends the poem with two bold, blunt rhymes: "hate"/"great" and "ice"/"suffice." These rhymes provide the final irony: The destruction of the world is described in perfect harmony.

Frost's brilliant little poem can show students a good deal about the vocabulary of English. First of all, French–Latin loan words are extremely useful: In all cases but "suffice," the loan words provide a richer, more suggestive meaning than do their possible native equivalents. On the other hand, native words are useful, as well—essential, in fact: No loan words could possibly replace *fire, ice, world,* or *hate.* Finally, the careful balance of native and loan words creates a believable and engaging voice. At the end of our discussion, when I asked the class for a final characterization of the speaker, a girl named Megan expressed it pretty well: "An old New England farmer who went to Harvard." Frost's speaker is indeed a complex mixture of tones and attitudes. He's shrewd, witty, ironic, playful, and profound—a fascinating character, much like his creator, Robert Frost himself.

Frost is, of course, a master in his use of words, but the rich and varied vocabulary of English is there for us all. One key, perhaps *the* key, to a successful writing style is a careful balance of native and French–Latin words. There are times that a predominately native or French–Latin style can work, but those times are comparatively rare. In most cases, a balanced style works best. I tried, in Chapter 6, to choose a subject *I* could handle well in an all-native style, but I still found that I needed a few loan words to express what I wanted. In the sample passages by Orwell and Thoreau, both writers use plenty of French–Latin words to praise the virtues of simplicity: Their styles are carefully balanced between French–Latin complexity and native directness. In *Fire and Ice* and in his poetry generally, Frost shifts back and forth between native and French–Latin words to create a voice that is both homely and intellectually subtle. The fact that English has two distinct registers, two kinds of words, is an enormous advantage to writers. Experienced writers can balance the two to express exactly the meaning and tone they seek. So can student writers, once they develop an awareness of what the two registers can do. Helping students develop that awareness has been the focus in these last three chapters.

Applications

1. Following is the conclusion of Abraham Lincoln's Second Inaugural Address. Look up the origins of the words and analyze how the two types of words are positioned within the paragraph.

What effects does this positioning achieve?

> With malice towards none; with charity for all; with firmness in the right, as God gives us to see the right, let us strive on to finish the work we are in; to bind up the nation's wounds; to care for him who shall have borne the battle, and for his widow and his orphan—to do all which may achieve and cherish a just and lasting peace among ourselves, and with all nations.

2. In Herman Melville's novella *Bartleby the Scrivener*, Bartleby refuses to do assigned work by stating "I prefer not to." This comment becomes his trademark. What would change if his trademark were an all-native "I won't do it" or "I choose not to"? Would he be a different character? Would readers view him differently?

3. In the following poem by William Wordsworth, try to determine what has happened and how the speaker feels about it.

A SLUMBER DID MY SPIRIT SEAL

A slumber did my spirit seal;
   I had no human fears:
She seemed a thing that could not feel
   The touch of earthly years.

No motion has she now, no force;
   She neither hears nor sees;
Rolled round in earth's diurnal course,
   With rocks, and stones, and trees.

The word *diurnal* in line 7 means roughly the same thing as the native word *daily*. How would the poem be different if Wordsworth had written "earth's own daily course" in line 7?

4. In this poem by Emily Dickinson, the speaker's attitude toward an early fall day seems to shift and change. Go through the poem, stanza by stanza, and try to figure out what the speaker is thinking and feeling at each point. Then, look up the origins of the words, identifying native words (broadly defined) and French–Latin loan words. Do you find any correlations between the kinds of words used and what's going on in the speaker's mind?

THESE ARE THE DAYS WHEN BIRDS COME BACK

These are the days when Birds come back—
A very few—a Bird or two—
To take a backward look.

These are the days when skies resume
The old—old sophistries of June—
A blue and gold mistake.

Oh fraud that cannot cheat the Bee—
Almost thy plausibility
Induces my belief.

Till ranks of seeds their witness bear—
And softly thro' the altered air
Hurries a timid leaf.

Oh Sacrament of summer days
Oh Last Communion in the Haze—
Permit a child to join.

Thy sacred emblems to partake—
Thy consecrated bread to take
And thine immortal wine!

9
Native and Borrowed Words in American Society

S*tudents* can learn a great deal about American society by exploring the kinds of words people use to describe the things they value. In this chapter, I set forth an activity that allows students to compare how native and French–Latin words are used in various areas of experience. In most areas, these two types of words are used to express a hierarchy of values. The French–Latin words usually express the more valued things, but there are many interesting exceptions. This activity requires some historical background and some knowledge of how to obtain etymological information from a dictionary. Ways to introduce those matters are described in Chapter 3, but for the purposes of this chapter we can assume that the class already has the necessary background knowledge.

Setting Up an Area Search

This activity, called an Area Search, involves looking up lots and lots of words, and it's important that the class not get bogged down in discussing whether a word is native or borrowed. To avoid such distractions, the definition of *native word* can be expanded to include any word with Old English or Old Norse in its etymology. This expanded definition includes native words strictly defined—words that can be traced back to Germanic or Indo-European—and two kinds of early loan words: early Latin loan words, such as *dish* or *street*, which were present in Old English; and loan words from Old Norse, such as *knife* or *take*, which were part of Old English, too, but rarely appeared in writing until the Middle English period. In terms of tone and social value, these words act exactly like native words, anyway. I also tell students to count as a French–Latin loan word any word that was borrowed into English from French or Latin at any time after the Old

English period. This definition lumps together words from different historical periods, as in the following list compiled from the *Oxford English Dictionary*, with dates for each word's first appearance: *substantial* (1380), *elegant* (1485), *discriminate* (1628), *cuisine* (1786), *ambience* (1889). Still, this kind of grouping makes sense in terms of tone and social value. What most French–Latin words defined in this way have in common is their feeling of special status: They name highly valued things or are used to confer special value on ordinary things.

An Area Search involves students exploring the kinds of words used in different areas or categories of experience. To begin it, you can suggest certain areas to explore or solicit suggestions from the class by asking these two questions: (1) "What are your areas of interest?" (The word *areas* works better than *interests* because *areas* elicits general categories, for example, sports, not just football.) (2) "What are some important institutions in our society?" Answers can be listed on the board. Personal interests are likely to include sports, food, clothes, and personal relationships. Social institutions will include government, schools, the legal system, churches, and the military. After a list is generated, you and your students can determine which areas to explore. At this point, you might want to explore one of the categories with the whole class, drawing out words and discussing them; or you might decide to skip the whole-class introduction and simply set up small search groups to explore the different categories. This activity works very well as a small-group inquiry. Each group should contain three or four students, and have at least one dictionary.

The students in each study group have a few basic tasks: (1) Generate as many words used in their area as they can find, (2) look up the origins of the words and identify the native and French–Latin words, and (3) explore the differences between the ways the two kinds of words are used. One way to explore differences is to ask what kind of thing a given word refers to: Does it refer to something ordinary or to something special—to a *game* (native) or a *tournament* (French–Latin)? A second way is to "translate" back and forth between the two types: from "We liked the show" (native) to "We enjoyed the performance" (French–Latin), and vice versa. Students who do the warm-up activities described in Chapter 5 will have a pretty good idea of what questions to ask, and they will certainly be familiar with this kind of translating.

After the small groups have done their work, each one can report to the rest of the class, which can, of course, suggest additional words and examples for each category. It's hard to predict how long this whole process might take. I allow one full class period (forty-five to fifty minutes) for the small groups to research and discuss their words, and I expect full-class discussion of a single category to last at least half a period, maybe even an entire period. Students like to talk about words, especially if the words involve categories in which they're personally interested. I suggest that your class start with only two or three categories at once, with two small groups working on each category. After the first run-through, you will have a clearer sense of how much time a given class will need to do this activity well. For the sake of illustration, I present some of the common categories here, pointing out the words and issues that are likely to arise. I also add some additional teaching applications at the end of each category.

Sports
Sports is a popular category and a fruitful one to explore. Native words in this area include *play*, *game*, *win*, *lose*, *beat*, and *team*. Common French–Latin loan words include *athlete*, *champion*, *compete*, *defeat*, *league*, *participate*, *sport*, *tournament*, and *victory*. It's clear that the native words convey the basic elements of any game or sport at any level, from sandlot baseball to the World Series. On the other hand, some of the loan words, such as *champion*, *league*, and *tournament*, refer to specialized, high-status forms of sporting activity and have no native equivalents. For the most part, though, the native words and loan words can be paired as synonyms: *game–sport*; *beat–defeat*; *play–compete*, *participate*, and so on. Once the pairing begins, a small group or a class can extend it indefinitely, translating simple native words into all sorts of elaborate French–Latin equivalents: a *game* is a *contest* or *sporting event*; a *player* is a *competitor* or *contestant*; the *winning team* doesn't just *beat the other team and win the game*, it *defeats*, *conquers*, or *vanquishes* its *opponent* or *adversary* to *gain the victory* or *emerge victorious*. It's clear that there are two entirely different styles involved: The same facts may be described in two different ways. There is a special, highly inflated rhetoric that people use to talk and write about sports. Looking at this rhetoric can open up many issues for extended class discussion. What's the effect of using military metaphors such as *conquer* and *adversary*? Is this rhetoric semi-playful, more mock-heroic than heroic, or is it deadly serious? Do Americans take sports too seriously? Isn't any sport really "just a game?" Shouldn't it be? Should school sports place less emphasis on competition and more emphasis on wide participation? Do females have a different attitude toward competition than males? Is one attitude "heathier" than the other? Most classes can really "get into" sports; it's a good category with which to begin this activity.

Follow-up Activities and Questions

1. Replace *beat* and *lost* in the following sentences with as many words or phrases as you can.

   1. (Your team) beat (the other team) 3–1.
   2. (Your team) beat (the other team) 10–1.
   3. (Your team) lost 3–1.
   4. (Your team) lost 10–1.

   Look up the origins and meanings of all your substitutes in a dictionary.

   What kinds of words did you use to replace *beat*? Did the scores affect your choices?

   What kinds of words did you use to replace *lost*? Did the scores affect your choices?

2. Why would it be unwise to say, "I like to play games," on an application to a college or prospective employer? Why would "I like to participate in sports" be more appropriate? Write a paragraph or two explaining your answers.

3. We often hear the term *competitive sport*. Is there such a thing as a *noncompetitive sport*? In your answer, consider and classify the following activities: A person hikes up a hill; two people play tennis without keeping score; two Little League teams play baseball without keeping score; a person goes skating on a pond. If you don't consider some or all of these activities sports, what would you call them? Games?

4. The following statement was made by a high school basketball coach. When you look up the origins of the words, you'll find that most of the key words are native. Try to translate the statement, substituting French–Latin loan words for the key native words. Then, compare the results. Is your translation saying the same thing? Does your translation have the same tone as the original? For which coach would you rather play—the one who made the first statement or the one who made your translation? (Note: The origin of *fun* is unknown; because it's a simple, familiar word, count it as native when you make your translation.)

   And you have to want to be good. You have to want to win. I don't know what the point of playing is if you don't want to win. I mean, people talk about playing for fun, but what's fun is winning, you know? You're not doing anybody a service by losing. The kids sure as shit don't want to lose.

—"High School Basketball Coach." (2000) In *Gig: Americans Talk About Their Jobs at the Turn of the Millennium.* Eds. John Bowe, Marissa Bowe, and Sabin Streeter. New York: Crown, 323.

Food

Food is also a popular category, and it is relatively easy to explore, although it involves some social attitudes that may not be familiar to all students. Strictly native words for food and cooking that come immediately to mind are *food*, *drink*, *eat*, *meal*, *bread*, *milk*, *meat*, *fish*, *salt*, and *oven*—a very basic list. To these can be added some equally basic Latin loan words, which appeared in Old English: *cook*, *dish*, *kitchen*, *pot*, *pan*, *cup*, *beer*, *wine*, *cheese*, *butter*, and *pepper*. Old English must have had many more words for food and cooking than the few that have survived, but the others were no doubt replaced in the large influx of French–Latin words during the Middle English period, words that reflect the more sophisticated attitudes of the French-speaking upper classes: *appetite*, *banquet*, *beef*, *beverage*, *boil*, *broil*, *chef*, *course*, *dine*, *dinner*, *feast*, *flavor*, *fork*, *fry*, *pastry*, *plate*, *pork*, *roast*, *sauce*, *season*, *soup*, *spice*, *supper*, *taste*. French words for food and cooking continued to be borrowed into English after the Middle English period, because French cooking has always had a strong influence in England and in much of Europe. More recent French loan words include *cuisine*, *gourmet*, *restaurant*, and just about everything connected with restaurants—the *menu*, the *entree*, the *salad*, the *dessert*, even the *bill* or *check*.

A good way to help students find a pattern in all of these words is to suggest that they start with the word *gourmet*, which many, or at least some, of them will know: What is a *gourmet* attitude toward food? What words reflect such an attitude? What's the opposite of a gourmet attitude? What words reflect that attitude? The words divide quite neatly into French–Latin *gourmet* words against native words, which reflect a much more utilitarian attitude—ask if the students would want to call it a *fast food* (native) attitude. The native words describe cooking and eating food as basic human functions, nothing more: People must eat to live; some food must be cooked before it is eaten. The French–Latin words convey a more discriminating, less utilitarian attitude: They define eating as a special pleasure and cooking as an art, not a basic skill. They name various kinds of cooking—*boil*, *broil*, *fry*, *roast*, *saute*—and various additions to make food more appealing and interesting—*sauce*, *season*, *spice*; they show a concern for *flavor* and *taste*. The French–Latin words name special occasions—*banquets*, *feasts*, *din-*

ing at *restaurants*, not just everyday *meals* (native); they even distinguish the most important meal of the day, *dinner*, from the more humble *breakfast* (native). In terms of actual food, French–Latin words name the more prestigious *beef* and *pork*, in contrast to the more affordable *chicken* (native). It's clear that the French–Latin words convey a higher regard for the cooking and eating of food. When native and French–Latin words are applied to the same thing, the loan word has a much higher tone: *dining* is a more gracious activity than *eating*; a *chef* has more status than a *cook*; people who want to become chefs go to *culinary institutes*, not *cooking schools*. Students might be interested to know that the United States has, in fact, a second CIA—the Culinary Institute of America, located in Poughkeepsie, New York.

Restaurants tend to reflect different attitudes towards cooking and eating. Some take the *gourmet* approach and feature *fine dining*. Some take a purely functional approach and offer *fast food*. There is also a third kind of restaurant, one that serves basic food prepared with care and pride; such restaurants offer *home cooking* (native) and *homemade* (native) items. Because most students are familiar with restaurants, although probably not with the gourmet kind, restaurant language is a good sub-area for them to explore. Interested students might want to compare the menus and advertisements from different restaurants in terms of the kinds of language used. Some might go on to write sample menus or ads of their own. I doubt that many American adolescents will have much sympathy for the gourmet attitude, especially if they're like the student who told me recently that the only purpose of a meal is to "pack protein." Still, they might enjoy exploring the language used to express that attitude.

Follow-up Activities and Questions

1. Animals are the sources of various meats. Sometimes, the name of the animal and the meat are the same: A live *chicken* becomes *fried chicken*. Sometimes, the names of the animal and the meat are different. Make a list of animals and the meats that come from them. When the names are not the same, try to figure out why. Looking up word origins will help, but current attitudes may be a factor, too.

2. Write a brief paragraph promoting a fancy French restaurant. Describe the kind of cooking, special dishes, and the setting. Tell who does the cooking. Use some well-chosen adjectives. Try to make the place as appealing as possible.

3. Write a brief paragraph promoting a restaurant called "Mom's Place."

4. Write an essay defending, or criticizing, the "gourmet attitude" toward food. Is it snobbish and elitist, or does it reflect a more positive human impulse? Do you ever have this attitude? If so, when, and why?

Clothing

Clothing is another popular area, and one where most students have attitudes that are anything but utilitarian. Almost all students are "gourmets" when it comes to choosing and wearing clothes. In this area, as in food and cooking, the French have long had tremendous, worldwide prestige. It's not surprising, then, that French–Latin words for clothing have had high status in English from the Middle English period up to the present. The *style* and *fashion* that students value in clothing are French–Latin words and express the classic French attitude.

Students will quickly find that the surviving native words for clothing are few and very basic: *clothes* and *clothing, cap, hat, shirt, shoe,* and *wear.* A few, equally basic native words survive for the making of clothes: *sew, stitch, needle, thread, thimble,* and *wool.* All of these words existed in Old English. Students will also find a few other words that were formed from native elements in Middle and Modern English: *necktie, stocking, sweater,* and *underwear.* These should be considered native as well.

In contrast to this small, utilitarian list, students will find a host of French–Latin loan words that reflect a view of clothing as something special, as a source of social prestige. This intense interest in the social aspect of clothing can be described only in French–Latin loan words; there are no native equivalents for *fashion, mode, style,* or *vogue.* Likewise, there are no native equivalents for the French–Latin names for many things we wear: *boot, coat, dress, gown, jacket, jeans, pants, suit,* and *robe.* Some of these items are ordinary, but several are special, *dress-up* items, and all of them are *dressier* than *underwear.* As students well know, there is a lot of *style* involved in the wearing of the common *jeans,* even if they're not *designer* (Latin) *jeans.* The French–Latin words for making clothes are much fancier and more specialized than the native ones: *embroider, lace, pleat, ribbon, satin, taffeta, tailor, tassel.* When native and French–Latin words are paired as synonyms, the loan words are much higher in tone. Students might explore how many ways "She was wearing her best clothes" could be translated into French–Latin words: For the native *clothes,* there are *attire, apparel,* or *garments;* instead of just *wearing* something, she could be *dressed, attired,* or *arrayed* in it. At some point in class discussion, students might get into larger issues: Why are clothes so important to us? Do clothes reveal or conceal the person beneath them? Interested students could explore such issues in research projects—there are fascinating books on the history of fashion. Other projects are to examine the language of high fashion in magazines such as *Vogue* or in newspaper wedding announcements. Advertisements for clothing stores are also interesting to analyze. Even the Yellow Pages can yield something interesting: Mine lists "Men's Clothing" and "Women's Apparel." Apparently, women are supposed to be more interested in fashion than are men. I wonder if your students would agree.

Follow-up Activities and Questions
1. Translate "The bride was wearing pretty clothes" into several different French–Latin versions. Pick the one you like best, and explain why you chose it over the others.
2. Look around town or in the Yellow Pages for the names of stores that sell clothes. Analyze the kinds of appeal these names make.
3. Write two ads: one for "Sam's Cut-Rate Clothes" and one for "Susanne's Fashion Boutique."
4. Try to describe the clothing of a business executive, using only native words. Then, try to describe the clothing of a construction worker, using only French–Latin words. Which was harder to do? What does this experiment tell you about the words for clothing in the English vocabulary?

Values and Relationships
The area of values and relationships can be interesting to explore, and a focus on common words helps to bring out personal opinions in a relatively impersonal way. You might open up this area by asking your class to consider the words used in significant personal relationships.

1. What qualities do you look for in a good friend?
2. What qualities do you look for in a good parent?
3. What qualities do you look for in a good teacher?

When your students ponder such questions, they'll find that native words have much more status in this area than they do in the areas of food, clothing, or sports. Native words I'd expect to find would include *caring, cool, fair, kind, loving, open, strong, tough,* and *truthful.* I'd also expect the Old Norse loan word *trust,* along with *trustworthy* and *trusting.* Some of the words in this group—*cool, fair,* and *open,* for example—were simply physical terms in Old English; they weren't applied to positive human characteristics until later. Still, these are native in origin, and they retain their down-to-earth tone, even when their meanings become more abstract. A list of common French–Latin words in this area is likely to be just as long and impressive. I'd expect it to include these nouns and their corresponding adjectives: *courage, honesty, honor, loyalty, respect, sincerity,* and *sympathy*; also at least a few other adjectives, such as *dependable, faithful, flexible, generous, reliable,* and *responsible.*

When I asked Elaine Burnham's senior English class to come up with ten words for a good friend, ten for a good parent, and ten for a good teacher, their choices were almost equally divided between native and French–Latin words. For a good friend, they chose, in order, *loyal, trustworthy, outgoing, honest, positive, respectful, open-minded, friendly* itself, *moral,* and *entertaining.* Six of these are French–Latin, and these four are native: *trustworthy, outgoing, open-minded,* and *friendly.* For a good parent, they chose, again in order, *understanding, responsible, loving, caring, giving, respectful* ("of me and my property"), *kind, well-mannered, cool,* and *youthful* (or *a child at heart*). Of these ten words, only three are French–Latin: *responsible, respectful,* and *well-mannered.* Elaine's students tweaked us a bit in their choices for a good teacher; nevertheless, after discounting *lazy* and *easy,* we did get them to agree on the following ten words or phrases, in no particular order: *smart, knowledgeable, laid back, flexible, helpful, honest, consistent, understanding, easy to talk to,* and *creates a good environment.* This list is equally divided between native and French–Latin words: *Smart, knowledgeable, laid back, helpful,* and *understanding* are native; the other five are French–Latin.

It's clear that, in the area of values and relationships, it's not the usual situation of a few humble native words matched against a host of powerful loan words. In this area, the two types of words are about equal in number and in status. When a native and French–Latin word are paired as synonyms, the native word is not always lower or weaker. It may, in fact, be stronger: In each of these pairings, for instance, the first word, the native one, could be seen as a fundamental quality, a virtue, not just an attitude or attribute: *kind/sympathetic; loving/compassionate; trustworthy/reliable.* Native words have such status and strength in this area because they tend to reflect basic human values, personal values, while French–Latin loan words tend more to reflect public values. The more personal a relationship is, the more likely it is to be dominated by native words.

To bring this personal–public distinction home to Elaine's students, I asked them to respond to three additional questions:

1. Would you use the word *loving* to describe a good teacher?

2. Would you use the word *sincere* to describe a good parent?
3. Would you call a good teacher or a good parent *just*?

I expected them to say that the native *loving* is too personal to apply to a teacher–student relationship, which is public and political; that the French–Latin *sincere* is too impersonal to apply to a parent; and that the French–Latin *just* is too public and institutional to apply to a person. I received pretty much what I expected for the first and third questions. Here are some responses to the first question: "No. Because a teacher doesn't love you the way a parent loves you"; "Teachers shouldn't be loving—it's too personal. They should, however, be caring"; "I wouldn't use the word *loving* for a teacher because it doesn't sound professional. Teachers and students should be friendly, but by no means loving." Here are some responses to the third question: "*Just* wouldn't be a quality that I would look for in a teacher—it's too serious. I would expect a judge to be just"; "People who are just in society should be police officers and the court"; "I would want a judge to be just, to follow the rules of America; if a teacher was just, you could never get away with anything."

The answers to the second question surprised me. The students tended to equate the words *sincere* and *honest*; they used *sincere* to mean "honest." I was impressed by how much students wanted their parents to tell them the truth: "I should hope that parents should be sincere. When parents idealize or shelter the child's opinion of themselves, it creates false opinions and misleading hopes. I hope my parents tell me when I'm stupid"; "I'm not sure if I would use sincere because most parents will tell their kids stuff just to support them. I hate it when I do something bad with music or art and my parents try to convince me that it's great." Here's a view which is more understanding of parents but still seems to define *sincere* as "honest": "No, I wouldn't. Sometimes when something bad happens, they can't tell you; it's for your own protection. They just don't want to hurt you." Reading such thoughtful answers made me feel like a cynic, because I never equate *sincere* and *honest*; I just assume that *sincerity* reflects a way of presenting one's self socially. I didn't try to "enlighten" Elaine's students on this distinction; I prefer idealism to cynicism any day.

Although the third question didn't work out quite the way I had expected, I still felt that most of Elaine's students did see how the personal—public distinction applies to the use of native and French–Latin words in the area of values and relationships. The public associations of French–Latin words will become more apparent to students if and when they examine the language of public institutions, the government, the military, and the schools.

Follow-up Activities and Questions

1. List ten qualities you'd look for in a good teacher, and ten you'd look for in a good coach. Look up the origins of the words on each list. Compare and discuss the two lists. Does one list have significantly more of either native or French–Latin words? If so, discuss why.

2. List ten qualities you'd look for in a good boss or employer. Look up the origins of each word on your list. Compare this list with the lists you or your class made for a good teacher and/or a good coach. Discuss similarities and differences.

3. Write a brief speech in support of a candidate for public office (for example, school board, mayor, governor, or president). Look carefully at the "value words" you've used to portray the candidate's relationship to the American people. Analyze how you've used native and French–Latin words.

4. Write brief answers to the following three questions. Share and discuss your answers with the class.

    1. Mrs. Brown doesn't play favorites; she treats all her students the same. Would you call her *fair* or *impartial*? Explain your choice.
    2. Would you prefer your brother or sister to be *kind* or *sympathetic*? Explain your answer.
    3. As a friend, would you prefer to be called *reliable* or *trustworthy*? Explain your answer.
    4. As an employee, would you prefer your boss to be *demanding* or *tough*? Explain your answer.

Government

As a result of the Norman Conquest (see Chapter 3), the government of England was completely taken over by a French-speaking ruling class. During the Middle English period, the Normans and their descendants developed and controlled the government and judicial system of England, giving French–Latin names to the forms they developed. They did leave the native words *king*, *queen*, and *kingdom*, probably because they were too basic to replace, but most of the native words for government simply disappeared. During the Renaissance, this borrowing of loan words continued when scholars introduced the political ideas of the Greeks and Romans into the English vocabulary. As a result of these developments, English acquired a wide range of French–Latin loan words for forms and principles of government. When the American founders established the political institutions of this country, they had these loan words right at hand.

An interesting way to introduce students to the modern American vocabulary of government is to ask them to explore a key paragraph in the Declaration of Independence. Here it is, with French–Latin words italicized and native words in brackets:

> We [hold] these [truths] to be [self]-*evident*, that all [men] are *created equal*, that they are *endowed* by their *Creator* with *certain unalienable* [Rights], that among these are [Life], *Liberty* and the *pursuit* of [Happiness]. That to *secure* these [rights], *Governments* are *instituted* among [Men], *deriving* their *just powers* from the *consent* of the *governed*. That whenever any *Form* of *Government* [becomes] *destructive* of these [ends], it is the [Right] of the *People* to *alter* or to *abolish* it, and to *institute* [new] *Government*, [laying] its *foundation* on such *principles* and *organizing* its *powers* in such *form*, as to them shall seem most [likely] to *effect* their *safety* and [Happiness].

In practice, I'd ask the students to look up the origins of all nouns, adjectives, and verb forms, but I've identified the loan words here for convenience. In the passage as a whole, French–Latin loan words outnumber native words by about two to one, but the proportion is almost one to one in the opening sentence and through the phrase "to secure these rights." I'd ask students to figure out why the first sentence is so different, perhaps by asking, "What is the subject of the first sentence?" and "What is the rest of the paragraph about?" The answer I'd hope to get is that the first sentence is talking about "men" as private individuals, in their relationship to God: The native words *truths* and *Rights* are used to express the religious belief that basic human rights, including *Life* itself, come from God, not from the laws and governments of men. The rest of the paragraph talks about "Governments," human institutions, and it is dominated by French–Latin words. Native words are used for the private or personal sphere; French–Latin words, for the public or political sphere. This distinction holds true in every area of experience, as I try to show throughout this chapter.

When students are asked to develop lists of words for government, they'll find the area totally dominated by French–Latin words, starting with the word *government* itself. French–Latin words name the political entity (the *country*, *nation*, *state*, or *municipality*), the political role of individuals (*citizen*, *taxpayer*, *voter*, the *people*), the kind of political structure (*democracy*, *elective office*, *representative*, *republic*), the branches of government (*executive, judicial, legislative*), and the levels of government (*federal, state, county, city, local*). If students explore the three branches of state and federal government in detail, they'll find many more French–Latin words: for the executive, *administration, cabinet, commissioner, department, governor, policy, president, secretary, treasurer*; for the judicial, *attorney, court, crime, defendant, judge, jurisdiction, jury, plea, plead, plaintiff, police, punishment, sentence, verdict*; for the legislative, *bicameral, bill, congress, congressional, enact, representative, senator, tax*. This listing could be continued almost indefinitely. However, you will need to ask your students to report on the meanings of the words they look up, not just the origins. Your students may be familiar with many of these words, but they may not really know what some of them mean: What, exactly, is the difference between a *democracy* and a *republic*?

There are very few native words still in use in the area of government. *Law*, which is really from Old Norse, is the most important one, but the abstract terms *freedom* and *right* are also widely used. If your students look at local government, they will have more success finding a few native words for political offices, such as *alderman, sheriff*, and *town clerk*, although French–Latin words tend to dominate even at the local level, with offices such as *constable, councillor, mayor*, and *selectman*.

Follow-up Activities and Questions

1. Describe the legal situation in the American Wild West: What were the Good Guys and the Bad Guys called? How was breaking the law punished, when it was punished? What kinds of words dominate the legal world of the Wild West, and why?

2. Explore the words used in your local town, county, or city government. How many native words can you find? Look up the original or root meanings of any native words you find and compare those older meanings with their current meanings.

3. Here are some crimes, described in native words. Translate them into legal terms: setting fires, lying under oath, killing someone, misleading someone, stealing, sleeping with someone else's husband or wife. Are any of your legal terms native, or are they all French–Latin loan words? Do you see any reason why native words for certain crimes might have survived in a legal system dominated by French–Latin words?

4. Following is the Preamble to the Constitution of the United States. Look up the origins of all the nouns, adjectives, and verb forms. Comment on what you find.

We, THE PEOPLE of the United States, in order to form a more perfect Union, establish Justice, insure domestic Tranquillity, provide for the common Defence, promote the general Welfare, and secure the Blessings of Liberty to ourselves and our posterity, do ordain and establish this CONSTITUTION for the United States of America.
—September 17, 1787

The Military

This military is an interesting area for students to explore. Although most teachers I know have fairly strong antimilitary attitudes, most secondary students I know—and not simply the male ones—tend to be quite interested in military matters. They like to read about wars, both historical and fictional, and some of them are planning, or hoping, to have military careers. This interest is not limited to White students. The American military has a good reputation for treating minority citizens fairly and giving them an equal chance to advance.

As an institution of government, the military is dominated by French–Latin loan words, from *military* itself onward. Students exploring this area will be hard-pressed to find native words, but they'll have no trouble finding loan words. The italicized words in the following list are all French–Latin loan words, and they name every aspect of military activity: *war* and its synonyms *action, battle, combat,* and *conflict;* the names of the *armed forces* or *services:* the *Air Force,* the *Army,* the *Marine Corps,* the *Navy;* the ranks of military *personnel: officer, soldier, general, colonel, major, captain, lieutenant, sergeant, corporal, private;* the names of weapons: *arms, artillery, bomb, cannon, rifle;* the names of military *operations* or *strategies: advance, assault, attack, barrage, bombardment, containment, defense, invasion, offensive, retreat;* and, of course, the results: *defeat, glory, peace, surrender, victory.* There are many more military loan words, but these are more than enough to show how common and numerous they are; many of them become even more familiar when they are used as metaphors in sports or politics, two other areas of organized conflict. In contrast to this large group of loan words, students will find only a handful of common native words: *die* (Old Norse), *fight, fire, gun* (Old Norse), *kill, shoot, wound,* and *weapon.*

Comparing the native and French–Latin loan words in this area can be quite revealing. The native words are both few in number and neutral in tone. None of them is exclusively associated with war. People *shoot guns, wound* or *kill* people with *weapons,* every day in robberies, murders, domestic disputes. The native words are ordinary and factual; we hear them on the nightly news. On the other hand, the loan words are used to describe large and important public events, conflicts between political entities, not private individuals. They convey an attitude of seriousness and respect. A *fight* can be merely two men punching each other, but, if a sportswriter calls it "a real battle," it becomes something special and worthy of regard. There is a whole rhetoric of admiration for military activity, and, when it is used metaphorically in areas such as sports or politics, it tends to increase respect for activities in those areas, too. Critics of the military object to this rhetoric, seeing this use of high-toned words to glorify war as a big lie; they claim that it's the native words that give the true picture—*wounds*, *killing*, and *dying*. As a teacher, I try to suggest to my students that both positions are right, and wrong. War can be glorious, but the fancy words can disguise terrible pain. Still, military rhetoric can also ease that pain and emphasize the value of courage and sacrifice. Would the relatives of a dead soldier prefer to hear "He died in battle" or "He died in a fight"?

Although what I've termed *military rhetoric* relies heavily on French–Latin loan words, there are occasions when the simple directness of native words can have rhetorical power, too. A famous example is Winston Churchill's repeated use of *fight* in his address to Parliament on June 4, 1940:

> We shall go on to the end, we shall fight in France, we shall fight on the seas and oceans, we shall fight with growing confidence and growing strength in the air, we shall defend our island, whatever the cost may be, we shall fight on the beaches, we shall fight on the landing grounds, we shall fight in the fields and in the streets, we shall fight in the hills; we shall never surrender . . .

In this speech, Churchill describes England as fighting, not for glory or honor, but for its very survival. Churchill's simple, native language conveys this basic resolve.

Follow-up Activities and Questions

1. Compare these three accounts of the same game. Which one do you prefer, and why?
   a. It was a great game, a tremendous battle between two worthy opponents.
   b. It was a great game, a long, hard fight between two strong teams.
   c. It was a great game, a long, hard fight between two worthy opponents.

2. One of the most famous war stories in American literature is Stephen Crane's novel, *The Red Badge of Courage*. This novel focuses on what a young man, Henry Fleming, learns about war and about himself during the Civil War. Following are two accounts of Henry's state of mind, one from the beginning of the novel, and one from the end. Look up the origins of the words used in each passage. What do the kinds of words used reveal about the change Henry has gone through?

   1. He had burned several times to enlist. Tales of great movements shook the land. They might not be distinctly Homeric, but there seemed to be much glory in them. He had read of marches, sieges, conflicts, and he had longed to see it all. His busy mind had drawn for him large pictures extravagant in color, lurid with breathless deeds. (from Chapter 1)

   2. . . . He found that he could look back upon the brass and bombast of his earlier gospels and see them truly. He was gleeful when he discovered that he now despised them.

      With the conviction came a store of assurance. He felt a quiet manhood, non-assertive but of sturdy and strong blood. He knew that he should no more quail before his guides wherever they should point. He had been to touch the great death, and found that, after all, it was but the great death. He was a man. (from Chapter 24)

3. A fight could be described as a battle, a brawl, a ruckus, or a rumble. What do these words mean and what attitudes do they convey? What kind of fight might be called a battle? Look at the gang fight in S. E. Hinton's, *The Outsiders*. Would you call it a battle? Why or why not?

4. Look up the names for all of the ranks in one or more of the military services. Are any of these names used in other areas of American life? If so, how are they used? Are they used seriously, semi-seriously, or humorously? You might start with Colonel Sanders.

Education

The institution students know best is, of course, the school. In the area of education, as in government and the military, the pattern of language use is the same. There is a small group of native words, surrounded by a very large group of French–Latin words, which dominate the territory. Many of these loan words were borrowed into English directly from Latin, rather than through the intermediary of French. Latin was the language of scholarship and higher learning during the Middle Ages and on into the Renaissance, and it had enormous prestige both in England and in Europe generally. Because of their closeness to Latin, loan words in the area of education may sometimes seem more formal and specialized than French–Latin loan words in government and the military.

While *education* looks and feels like the loan word it is, the word *school* is short, simple, and down to earth, that is, native in look and tone. It's a shock to discover that *school* came into English from Latin and ultimately from Greek. Still, it's an ancient English word, already present in Old English, and I consider it a native word in this chapter: *School* is as far from *education* in tone as the native *teacher* is from *educator*. Students get an ironic laugh at the root meaning of *school*, if and when they look it up: In the *AHD* Appendix under **segh-**, Greek *skhole* is defined as "holding back from work" and "engaging in leisure activity." Today's students tend to define it the opposite way!

When your students explore the words used in schools, they'll find a small core of native words to describe things people do: *teach, learn, read, write, think, know.* (They might note, however, that only *read* and *write* are strongly associated with actual schools.) They'll also find a few other common native words for physical objects and places: *board, book, building, high school, home room, locker, middle school,* and *shop.* While these words name very ordinary things, there are a few native words that name significant concepts: *knowledge, learning, teacher,* and *skill.* These words are positive and dignified in tone. *Skill* is from Old Norse, and the *-ledge* in *knowledge* may have been borrowed, but these are still ancient English words that can be considered native.

In contrast to this small, but significant native group, your students will find a much larger group of French–Latin loan words. These loan words, which I italicize when I first mention them, dominate the structure and content of schools and schooling: Schools have *faculty, principals, students* (and *superintendents* and other *administrators* in the *central office*); the school for the youngest children is called the *elementary, grammar,* or *primary* school; the middle and high schools are called *secondary* schools; schools have different *curricula* or *courses* of *study*; students can take *college-preparatory, general,* or *vocational* courses; students have *classes* or courses in different *subjects*; *academic* subjects may include the broad categories of *foreign languages, mathematics, social studies,* and *science,* along with the specific subjects within each category; subjects include *art*, *biology*, *history*, *physics*, and so on—the only common subject with a native name is *English* itself; successful students *pass* from one *grade* to the next, receiving a *diploma* at *graduation* or *commencement*; outstanding students also receive awards for *academic achievement*. After graduating, students can take the French–Latin route and *enroll* in a *college* or *university*, or they can follow the native road and *go to work* (native).

Many of these loan words are special and necessary; there are no native equivalents for them. There are, however, some areas of overlap that your students could explore. The native verb *teach* has at least two French–Latin "synonyms": *instruct* and *educate*. Your students might write some sample sentences, insert the three synonyms in them, and discuss the results. They might try the same thing with *teacher*, *instructor*, and *educator*. I think they'd find that the native words sound more personal and down to earth, while the loan words reflect a concern for public status or "image." Good secondary teachers call themselves *teachers*, not *educators*, but an image-conscious school might announce that "our faculty are *professional educators*, many with *advanced degrees*" (French–Latin words italicized by me.).

Like all institutions, schools have their special jargon, their official rhetoric, and, like all institutional rhetoric, it is dominated by French–Latin words. Students have probably encountered enough of this official school language to be quite good at writing it. They might enjoy translating back and forth between the official school version and the "real" version of the same basic facts. They might try writing mock report cards, sugar-coating facts such as these for parental consumption:

> John sleeps through every class.
> John swears at his teachers.

Then again, you might bring in some educational jargon and ask your students to translate it into plain, native English:

> We want our students to relate positively to printed texts.
> We want our students to develop their social interaction skills.

Although your students can have some fun mocking the excesses of school language, you may not wish to let the mockery go too far. Some school language is silly and pretentious, but much of it is valuable and necessary. Without French–Latin words and concepts, serious academic work would be almost impossible. With native words, we can ask our students to *think*; with French–Latin words, we can be more specific and more helpful.

We can ask them to *analyze, classify, compare, contrast, define, evaluate, interpret*, and so on; we can identify a whole host of intellectual strategies and help our students learn how to use them. Furthermore, a proper use of prestigious French–Latin words can confer respect for education itself. In our society, it really *is* an *honor* to be an *honor student*; people celebrate it on their bumper stickers! High school *commencements* are formal occasions when whole communities listen to French–Latin rhetoric in praise of *academic achievement*. There's too much political posturing about education in the United States today, but, beneath it all, *education* remains one of our society's most respected words and values.

Follow-up Activities and Questions

1. In Avi's young adult novel, *Nothing But the Truth* (Avon, 1993), a fairly typical high school student named Philip Malloy has a good deal of trouble at Harrison High School. The novel features a number of letters from school administrators, written on official school stationery. At the top of this stationery is the slogan "Where Our Children Are Educated, Not Just Taught." On the basis of this slogan, what do you expect the school administrators to be like? You might like to read this novel—it has lots of good insights into the politics of high school life. If you do read it, take a close look at the language used in the letters themselves.

2. Here are several verbs often used in school assignments: *analyze, classify, define, interpret*, and *summarize*. All of these are French–Latin in origin. Try to capture their meanings by translating them into native words. Share and discuss what you come up with.

3. What's the difference between *education* and *training*? Are there some areas in which one term might be more appropriate than the other? Look up the root meanings of each verb. Then, write a brief essay in answer to these questions.

4. Here, from W. E. B. DuBois' *The Souls of Black Folk*, is his description of the first colleges established for the newly freed slaves after the Civil War. What does DuBois praise about these schools? Look at the key words he uses. Are they native, French–Latin, or a mixture of both? What values are associated with each type of word?

> The teachers in these institutions came not to keep the Negroes in their place, but to raise them out of the defilement of the places where slavery had wallowed them. The colleges they founded were social settlements; homes where the best of the

sons of the freedmen came in close and sympathetic touch with the best traditions of New England. They lived and ate together, studied and worked, hoped and harkened in the dawning light. In actual formal content their curriculum was doubtless old-fashioned, but in educational power, it was supreme, for it was the contact of living souls. (from Chapter VI)

What Students Can Learn About Our Language and Culture

There are many other categories that your students might like to explore: arts and crafts, popular culture and entertainment, religion (in the right school climate), and science. Some areas, like carpentry or farming, will show considerably less French–Latin influence and more native survivals. I hope that, after exploring a few categories, your students might want to do more.

This kind of investigation has many benefits. First of all, it can give your students a stronger sense of the differences between native words and French–Latin loan words. They'll find that, in every public area, French–Latin words tend to name the things that have power and prestige, the things that are more highly valued in our society. They'll also find some significant exceptions: native words, such as *love, right,* and *learning,* that name highly valued things or concepts. In terms of rhetoric or writing style, your students will find that French–Latin words have a dignified and impressive tone, which can confer value on things, such as sports or warfare, that might be viewed less positively if described in more ordinary terms. If they respond critically, but not cynically, your students will see that French–Latin words can be used for good or for ill: They can be used to celebrate some of our highest ideals and values (*courage, education, liberty*), but, in the language of advertising or bureaucracies generally, they can also be used to inflate or deceive. To sum it all up, I'd claim that students who do this activity will learn a great deal about our language and our culture, and about the relationship between the two.

10
Words and Gender

Words reflect social assumptions and attitudes that may not be fully apparent, even to people who use them. A careful study of the words used in a given area can make students more aware of the attitudes behind common words and more careful in their own word choices. Discovering that innocent-looking words may reflect unconscious bias can be quite an eye-opener for students. When I ask White students what color *flesh-colored* Band-Aids are, they are often stunned by the casual assumption that everyone's skin is the same color as theirs: "Oh my God, I never realized I was being a racist without even knowing it!" is the kind of reaction I usually get.

In this chapter, I set forth some ways that you can engage your students in a close look at the attitudes and assumptions embedded in common words involving gender differences. Gender is an engaging and timely area to explore. All students are interested in it, and it is, of course, an area in which important social changes are occurring. A close study of the common words used can lead students to an informed discussion of those changes. Because discussion of gender differences leads quite easily to the issue of sexual orientation, I provide some ideas for engaging students in a study of that topic, too, both in this chapter and more fully in Chapter 11.

Gender Assumptions and Attitudes: Results of a Questionnaire

I am using some recent classes I spent with Donna Bakke's senior writing students to illustrate some teaching approaches. Donna and I began the first session by passing out the handout in Figure 10.1, duly expanded with writing spaces after each question. I had used most of the questions before, in both high school and college classes, but there were a few new ones I was eager to try out.

FIGURE 10.1
Language and Gender Questionnaire: Assumptions and Attitudes

1. What's the male counterpart of a **tomboy**? Is it a positive term? Is **tomboy** a positive term?

2. What's the female counterpart of **bachelor**? Is it a positive term? Is **bachelor** a positive term?

3. Write two sentences: use a form of **father** as the verb in one; use a form of **mother** as the verb of the other. What do the words **father** and **mother** mean in these sentences?

4. Compare the ways boys and girls use the words **girlfriend** and **boyfriend.** Explain any differences you see.

5. Which of the following words would be considered a compliment when applied to one gender but not to the other? Which would be considered a compliment by both genders? Put **F, M,** or **B** after each word, or **N,** if you don't think either gender would consider it a compliment.

Kind:	Brave:	Sweet:	Polite:	Tough:
Aggressive:	Gentle:	Sensitive:	Nice:	Competitive:
Bubbly:	Perky:			

6. Is there a female counterpart to **macho?** Is **macho** a positive term?

7. Is **lady** a positive term? All the time? Consider these examples: "She is always a lady," cleaning lady, lady wrestler, lady poet.

8. In Shakespeare's day, the lord of the household was referred to as **sir** or **master,** while the lady of the household was referred to as **madam** or **mistress.** Have all of these words kept their status?

9. What metaphor do **straight, deviant,** and **perverted** have in common? What social attitudes and assumptions determine how these words are applied to people and behavior today?

©2001 by Thomas Carnicelli from *Words Work*. Portsmouth, NH: Heinemann.

The class wrote out their answers, while Donna and I circulated to answer questions. Students needed the most help with numbers 3 and 9. It was a ninety-minute session. The students wrote their responses during the first half hour, and we discussed the questions as a class during the next hour. I'll go through the questions one by one, focusing on what this one group of students said and wrote, but also reflecting more generally on the issues these questions raise and the other teaching opportunities they could provide.

Question one. *Tomboy* was regarded as a positive term; students agreed that it's OK for a girl to act like a boy. The reverse, however, was definitely not OK. A boy who "acts like a girl" was viewed negatively, and the class produced a rich list of disapproving terms: *Momma's boy* and *sissy* were the most common, followed by *fag, fairy, fruitcake, girly, sally-swanker,* and *wimp.* I must admit I wasn't prepared for this barrage of antihomosexual terms. Nor was Donna, who is a good deal younger than I. We told them that, in our youths, when consciousness of homosexuality was not so widespread, only the first two words were used. Society took a negative view of boys who "act like girls" even then, but such boys were not described as homosexuals, although I suppose the negative values attached to *momma's boy* and *sissy* reflected a suppressed fear that such boys might be or become homosexual. In any case, discussion of question 1 led us to two larger questions: Why does society approve of girls acting like boys but not vice versa? Why is the very possibility of homosexuality violently attacked in males but essentially ignored in females? Our class didn't get too far into these questions in our discussion, but the questions were clearly raised. The answers seem to involve two interrelated social assumptions: (1) males are superior to females; hence, it's only natural for girls to try to act like boys. (2) Homosexuality is a bad thing, especially in males, the dominant gender, because it leads males to take on characteristics of the supposedly inferior gender. These assumptions became clearer to the students as we worked through the other questions on the handout.

Question two. I hoped that this question, like the first one, would show students an underlying social assumption that women are inferior to men: A *bachelor* is a positive term; a man does not need to be married to have a good, valuable, maybe even enviable life. An unmarried woman is, however, widely regarded with pity or contempt; she is branded with the negative terms *spinster* or *old maid.* The assumption is that a woman's life acquires worth and status only through marriage with a man. All the students in our class saw *bachelor* as a positive term, especially if it referred to a younger unmarried man. A few expressed negative feelings towards the idea of an old unmarried man: "*Bachelor* can be negative if you're old or positive if you're young." The strongest negatives were, predictably, for old unmarried women, usually called *spinsters* and variously described as "old," "decrepit," "crabby," "mean," and "unuseful." Five students used the term *bachelorette*, which they tended to define positively (not surprisingly, because they said they got the word from the television show, "The Dating Game," where the unmarried women would hardly be considered spinsters!). I had the impression that this question was too far outside the life experience of most of the students for them to have much insight into it. Basically, they just preferred young people to old people and expected everybody to get married sooner or later. Most didn't fully see the social prejudices involved. There were, however, some nice exceptions, as in this written comment: "A spinster. A woman is looked down upon for not having been married by the age of 40 whereas men are rarely questioned or commented on if they are not married." And this one: "A woman who is not married is an old maid. Most women get married, and *old maid* is a negative term because most people think women should get married and have a family."

Question three. The point of question 3 is that society has traditionally had very different expectations for male and female parents. As a verb, *father* has traditionally meant simply to beget a child physically, whereas the verb *mother* has meant to nurture and care for a child. The students were familiar with the meaning of *mother* as a verb, but only a few knew the meaning of the verb *father* as well: "To father a child usually means to be the one who impregnates a woman, whereas to mother a child means to be the lifelong caretaker of the child." Several students defined the verb *father* as performing a father's distinctive caretaking role: " 'The dad fathered the child.' 'The mom mothered the child.' In the first sentence, the word *fathered* means that the dad set down the rules of the house. He also punished the child and didn't care as much about the feelings of the child. The word *mothered* means that the child's emotions were considered more." It's possible that the verb *father* will grow to have this meaning, but I don't believe this meaning really exists now. This student is inventing this definition by analogy with the verb *mother*, but society at large is tending in another direction, using the nongendered *parent* as a verb to describe the nurturing or caretaking function. Several students mentioned that the verb *mother* can have a negative meaning, like "spoiling the child" or trying "to protect the child from the world." I tried to point out that mothers just can't win in society's eyes: They're expected to do all the caretaking but are criticized for doing it too zealously. Both *momma's boy* and the negative meaning of the verb *mother* express the same underlying assumption: Mothers shouldn't dominate their children, especially their male children; males should not be subject to too much female influence.

Question four. This question, like question 1, gets directly into the life experience of teen-agers. It was the one to spark the best discussion and the best insights. This written comment, when read aloud, provoked some strong reactions: "Girls are more comfortable with their sexuality (as a whole). We are able to refer to our women friends as 'girlfriends' without fearing that people take it in a sexual way. Men, however, can't refer to their male friends as 'boyfriends' for fear of being thought of as gay." Nobody disagreed that the words are used in exactly this way, but the males denied that they felt personally insecure; they argued that they were merely adhering to a social taboo. The question raised in question 1 arose again here. Why does society not want boys to "act like girls," not to express any special affection for their same-gender friends? The answer would seem to be society's strong aversion to homosexuality, especially among males. And why does society have such a hostile attitude toward homosexuality? We didn't go into that question here, but we did touch on it in discussing question nine.

Let's pause for a moment to reflect on the issues raised in the first four questions. In one sense, traditional social attitudes are quite negative toward females, yet they also allow females certain freedoms that males are not allowed. By the same token, males are regarded as superior in some ways and granted certain freedoms, but they are also severely restricted by traditional expectations. A good question to ask at this point would be something like this: "Given our society's traditional assumptions about gender roles, which gender is better off—males or females?" I didn't have the chance to ask Donna's class to write in response to this question, but it would have been a fruitful way to bring things together.

Note: Question 5 is addressed in the section, Is This Word a Compliment? The results of question 5 were so interesting, I used them to develop a whole new series of questions and activities. So, on to question 6.

Question six. Question 6 was just a fishing expedition on my part. I'd never used this question before and I didn't know what I'd get, because I don't know of a female counterpart to *macho*. The question worked much better than I'd hoped. The answers were extremely varied and extremely revealing. The concept of a macho woman inspired both hostility and admiration, and the attempts to define it were often unusually thoughtful. The most colorful term students came up with was *hoochie* or *hoochy*, a term that some saw as positive, some as negative: "Someone who wears revealing clothes, is self-assertive, and goes for what she wants—a babe, spice girl, feminist, hoochie"; "Macho men I have encountered have been overly confident in their looks and personality. Hoochies are also that way; they walk around thinking every man wants them. So, overall, *macho* and *hoochie* are negative." Some of the female students liked the out-front sexiness that a female version of *macho* implies and connected it with feminism: "Radical Feminist—strong, female, sexy, and aggressive." Another female student, though, felt that such a woman would be described negatively by society at large: "The female counterpart to *macho*, and please excuse my language, would be considered a bitch. If a woman came across as aggressive and outspoken, society would look upon her as a bitch. She might also be called *butch* if she had muscles and was outspoken to men." This student was more right than she realized, because four of her classmates did use *butch* as the answer to this question. Apparently, they couldn't conceive of a positive image combining aggressiveness, sexiness, and heterosexuality: "Butch, and this is anything but positive. If a woman is referred to as a butch, she is thought of as a manly lesbian." A macho man is the very opposite of homosexual (despite the Village People!), yet a macho woman somehow has to be a lesbian! We didn't get a chance to discuss these various terms much in Donna's class. I really wish we had. The more I read the written comments, the more fascinating they become. Clearly the concept of a macho woman is an attempt to combine the stereotypes of the two genders—it's the *sensitive male* in reverse. No wonder the responses were so varied.

Question seven. We did have a chance to discuss question 7. In their written answers, most students regarded *lady* as a positive term, associating it with dignity and refinement, "the stereotype of what a woman should be." Most derived this concept from the sentence, "She is always a lady," and had little to say about the other examples. In class discussion, I told them that early feminists hated the word *lady* because it set forth a "proper," but passive and traditional role for women, the very stereotype the students were praising. I asked the students to compare *lady* and *woman* and to decide which one is stronger. Most students agreed that *woman* is the stronger term, but they continued to value the concept of a *lady*, too. When we came to discuss the other examples, the students saw that *lady* was being used in rather bizarre ways: *Cleaning lady* is an attempt to dignify a menial job; *lady wrestler* is deliberately ironic; and *lady poet* is, in the written comment of one perceptive student, "kind of sexist because 'lady poet' makes the point that all poets are male except for 'lady' poets."

Question eight. Students recognized *sir* and, to a much lesser extent, *madam* as polite and respectful forms of address, but they generally saw the other two terms as negative: "*Sir* and *Madam* still have retained their regality, whereas *master* has a controlling undertone and *mistress* refers often to adultery." They realized that *mistress* had gone down in status, but they didn't realize how far *madam* had fallen, too, because none of them knew its common connection to the brothel. The point of this question is to show how female words of power tend to lose status while male words of power retain status. There are, of course, plenty of positive senses of *master* still in use, but I doubt whether there are any positive senses of *mistress* left, at least in contemporary America. If you would like to pursue this kind of inquiry, you could invite students to consider other male–female pairs: *patron/matron, governor/governess, lord/lady, wizard/witch*. In all cases, the male term retains power and prestige, while the female term has considerably less power, or, like *witch* or *madam*, power in a socially disapproved area.

Question nine. To answer this question 9, students needed a certain amount of prodding from Donna and me. We asked them what action or picture lay behind the three words *straight, deviant,* and *perverted* and directed them to look up word meanings and etymologies. The etymology of *deviant* in the *AHD* is the best clue: "Lat. *de-* 'off, from' and Lat. *via* 'road, way.'" Once they got the picture of a path, the students connected the three words easily: *Straight* means "going in the right direction"; *deviant* means "leaving the beaten path"; *perverted* means "turning around completely," "going the wrong way," or "walking a twisted path." The students clearly saw the applications of this metaphor to sexual behavior, to drug use (to be *straight* is to be "free of drugs"), and to criminal behavior (criminals try to *go straight* and obey the laws of society). They also concluded that there seems to be a strong element of religious morality behind society's aversion to homosexuality: Like criminals, homosexual people have strayed from the religious ideal of following "the straight and narrow path."

Is This Word a Compliment?

The responses to question 5 proved remarkably fruitful. The students marked their responses to it during the first class meeting, and we discussed those responses during most of a second ninety-minute period. I had tallied all of their responses and passed out the table in Figure 10.2 prior to the discussion.

Before I discuss these results, let me set forth what I was trying to do with this question. I devised question 5 to test how strong traditional gender stereotypes are in the group. I put in five "hard" words, which reflect the traditional male image: *aggressive, ambitious, brave, competitive,* and *tough.* I balanced these with five "soft" words, which reflect traditional female images: *bubbly, gentle, perky, sensitive,* and *sweet.* I then added in three words I didn't expect to be strongly associated with either gender: *kind, nice,* and *polite.*

Donna and I set up the class discussion with a series of questions. After reaching an easy consensus as to which words would traditionally be associated with males and females, we then asked the class whether, in their survey responses, they had reinforced or contradicted the stereotypes. The students found a considerable departure from traditional gender stereotypes on the part of both male and female respondents. Both groups had strongly agreed that two traditional male words, *ambitious* and *brave,* are now commonly applied to both genders. Although there were clear traces of the more traditional view for *brave,* which had 4 1/2 votes for M, *ambitious* got only 2 M votes. The two groups had also agreed that one of the "softer," more female words, *sensitive,* is now commonly applied to both genders, although the word did get 4 F votes, which reflects the more traditional view.

That part was easy enough to establish. The next part was a bit more of a challenge. We asked the males and females to form separate groups and asked them these two questions:

1. How did your group define itself? What qualities did it value? What qualities did it resist or reject?
2. How did your group define the other group? Did you make any false assumptions about the other group?

Answering the first one involved adding the B's and F's for the females, and the B's and M's for the males. Both groups found that they defined themselves in ways somewhat beyond the traditional gender stereotypes. In their survey answers, the females were comfortable enough with all of the traditional "soft" words, but they added the "harder" *ambitious* and *brave* as well; they were, however, not generally comfortable with other traditional

FIGURE 10.2
Is This Word a Compliment?

For Males (M), for Females (F), for Both (B), or for Neither (N)?

Word	Difference	Male Group (8)	Female Group (8)	Total
kind	0	7B, 1F	7B, 1F	14B, 2F
nice	½	7½B, ½F	8B	15½B, ½F
brave	½	5½B, 2½M	6B, 2M	11½B, 4½M
tough	½	6½M, 1½B	6M, 2B	12½M, 3½B
perky	1	7F, 1B	6F, 1B, 1N	13F, 2B, 1N
aggressive	1½	5M, 3B	4½M, 2B, 1½N	9½M, 5B, 1½N
ambitious	2	8B	6B, 2M	14B, 2M
polite	2	8B	5B, 2F	13B, 2F
sensitive	2	7B, 1F	5B, 3F	12B, 4F
sweet	2	4B, 3F	3B, 5F	7B, 8F
gentle	2	4B, 4F	5B, 2F	9B, 6F
competitive	3	6B, 2M	3B, 3M, 2N	9B, 5M, 2N
bubbly	3	4N, 3F, 1B	1N, 6F, 1B	9F, 5N, 2B

The differences are between the male and female groups. When there are only seven votes counted for a group, one of the eight group members did not vote. Fractions indicate split votes (i.e. B/F).

male words, such as *aggressive, competitive,* or *tough,* although those words did get a few female votes. The males were comfortable enough with all of the traditional male words, but they were also surprisingly comfortable with the "softer" female words *sensitive* and *sweet,* and they certainly wanted to be considered *kind, nice,* and *polite.* The only soft word they resisted, slightly, was *gentle.* On the basis of this analysis, the groups concluded that the males had broadened their conception of their gender somewhat more than the females had broadened theirs.

To answer the second question, the two groups were told to focus their attention on the last seven words, the ones in which the differences between the two groups were greatest. It's clear that each group made some false assumptions about the other. The males assumed that the females were more comfortable with being called *ambitious* and *competitive* than the females actually were. The females were, in fact, deeply conflicted about the ideal of being *competitive*: Only three out of the eight female respondents considered it complimentary to their gender, and two of the eight didn't consider it a compliment to anyone. Four of the eight males assumed that no one would like to be called *bubbly*, but seven of the eight females seemed to feel comfortable enough with it. On the basis of their responses to these three words, the females turned out to be more traditional than the males had assumed.

On the other hand, the males turned out to be somewhat less traditional than the females had assumed. The female respondents assumed that males would be more opposed to "soft" compliments than the males turned out to be. The females voted, 5F–3B, to consider *sweet* a female compliment, but the males voted, 4B–3F, to consider it complimentary to both genders. The males were much more positive about being called *polite* or *sensitive* than the females had assumed they would be. Only in response to the "soft" word *gentle* were the males a little more traditional than the females expected: The females voted, 5B–2F, to consider the word equally complimentary to both genders, but the males split, 4B–4F, on the word.

After a careful analysis of the survey results, the class went on to discuss what the results might mean. All kinds of interesting questions arose:

1. Why do females tend to resist the idea of being *aggressive, tough,* or *competitive*? Are they right to resist these ideas, or are they being too passive and timid?
2. Why do females accept *bubbly* as a compliment? Don't they want to be taken seriously?
3. Why do males resist *gentle* as a compliment but accept *sensitive* and *sweet*?
4. Males seem to have moved away from the traditional male image. Have they moved far enough? Should they try to become less *competitive, aggressive,* and *tough*? Or have they moved too far already?

These questions provoked lively discussion, just as they would in any class. The most heated debate centered around the value of being *competitive*: Is competitiveness a good or bad thing? The group moved inevitably to the largest question of all: "Should society work toward breaking down traditional gender stereotypes, or do these stereotypes represent important truths about the natures of males and females?" That, of course, would be a perfect topic for an essay to conclude this brief inquiry into gender stereotypes.

Strong, Hard Words and Weak, Soft Words

Answering and discussing the initial written questions and then analyzing and discussing the responses to question 5 took our class almost three hours of class time. We did, however, find time for one more thing. Ever since I first heard of it, I've been intrigued by the "semantic differential" technique developed by the communications scholar Charles E. Osgood. This technique consists of getting respondents to mark their reactions to a given word on a series of scales between opposing adjectives. The word in question is put at the top and the opposing adjectives are set at opposite ends of the scales. The format looks like the following, with *tough* as the word to be scrutinized:

tough

strong	_	_	_	_	_	weak
cold	_	_	_	_	_	warm
serious	_	_	_	_	_	silly
hard	_	_	_	_	_	soft

The positions on the scales could be labeled *very, quite, neutral, quite,* and *very*. Thus, if I felt that *tough* has the connotation of being very strong, I'd mark the far left position on the strong/weak scale. On the other hand, if I felt that *tough* does not give a distinct impression of either seriousness or silliness, I'd mark the middle position on the serious/silly scale.

I set up some simple scales for some of the more controversial words identified in the survey. Osgood usually had seven positions, but I kept it to five. Osgood usually had ten or more opposing traits, but I limited it to just four. I chose the words to contrast qualities traditionally found in the male and female stereotypes. The results of this little experiment allowed our class to understand the survey responses a bit better. Figure 10.3 shows the class reactions to some of the key words. There were twelve respondents in all, six male and six female.

These results shown in Figure 10.3 confirm my initial assumption that *aggressive, ambitious, brave, competitive,* and *tough* are "hard" words. All five are marked very heavily in the two left-hand columns, next to "hard" and its related qualities "strong," "serious," and "cold." The word with the most marks in the two left-hand columns was *tough*, which received 45 out of a

FIGURE 10.3
Semantic Differential Scales

Aggressive

strong	10	1	1	0	0	weak
cold	6	4	2	0	0	warm
serious	6	2	2	2	0	silly
hard	8	4	0	0	0	soft
	30	11	5	2	0	

Ambitious

strong	5	7	0	0	0	weak
cold	0	4	8	0	0	warm
serious	8	3	1	0	0	silly
hard	6	2	4	0	0	soft
	19	16	13	0	0	

Brave

strong	12	0	0	0	0	weak
cold	2	4	4	0	0	warm
serious	8	2	1	1	0	silly
hard	6	3	3	0	0	soft
	28	9	8	1	0	

Gentle

strong	0	0	2	5	5	weak
cold	0	0	0	2	10	warm
serious	2	3	5	2	0	silly
hard	0	0	1	0	11	soft
	2	3	8	9	26	

Tough

strong	12	0	0	0	0	weak
cold	8	2	2	0	0	warm
serious	10	1	1	0	0	silly
hard	10	2	0	0	0	soft
	40	5	3	0	0	

Competitive

strong	11	1	0	0	0	weak
cold	5	4	3	0	0	warm
serious	10	1	1	0	0	silly
hard	8	3	1	0	0	soft
	34	9	5	0	0	

Sweet

strong	0	0	7	4	1	weak
cold	0	0	0	1	11	warm
serious	1	2	5	2	2	silly
hard	0	0	1	0	11	soft
	1	2	13	7	25	

Sensitive

strong	0	1	2	4	5	weak
cold	0	0	1	1	10	warm
serious	4	0	7	0	1	silly
hard	0	0	2	1	9	soft
	4	1	12	6	25	

Bubbly

strong	0	2	2	3	5	weak
cold	0	1	3	1	7	warm
serious	0	0	0	2	10	silly
hard	0	0	2	3	7	soft
	0	3	7	9	29	

possible 48. It was followed by *competitive* (43), *aggressive* (41), *brave* (37), and *ambitious* (35). These figures shed light on the results of the earlier survey. In that survey, the eight male respondents unanimously accepted all five of these "hard" words as complimentary to them; the eight female respondents regarded only two of the five—*brave* and *ambitious*—as complimentary to them, and with two dissenting votes in each case. They rejected the three "hardest" words and felt comfortable only with the slightly "softer" two of the five—*brave* and *ambitious*. They obviously felt that they did not want to identify with the "harder," more combative aspects of the traditional male stereotype.

The results of this semantic differential experiment also shed light on other questions raised in the earlier survey. The words *bubbly*, *gentle*, *perky*, *sensitive*, and *sweet* did prove to be "soft," with a majority of marks in the two right-hand columns, next to "soft" and its related qualities, "warm," "silly," and "weak." The word with the most marks in the two right-hand columns was *bubbly*, with 38, followed by *gentle* (35), *sweet* (32), and *sensitive* (31); *perky*, not listed in Figure 10.3, had 26. The two with the most votes, *bubbly* and *gentle*, produced some unusual results in the survey, and these figures may help to explain those results. In the survey, a majority of the male respondents felt that *bubbly* is not a compliment to either gender, but seven of the eight female respondents regarded it as complimentary to them. When the marks for *bubbly* are compared with the marks for the other "soft" words, the big difference is found on the serious/silly scale. *Bubbly* was clearly regarded as the silliest word by both males and females; all twelve respondents marked it as quite (2) or very (10) silly.

It seems clear that females are more accepting of "silly" qualities than are males. Females don't mind these qualities, and even like them. Why don't males feel the same way? Is it because males feel more obliged to maintain a "cool" or "strong, silent" image? In the survey, a majority of the male respondents considered the "soft" words *sensitive* and *sweet* as complimentary to them, but they were more resistant to *gentle*. A look at the figures might explain why. *Gentle* is ranked the "weakest"; it is slightly weaker than *sensitive* and considerably weaker than *sweet*. It is tied for "softest" and "warmest" with *sweet*. It has slightly more of these three traditional female qualities than any other word, including *bubbly*, which has more right-hand marks over all. Perhaps that's the problem; perhaps *gentle* is just a little too "soft" and female for the males to be entirely comfortable with it.

These semantic differential scales are fun to play with, and they can, as in this case, confirm and clarify intuitions and assumptions about people's reactions to words. They have many uses in contemporary society. Advertisers and political consultants use them to craft messages to appeal to various segments of the population. Teachers in turn can use them to help students analyze the language of advertisements and political speeches. In fact, teachers can use them to explore the connotations of any word.

These activities were done in two ninety-minute class periods and part of a third. In the first period, the students wrote responses to the nine questions on the initial handout for about thirty minutes; then, the whole class discussed the questions for the next four. Before the next meeting, I compiled the results from question 5 and presented them as a chart. Interpreting and discussing these results took up most of the next ninety-minute session. At the end of that second session, students filled out semantic differential scales for all the words used in question 5. I compiled the results and presented them briefly at the start of a third class period, which was mostly devoted to other activities.

This unit was highly compact, and it could easily have been extended over another full week or so. The two statistical activities could, for instance, have been done by the students themselves. Compiling, interpreting, and presenting information in clear graphic form are valuable skills that all students need to acquire. I recognize, of course, that not all teachers will choose to use these rather technical activities—although I do want to urge every teacher to try semantic differential scales at some point. Without the statistical work, the unit still offers plenty of opportunity for fruitful discussion. It also offers endless opportunities for writing assignments, including two topics I've mentioned before but want to repeat here:

1. Given our society's traditional assumptions about gender roles, who is better off—a male or a female?
2. Should our society continue to try to break down traditional gender stereotypes, or have we gone far enough? Are these stereotypes simply social conventions, or do they reflect important truths about the natures of the two genders?

At the end of a unit like this one, writing essays on either of these topics would help students assimilate and connect the points raised in earlier discussions of specific words.

A study of the words used for gender in our society leads inevitably to the issue of homosexuality. In Donna's class, I asked only one question directly related to attitudes toward homosexuality: the one involving the common metaphor behind *straight*, *deviant*, and *perverted*. Nevertheless, almost every other question led us to confront the issue: Why is *tomboy* a positive term, while *sissy* is highly negative? Why do we praise a male for being *his father's son* but criticize a male for being a *mother's boy*? Why can a girl call her female friend her *girlfriend*, while a boy would never be caught dead calling a male friend his *boyfriend*?

We raised and discussed these questions in Donna's class, but my primary focus there was on gender stereotypes. I wish we'd had the time to explore social attitudes toward homosexuality in greater depth. It's a tricky topic, but Donna's students could have handled it; they were mature and comfortable discussing sexual issues. For teachers who have a suitably mature class, and who want to tackle an explosive but highly important topic, I've developed a detailed unit on the words people use to talk about homosexuality; that unit appears in the next chapter. It can be taught in conjunction with parts of this chapter, but it can also be taught by itself.

11
Homosexuality
The Words We Use to Talk About It

While I'm strongly, even viscerally, opposed to teachers trying to impose a social or political agenda on their students, I do encourage teachers to address issues of outright prejudice. I think it's highly appropriate for teachers to address the prejudices inherent in female, and male, stereotypes. In this chapter, I encourage you to do something more risky: Address the widespread prejudice against homosexuality.

Prejudice against homosexuality has led to some very bad things in our secondary schools: taunting and social ostracism of any student suspected of being homosexual; savage beatings of boys who are, or are suspected of being, homosexual; suicides of boys or girls who feel, accurately or not, that they are homosexual. It is high time that our schools began to combat such horrors by asking our students to think seriously about homosexuality and about the way it is regarded in American society at large. To that end, I developed a unit that focuses on the words people commonly use to talk about heterosexual and homosexual behaviors. Whenever I've discussed this topic with classes, I've found that a focus on the common words used gives everyone something "out there" to talk about, so that the discussion doesn't get bogged down in personal opinions and arguments.

I'm well aware of how explosive discussions of homosexuality can be. Several years ago, when I was discussing attitudes toward homosexuality with a class of Black high school students, things often got pretty tense. One of the male students was openly homosexual, and, at one point, another Black male called him "a traitor to the race." Another student, from a conservative religious background, thought homosexuality was sinful and wanted to leave the class until we moved to a new topic. Nevertheless, the group stayed together, talked together, and did, I think, develop more tolerant attitudes.

Increased tolerance is the avowed goal of the following unit. This unit is something I put together specifically for this book, but it is based on many of my teaching experiences, at both the high school and college levels. This approach has worked for me in the past, and I feel confident in recommending it to other teachers. I do, however, want to issue two warnings: (1) The class must be mature enough to handle the topic, and (2) the teacher must be careful not to come on too strongly against students with initially prejudiced attitudes. Tolerance has to work both ways!

Defining Assumptions: What's Wrong with Homosexuality?

I like to initiate discussion by giving the class some basic definitions, taken from the *AHD*:

> **morality:** 2. A system of ideas of right and wrong conduct: *religious morality; Christian morality.*

> **natural:** 1. Present in or produced by nature; . . . 4a. Not acquired, inherent.

> **normal:** 2. *Biology.* Functioning or occurring in a natural way.

> **pathological:** 2. Relating to or caused by disease.

In discussing these concepts with students, I'm especially interested in their thoughts on where our ideas of right and wrong come from: Do these ideas all come from religion, or are there moral values that aren't derived directly from religion? Do atheists, for instance, have a sense of right and wrong? At some point, I like to connect this philosophical discussion to a larger question: Where does opposition to homosexuality come from? After discussing the matter, classes generally agree that there are three basic positions against homosexuality: the moral/religious view, the medical view, and the biological view. When people say homosexuality is *sinful*, they're expressing the moral/religious view. When people call homosexuality an *abnormality* or a *disease*, that's basically a medical view, although the word *abnormal* often seems to interchange with *unnatural*. When people say that homosexuality is *unnatural*, they seem to be taking a broader view, to claim that homosexuality is contrary to the biological laws of nature itself. This might be called the biological view, although it often tends to have a moral component, as when people call homosexuality "a sin against nature."

After the class has identified these various positions, I pass out a list of words: *heterosexual, straight, homosexual, lesbian, gay, sodomite, deviant, pervert,* and *perverted*, *queer*, *fairy*, *fag* and *faggot*, and *unnatural*. I then assign the words to student teams. Each team must report five things about their assigned word:

1. The word's sexual meaning, if it has one
2. Any other significant meanings it has
3. Its origin or root meaning
4. The word's current social status
5. The kind of standard the word expresses

For the fourth part, I tell them to use these questions: Is the word's current sexual meaning positive, neutral, or negative? Is its sexual meaning classified as "offensive slang," or is it a meaning that could be used in polite society, in school, and in the public media? For the fifth part, I tell them to use these questions: Does the word make a positive or negative judgment? If so, is the standard for that judgment religious/moral, medical, biological, or some combination? The teams gather this information and report it to the class, where it provides the basis for whole-class discussion. The word list determines the order of the class discussion. The following sections focus on the words in the list, along with the information and ideas the list can generate.

Straight *and Its Opposites*

The word list has a certain logic to it, as you will discover. It begins with relatively neutral, inoffensive words, both to establish certain facts and to build a constructive atmosphere. It begins, in fact, with two words for heterosexuality: *heterosexual* itself and *straight*. Most students know the word *heterosexual*, but they know it more precisely when they learn its origin or root meaning: *hetero-* is a Greek root meaning "other" or "different"; a heterosexual person is a person of one sex who is oriented sexually towards persons of the other sex. The word itself is neutral and nonjudgmental; it's a scientific description of the facts. *Straight* is obviously a much more judgmental term. Students know that *straight* is the most commonly used synonym for *heterosexual* and that it is a generally positive word. If asked to come up with other current uses of *straight*, they can come up with quite a few: A moral person stays on "the straight and narrow path"; a straight person is honest and fair; a straight talker tells you the truth; a former drug user is straight when free of drugs; a criminal reforms and "goes straight."

Once these various uses of the word have been established, students can go on to discuss the standard used in each context: Is the standard moral, medical, biological, or some combination? The standard is clearly moral in most cases, but not in all of them. For example, is the word *straight* moral when applied to the former drug user? Most students say "no" and decide that *straight* in that case involves a medical standard: The drug user has returned to healthy behavior. When asked what *straight* means when applied to heterosexual behavior, classes tend to split into several factions. Some see the word as not conveying any positive judgment at all; they take it as a neutral synonym for *heterosexual*. Others, especially those from conservative religious backgrounds, see it as meaning "morally right." Still others say that, to them, *straight* does convey a positive judgment, but that it just means "normal." When asked what *normal* means, they say "common" or "usual" but not necessarily "morally right." When pressed to choose whether the meaning of *normal* is closer to "moral" or "natural," they hesitate and usually choose the latter.

This position, which resists moral judgment made on religious grounds, and which tends to equate *normal* and *natural*, is where many people are today, and it's useful to try to define it as clearly as possible. It's essentially a biological view, yet it may have more traditional morality in it than people realize or want to admit. To explore this position further, I ask the class to brainstorm lists of words that are opposites of *straight*, and we then discuss how those words are used. (*Note*: It's not surprising that *straight* should tend to mean "right" and its opposites tend to mean "wrong": *right* derives from the Indo-European (I-E) root *reg-*, which actually means "move in a straight line," while *wrong* derives from the I-E root *wer-2*, which means "turn" or "bend.") Students quickly come up with words like *crooked*, *curved*, *bent*, or *twisted*. When applied to human behavior, two of these words, *crooked* and *twisted*, clearly convey a strong note of moral disapproval, but neither is strongly connected to sexual behavior, although *twisted* has at least some sexual connotations for most students. *Bent* is, in fact, a slang synonym for *homosexual* in England, but it's not commonly used in the United States, and very few American students know it. There are, however, two other opposites of *straight* that are frequently applied to sexual behavior, and most often to homosexuality: *deviant* and *perverted*. Because these two words appear later on the list, the teams responsible for them can be called on at this point. If they've done their work carefully, these teams will have discovered that the root meanings of these two words contain a road metaphor: *Deviant*, from Latin *de-* ("off," "from") and Latin *via* ("road," "way")", conveys an image of turning off the direct road; *perverted*, from Latin *per-* ("completely") and Latin *vertere* ("turn," "change"), has a root meaning of turning completely around or of walking a twisted path. Most students know that both of these words are commonly used to convey a negative judgment of homosexuality. *Deviant* is not, however, all that familiar to most students. If they're unsure of its current use, I give them my opinion of it: To me, *deviant* seems to represent a medical, rather than a moral, view; calling homosexuality *sexual deviance* is to describe it as a pathological condition. Students do, of course, know *pervert* and *perverted*, and they know that these terms express a strongly negative judgment of homosexuality. The team studying this word should be able to see the traditional moral standard behind it: The first meaning of the verb *pervert* in the *AHD* is "To cause to turn away from what is right, proper, or good; corrupt." Thus, even though *straight* sexual behavior may not be judged as morally correct in and of itself (perhaps sex itself is a necessary evil?), deviations from heterosexual behavior seem to be regarded with strong moral disapproval. Exploring *straight* and its opposites gives students a lot to think about.

Mainstream Words: Homosexual, Lesbian, Gay

The next two words on the list, *homosexual*, and *lesbian*, can be discussed together. Students are familiar with these words, but they usually don't know much about them. I want them to know the origins or root meanings of these words: *homo-* is a Greek root meaning "same." I try to point out, whether or not someone asks, that the Greek root *homo-* is not related to the Latin word *homo*, which means "man" in the generic sense, although people often interpret it as meaning simply "male." For whatever reason, male homosexuality has received the brunt of social disapproval over the centuries, while female homosexuality has been relatively ignored. Hence, I think the word *homosexual* might evoke less hostility if people were more aware of its root meaning: It refers to a person of either sex who is sexually oriented toward persons of the same sex; it doesn't refer only to males.

The team assigned to *lesbian* can easily find that the word derives from Lesbos, the island home of the great Greek female poet Sappho, whose lyrics appear to celebrate sexual love between women. It won't hurt students to know that there were great female poets in antiquity, and that some famous people in history were homosexual. In regard to the current use of *homosexual* and *lesbian*, some students consider both words as neutral, nonjudgmental terms, and that is, in fact, their current status. Other students, however, see one or both words as negative. I ask these students whether they've ever seen or heard the two words used in the media or in places where negative terms would not be tolerated. If they still say "no," I don't try to argue with them, especially if I know they're coming from very traditional religious backgrounds. I just invite them to look around and notice how the words are used in mainstream society.

It's never easy to predict the reaction the word *gay* may provoke. I consider it similar to *lesbian* as a widely used, nonjudgmental term; the *AHD*, for instance, uses it as such in its definition of *homosexual* as a noun: "A homosexual person; a gay man or a lesbian." I don't think *gay* has achieved a neutral status yet with too many young people. It still tends to arouse the same negative reactions that *homosexual* and *lesbian* can arouse, and I treat such reactions accordingly. When it looks up *gay*, the student team will find several meanings in addition to the sexual one. The *AHD* gives the meanings of "Showing . . . cheerfulness and lighthearted excitement" and "Bright or lively, especially in color" prior to the sexual meaning. These are, of course, the older meanings of *gay*, the ones that have been overshadowed by the sexual meaning. I'm always curious to know whether the team members are even aware of these older meanings, and they usually aren't. Hence, I've concluded that, for most students today, the word *gay* really has no meaning except its current sexual one.

At some point, I like to tell my students a bit about the recent history of the word *gay*. I'm fully aware of how complicated this topic is, but, for students, I want to emphasize three points: (1) Homosexual people *chose* this word as the way they want to be identified; (2) they chose it when the two older meanings were still very much alive; and (3) they chose it as part of a concentrated political effort to gain greater respect and political power. Now *gay* is certainly not a very powerful word; it would be far to the "weak/warm/silly/soft" side of the semantic differential scale described in Chapter 10. "Why would any group want to choose a word that means 'light-hearted' and 'bright-colored' as a political rallying cry?"—that's the question I always raise if no student does. After I ask it, I watch where the discussion goes, often helping it along with this question: "Are 'light-hearted' and 'bright-colored' qualities you associate with a traditional image of homosexual people?" The answer is usually positive: The words evoke the effeminate image of the homosexual man, dressed in gaudy clothes, chattering away excitedly—the *airy-fairy*, the *swishy fag*. This is, I tell them, a false image, a stereotype; many, indeed most, homosexual men do not dress and act in this manner. And that, I then argue, is part of the political point. By adopting a word that evokes a traditionally negative image and *flaunting* it in the face of the serious and somber straight world, the homosexual community is saying something like this: "If you want to reduce us to this false stereotype, go ahead. We'll accept it, anyway. We're not ashamed to be different. We like who we are." I know there's a lot more to it, but a discussion along these lines can at least get students thinking.

If there are Black students in the class, or if the class is interested in Black history, it's fruitful to explore the connections between the language used by the Black and homosexual political movements. Blacks used to be called *Negroes* in mainstream American society. *Negro*, from the Spanish or Portuguese word meaning "black," was a polite euphemism; the word *black* itself was thought to be somehow too graphic or too negative. The Black Power movement considered *Negro* a weak, patronizing term; adopted the supposedly negative term *black* instead; and made the use of the word *black* a statement of pride, as in the famous slogan "Black is beautiful." I see the homosexual movement, with its slogan, "Gay Pride," doing essentially the same thing with the word *gay*.

Negative Words: from Sodomite *to* Fag

Having discussed the neutral words for homosexual people, the class can then examine words that are clearly negative: *sodomite, queer, fairy, fag,* and *faggot*. The students who look up *sodomite* find that it has been a condemnatory term for homosexual men since the late Middle Ages. They also become aware of one of the key sources of the long antihomosexual tradition of Christian churches: the biblical story of Sodom and Gomorrah (Genesis 19:1–28). I like to include this old word on the list because it gives students some historical perspective: Religious opposition to homosexuality has been around for a long time and still has a major influence on current social attitudes.

As the student team will discover, *queer* can mean simply "deviating from the expected or normal; strange" (*AHD*). I find that most people agree that *queer* can still be used with this general, nonsexual meaning, that it's not like *gay*, which is rarely used with its older meanings. All students know, of course, that *queer* is widely used as a negative term for a homosexual person; as evidence, the student team can cite the *AHD* entry for *queer*, definition 6: "*Offensive Slang* Homosexual." When the team checks the origin of this word, they will make an interesting discovery: It derives from the I-E root *terk-w*, which means "twist." Still another deviation from the straight path! In discussing the attitudes behind the disparaging use of this word, I like to call attention to its primary meaning—"deviating from the expected or normal"—and ask students this question: "Why do we humans tend to dislike or distrust anything that strikes us as strange or different?" This question often provokes an interesting discussion: This instinctive suspicion of difference can be seen as both a useful defense mechanism and a source of all kinds of prejudice—racial, religious, and sexual. In addition to this instinctive suspicion of any departure from social norms, students tend to find the biological view of homosexuality behind the negative use of *queer*: A *queer* person is seen as deviating not only from social customs, but also from the biological laws of human nature. If students checked the usage note after the entry for *queer* in the new, fourth edition of the *AHD*, they'd learn that some members of the gay community are trying to reclaim *queer*, just as they did *gay*. It might be interesting to ask a class whether they think this reclamation project will be successful. I suspect they'd say "no," and I'd tend to agree: *Gay* had some positive meanings before it was reclaimed; *queer*, at the moment, does not.

It's hard to assess the strength of the negative feeling behind the use of words like *queer*, *fairy*, *fag*, and *faggot*. All of these words are used primarily to refer to homosexual males, who seem to be our society's favorite targets. They all evoke and invoke the stereotype of a homosexual male as an effeminate man, a man who flounces around like a "bubbly" woman. If, for instance, students were asked to rate these words on the semantic differential scales described in Chapter 10, they'd no doubt rank all of these words on the weak/silly/soft side of the scales. *Fairy* would probably be ranked as the weakest of all. If they knew anything about fairies, students would know them as tiny, winged creatures who fly though the air—not a formidable image. When students look up the word *fairy* and find its root connection to the concept of *fate*, they can get a hint that the ancient fairies were creatures with considerable power, but that image is not really operative in our current society. The effeminate stereotype always provokes laughter, and, when the issue comes up, I like to ask my students about that laughter: Are they laughing with or at the effeminate male? Clearly, the answer is "At," and the laughter is not as innocent as it might seem. In discussing it, I sometimes tell my students about Amos and Andy: Whites were perfectly happy to laugh at lovable, nonthreatening "Negroes" who knew their place. This *Cage aux Folles* kind of laughter makes me nervous: It does evoke a certain affection for homosexual males, but only if they act according to the funny and harmless stereotype. There's a good reason why the sexual meanings of the words *queer*, *fairy*, *fag*, and *faggot* are all marked as *"Offensive Slang"* in the *AHD*. The effeminate stereotype is, ultimately, belittling and offensive.

Students who look up *faggot* and its shortened form, *fag*, won't get far by consulting the *AHD*. They'll simply confirm what they already knew—that it is a negative, disparaging term for a homosexual male. The *AHD* is non-committal as to the origin of this word, saying it might be from *fagot (faggot)*, "a bundle of twigs, sticks, or branches bound together." I don't understand why the *AHD* didn't add two salient facts: The bundle of sticks was used for firewood, and the firewood was used to burn heretics in the Middle Ages and beyond. To get at those facts, students would have to consult the *Oxford English Dictionary (OED)*, in which they are clearly stated. Heretics were burned alive, or put on the faggots, and those who recanted had to wear a faggot-symbol on their clothing. That much is history. How the word *faggot* became associated with homosexuality is not so clear. Homosexual activists claim that homosexual people were burned alive during the Inquisition, along with heretics, but there's not much historical evidence to support that claim. It seems to be a plausible enough legend, given the Church's hostility toward homosexuality, but no more than a legend. My hunch is that some party, either a friend or a foe to homosexual people, may have fostered this legend for political purposes; it can be used to create sympathy or hostility toward homosexual people. In any case, as the *OED* illustrates, extremely hostile references to homosexual males as effeminate *faggots* began to appear in America early in the twentieth century, and they've been appearing ever since. I like to share these facts and surmises with my students and then ask them this question: "If you believed the story of homosexual burning as an historical fact, how would being called a *faggot* make you feel?" If students retort that this is all just a bunch of made-up history, I invite them to ponder two historical facts that are beyond dispute: (1) the Nazis did imprison, torture, and burn thousands of homosexual people during the Holocaust, and those people were not Jews; and (2) in many of the United States, there are laws against homosexual practices. These laws are not enforced, but they're still on the books. Hence, even in twenty-first-century America, the state has the legal right to punish homosexual behavior, not by burning but by imprisonment. Whatever the precise historical facts, *faggot* is a hate-filled word to homosexual people. I hate to hear my students use it, and I hope that knowing some of the facts about its history might lead them to stop.

The Final Question: Is It Fair?

I chose to end the list with the word *unnatural*. This word expresses what is probably the most widely held objection to homosexuality. It is based on what I've called the biological view, the view that homosexuality violates the biological rules of human existence. People who don't have strong religious or moral objections to homosexuality may still consider it unnatural, arguing that, if everyone were homosexual, the human race couldn't survive: The natural law of survival is against homosexuality. This is a powerful argument in theory, but, if and when my students raise it, I just ask them whether they think homosexuality really poses a practical threat to human survival. Unless they're being obstinate, most of them say "no." Most are aware that overpopulation is a far more immediate and real problem, and I sometimes tell them that the number of homosexual people on the earth, even with the most extreme estimates, has never exceeded 10 or 12 percent of the total human population.

I address this purely hypothetical argument if it is brought up, but I try to move fairly quickly to a discussion of word origins. The students assigned to look up the root meanings of *unnatural* can report that it, and its opposite *natural*, derive from Latin *natus*, the past participle of Latin *nasci*, meaning "to be born." I then ask them whether they think this root meaning is still present in the current uses of both words: "Can *natural* refer to something you're born with, and *unnatural* to something you're not born with?" They usually say "yes," and, when they do, they've fallen into the trap that viewing homosexuality as *unnatural* inevitably leads to. I go on to tell the students that most homosexual people believe they were born that way, and that there's good scientific evidence to support this view. I then ask them how homosexuality can be unnatural if people are born homosexual: "How can something be natural and unnatural at the same time?" I purposely lead my students into this logical dilemma and let them wrestle with it for a while. Some simply maintain that people are not born homosexual, even if they think they are. In response, I say that the origin of homosexuality is highly controversial and that neither side has definitive proof at this point. "What if," I ask, "homosexual people really *are* born that way? Let's consider that a real possibility. How should homosexuality be regarded then?"

Some students may argue that homosexual people are "freaks of nature," but this is an easy position to refute. I look first to other students to refute it, but, if no one volunteers, I offer this counter-argument: A *freak* is, by definition, exceedingly rare, but homosexual people are certainly common and visible in American society. If all of those homosexual people are "freaks," then Mother Nature must be losing her grip. I then bring up the issue of left-handers and redheads: Left-handers and redheads are certainly not considered freaks, but there are probably just as many left-handers and redheads in the world as there are homosexual people. I then ask, "Why aren't left-handers or redheads considered *unnatural* while homosexual people are? Why are the traits of left-handedness or redheadedness seen as *natural variations* or *natural differences*, while homosexuality is considered an abnormality, a variation from nature, not of nature?"

I don't expect a bunch of young people to come up with strong answers to questions that American society at large is struggling with. Nor do I seriously try to convince them that homosexuality is really no more different than left-handedness. After provoking them with these questions for a while, I end with an appeal to their sense of justice. Young people have a very strong sense of justice, and I've found that the best way to get them to reconsider their unexamined prejudices is to appeal directly to this sense. Hence, I try to leave a class with this final question: "If people are born homosexual, then is it fair to put them down for it?"

This unit has an avowed political aim: It is designed to increase tolerance for homosexual people. Its method is to focus on the words commonly used to express opinions about homosexuality. My hope is that the focus on the words will lead the class to discuss general social attitudes, not just personal opinions about behavior. I've tried to portray the teacher as a poser of questions and provider of information, as a moderator, not an advocate. The great challenge in teaching a unit on such a potentially explosive topic is to keep the discussion from degenerating into highly personal arguments. Hence, it's crucial that the teacher be even-handed, allow all students to speak their minds freely, and never try to argue students out of their positions. If this unit works, the information and the discussion will lead students to reconsider their positions and attitudes for themselves.

12
Kinds of Intelligence
Words and Metaphors

The idea that there are different kinds of intelligence is widely accepted. Brain researchers have found that the two sides, or hemispheres, of the brain specialize in different functions. Researchers have also determined that individuals tend to favor one hemisphere over the other, that is, to be predominantly *left-brained* or *right-brained*. Hence, there is a sound scientific basis for identifying at least two main types of intelligence. Neuropsychologist Howard Gardner has gone even farther, speculating that there may be as many as seven types.

This neurological research only confirms what common sense suggests. Without giving the matter much thought, most of us seem to sense that there are different kinds of intelligence. We recognize that individuals are better at solving some types of problems than they are at others. We use many different words to describe intelligence: *brilliant*, *clever*, *shrewd*, and so on. These words may overlap, but they are not synonyms. We use them in distinct ways, to describe the kinds of intelligence employed in different occupations or activities, in different spheres. Albert Einstein is probably a universal choice as a very intelligent person. Most English speakers would call Einstein "brilliant," rather than "clever" or "shrewd." Why? That's the kind of question explored in this chapter.

This chapter sets forth an inquiry that can help students identify the different conceptions of intelligence embodied in the English words they use. This inquiry combines the study of language and the study of culture. As students explore the words used for intelligence, and lack of intelligence, in current English, they can become more attentive to word meanings and to the metaphorical dimension of language. As they explore how the prevalent metaphors for intelligence are applied in society, they can uncover the cultural values expressed in those metaphors. I would hope that, in the end, students are aware that there really are different kinds of intelligence and are more respectful of intelligence in all of its forms.

This is a challenging activity. It requires some sophisticated linguistic analysis, and it raises some heavy philosophical questions. It also may require a good deal of guidance from you. Although part of it could work with younger students, I see the full inquiry as appropriate for high school juniors or seniors in English or Humanities classes. I present the whole thing here in a kind of ideal form, a composite of my best experiences with this inquiry over the years. Needless to say, the actuality has always been a lot more chaotic than this orderly presentation. This inquiry can shoot off in all sorts of interesting directions—that's part of its value.

Finding the Master Metaphors: Bright, Quick, Sharp

The full inquiry consists of two main parts. Each part takes about two classroom hours, depending on how much of it is assigned as homework and how long the discussions are. The first part involves identifying and classifying the common words for intelligence used in current English. To draw these words out for study, I like to ask the students to make lists or fill in semantic frames. Here are three starter tasks that have always generated lots of words to explore.

1. List some synonyms for the word *intelligent*. Try to list words you actually use, or words you have actually heard or read.
2. Make a list of common words or phrases for "lack of intelligence."
3. Fill in the blanks with appropriate verbs or verb phrases. Use as many as you can find for each blank:
   a. "An intelligent person has a ___ mind."
   b. "An intelligent person really ___ a subject."
   c. "The teacher ___ the issue for us."
   d. "I found her explanation very ___; I finally understood."

The tasks are assigned as homework. When the students come to class, I ask them to prepare composite lists in small groups. After the groups are ready, they report their answers while I frantically write the words on the board. In short order, the board is covered with a large array of words and phrases. Then, we start talking about them all. Sorting through them as a whole class can be interesting and amusing: Task 2 in particular always generates a wealth of colorful images. Some of these images are genuinely funny (I have a large collection of *-head* and *-minded* phrases); some, like *moron*, *idiot*, *imbecile*, or *retard*, aren't so funny to the students after we've discussed them for a while. In the course of discussion, the concept of metaphor always becomes prominent; students see (there's one!) that people have to resort to metaphors to talk about something invisible or abstract like intelligence.

Eventually, the class needs to try to identify some common metaphors among all of the words and phrases. The words *quick*, *sharp*, and *bright* will certainly be on the board somewhere, and these are, in fact, the three common metaphors that our culture uses to talk about intelligence: In almost every common word or phrase, intelligence is described in terms of quickness, sharpness, or brightness. With perhaps a little strategic prodding, the students soon begin to see that quite a few of the items on the board can be grouped around these three metaphors. At this point, I like to write the words *quick*, *sharp*, and *bright* in three columns somewhere on the board and encourage the class to arrange the other words and phrases under them. When some of the most obvious connections are made, the three columns look something like this.

QUICK	SHARP	BRIGHT
slow	dull	brilliant
not too swift	obtuse	dull
quick-witted	acute	in the dark
		shed light on
		clarify
		enlighten(ed)
		dim-wit(ted)

When the class has gone as far as it can, it's time for the students to return to small working groups and hit the dictionaries (at least one dictionary per group). Each group should look up all the words on the board: the words already in the three columns and the other words, too. Their task is to determine which words will fit in which column, and which words won't fit into any of the three. There are fewer of this last type than might first appear. Through a careful dictionary search, students will find that some common words, such as *stupid*, *smart*, *dumb*, are connected to one of the three core metaphors, even though they don't appear to be at first. If students pay careful attention to etymologies in their searches, they'll discover unsuspected relationships between words. If they pay close attention to synonyms, they'll discover more words for intelligence than they had originally considered.

To keep things focused, I leave the original columns written on the board until the search is over. I also put them on a handout for every student to use. When the groups start using their dictionaries, they quickly find more words for each column. Each group writes the new additions on their handouts, and, when the groups report, I update the columns still on the board.

The following is a description of what should happen to the *quick* column if the students conduct a skillful dictionary search. When students look up *quick* in the AHD, they'll see that it used to mean "alive"; some of them may then be reminded of the phrase "a lively mind" or "a lively discussion." The *AHD* (Third Edition) entry for *quick* directs readers to "See Synonyms at *nimble*." If students do that, they'll discover that *nimble*, too, is often applied to the mind. If they pursue the association of intelligence and liveliness further, they'll discover that lack of intelligence is often correlated with deadness or inertia. Unintelligent people are *deadheads*, *dead from the neck up*, or *blockheads*, their heads like inert blocks of wood or cement. They have *rocks in their heads* in place of brains; they are *clods* or *lumps* of inert matter. They are *meatheads* or *boneheads*, with unresponsive flesh or bone where the "gray matter" should be.

If students look up *stupid*, *dumb*, and *dull* in the AHD, they'll find that these words, too, are connected to lack of quickness. The common link is slowness or inability to respond. Stupid people are so "slow to learn or understand" that they seem to be "in a stupor." Dumb people are not just slow to respond; they can't respond at all—as the students will cheerfully illustrate, dumb people just go "Duuh" when asked to think. A dull person is "lacking responsiveness or alertness" and "sluggish" in response. (Students will eventually realize that *dull* thus fits into all three columns; it can mean "not quick," "not bright," and "not sharp.") When the groups reconvene, the column under *quick* will clearly have a lot more entries.

The *sharp* column will fill up, too, if the dictionary search is conducted well. This column is likely to have *sharp*, *dull*, *acute*, and *obtuse* in it as the result of the initial class discussion. Finding additional words for it will require some clever and persistent searching of synonyms and etymologies. A look at the synonyms under *sharp* in the AHD will uncover the connection of *keen* to intelligence, as in the phrase "a keen mind." Three widely used words for intelligence are also associated with cutting: *smart*, *clever*, and *shrewd*. Students can find the association if they look up the etymology of each word in the AHD. *Smart* used to be associated with "sharp" or "stinging" physical pain. Students might ponder how *smart* became associated with intelligence. The AHD suggests that the link was "vigor or quick movement"; I'd suggest that clever and hurtful speech, as in the phrases "a sharp tongue" and "a cutting remark," may also have something to do with it. Students who come up with the familiar phrase "smart as a whip" will recognize this complex connection of intelligence, cutting, and pain. *Clever* and *shrewd* no longer suggest cutting, but their ancestors and relatives do. *Clever* derives from I-E *gleubh*, meaning "cut" and "cleave," which is also found in *cleaver*, *cleavage*, *cleft*, and *cloven*. *Shrewd* derives from I-E *sker*, meaning "cut," which also appears in *sharp*, *shears*, and *shrew*, a little animal with a sharp, pointed snout, or a person with a sharp tongue, as in Shakespeare's *Taming of the Shrew*.

Students might pick up a few more cutting words for mental action if they are asked to explore the physical part of the metaphor in detail: What, exactly, does a sharp mind *do*? What does it cut? How does it cut? Why does it cut? What kind of cutting is going on? When students start dissecting the metaphor, they should find that the core meaning is going beneath the surface to get at something inside. A sharp mind "cuts into" or "cuts through" the surface to get at the truth within; synonyms for *cut into* or *cut through* are *penetrate* and *pierce*, both of which can be used to describe a good mind in action. Where, in the actual world, could this kind of cutting operation take place? Students who take biology will recognize that it takes place in the laboratory: they have probably used the word *dissect*, but, once they check its etymology (from Latin *dissecare* ["cut apart"]), they'll be able to see its connection to the cutting group. If they look *dissect* up in the AHD, they'll find that the word is used metaphorically to describe mental activity. Another place where this kind of exploratory cutting takes place is in the operating room. Students will know the word *incision*. When they check its etymology (from Latin *incido* ["cut into"]), they'll see how it relates to the other cutting words. They may also pick up the word *incisive* (one word down from *incision* in the AHD), which is often used to describe intelligence in the phrase "an incisive mind." Clearly, the association of cutting and intelligence is strongly established in the English vocabulary. The mind as a cutting instrument is one of the dominant metaphors for intelligence in our culture.

The other dominant metaphor is the mind as a source or recipient of light. The association of light and intelligence pervades our vocabulary. Students should be able to spot this metaphor in their responses to all three of the opening tasks: for task 1, *brilliant* and *bright*, and possibly *enlightened*; for task 2, *dull*, *in the dark*, maybe *dim* and *dim-wit(ted)*. Task 3 in particular should draw out some familiar light images. An intelligent mind or person *sheds light on* a problem, issue, or situation and *illuminates*, *elucidates*, or *clarifies* it. A good explanation is one that is *lucid* or *clear*, and also *enlightening* or *illuminating*. The light images in most of these words are perfectly clear. As for *clear* itself and *clarify*, these words, too, are usually closely associated with light. I would expect all of these words to be added to the *bright* column on the board before any dictionary work even begins.

The dictionary isn't as essential in dealing with the *light* words. What is important is figuring out the metaphors involved. Students need to discuss some basic questions: What is the light? Where does it come from? Does the mind give it or receive it? I usually have to give a class some help in framing these basic questions, but the students normally take it from there. The positive light images seem fairly straightforward; they define the mind as the source or giver of light. The intelligent person is *bright* or *brilliant*, has *a brilliant mind*, which *sheds light on* a subject, issue, or situation, thus providing light for—*enlightening*—other minds. The light itself seems to be intellectual power, a kind of searchlight that spots the truth and helps others to see it.

Yet, the light sometimes seems to be conceived as knowledge itself. If one person can *enlighten* another, then one mind is the light-giver and the other mind is the receiver. Is the mind the giver or receiver of light? Is light the intelligence that discovers truth, or the truth that the intelligent mind discovers? The answer seems to be "both" or "all of the above!"

The complexity of the issue becomes apparent when students start trying to unpack the many words and images for lack of intelligence. Some of these seem to convey the notion of the mind as a source or giver of light: An unintelligent person is *dull*, as in *not too bright*, or a *dimwit*, whose mind emits very few lumens. Others seem to define the light as something outside of the mind itself, something the intelligent mind can perceive (as in the phrase "see the light"), while other people remain *in the dark*. Students may use the phrase "light cannot penetrate" to refer to lack of comprehension. If they examine the words *foggy* or *fog-bound*, they will probably picture a head so surrounded with fog that light cannot get through to it. If they examine *muddled thinking* or *muddled-headed*, they'll find an image of the mind as muddy water, water that light, indeed, cannot penetrate. *Foggy* and *muddled* are likely candidates for the *bright* column, if they're not already there.

After this kind of discussion and analysis, the three columns on the board will look something like the lists in Figure 12.1.

There are still two very common words to consider: *dense* and *thick*. Students may decide to put them in the *quick* column: a *dense, thick skull* seems as inert as a *blockhead* or a *bonehead*. Then again, students might put them with *foggy* and *muddled* in the *bright* column, arguing that *light cannot*

FIGURE 12.1
Words for Intelligence (or Lack of Intelligence)

quick	sharp	bright
slow	dull	brilliant
not too swift	obtuse	dull
quick-witted	acute	in the dark
lively	keen	shed light on
nimble	smart	clarify
deadhead	clever	enlighten(ed)
blockhead	shrewd	dim-wit(ted)
clod	penetrating	illuminate
lump	piercing	elucidate
bonehead	dissect	lucid
meathead	incisive	clear
stupid		see the light
dumb		foggy
dull		muddled

penetrate the *dense, thick* walls of an unintelligent mind. While both of these interpretations are good and plausible, I try to argue that *dense* and *thick* embody a somewhat different conception of the acquisition of knowledge. The quick or sharp or bright mind is an active seeker. Even when *light* refers to an outside source, not to the mind itself, the mind is still active; it must "see the light." In the metaphor embodied in *dense* and *thick*, the recipient of knowledge is entirely passive. As students discuss these words, they'll quickly come up with the phrases "pound it into your thick skull" or "get it into your head." In these phrases, the head is viewed as simply a physical skull, with dense, thick walls and no active faculty inside of them. If the mind even exists in this grossly physical image, it gets no credit at all for the acquisition of knowledge; the mind (or simply the head?) is reduced to a passive receptacle, a container into which knowledge is crammed by someone else.

It would be fruitful for students to ponder the implications of this (to me, appalling) metaphor. Do they accept it? Do they think of themselves, and their schooling, in these terms? They will say "no," but many of them have probably defined themselves as students in exactly this passive way. Discussion of this metaphor could lead students to explore a whole host of important questions. Is knowledge the same thing as information? Can knowledge be acquired passively? Would the passive receipt of knowledge involve intelligence? Is possession of knowledge a sign of intelligence? Is lack of knowledge a sign of lack of intelligence? Students can recognize that knowledge and intelligence are logically distinct, but, if they look at their own words for lack of intelligence, they'll surely find *ignorant*, *ignoramus*, or *clueless*. Clearly, in popular usage, lack of knowledge is often equated with lack of intelligence. Is this fair? Do they want to strike these words from their lists, or is there some reasonable way to connect knowledge and intelligence? As mentioned at the outset of this chapter, this inquiry can lead into some pretty deep waters.

Einstein, Your Auto Mechanic, and Grandma

Once the three master metaphors—bright, quick, sharp—have been identified, the class can go on to consider how these metaphors are used in our current society. In what spheres do these different metaphors appear? To have a class to explore this question, I set up another experiment. I invite the students to describe intelligent people in different occupations or roles. Here are the instructions I use:

> Here are seven categories of people:
>
>> Scientist
>> Student
>> Politician
>> Con-man
>> Auto mechanic
>> Athlete
>> Grandmother
>
> List three adjectives to describe an intelligent person in each category, without using the word *intelligent* itself. In other words, "An intelligent student is ___"; "an intelligent athlete is ___." Try to rank the three words within each category.

Choosing the categories is tricky. This activity draws out social stereotypes, and some of those provoke anger. I've had some nasty arguments over *secretary* when I've used it ("A secretary doesn't need intelligence"; "My Mom's a secretary, and she's smarter than you'll ever be!"). I've also seen hurt feelings from the children of used car salesmen when I used that category. It's useful to get a few slightly disreputable categories, but ones that are general types rather than specific jobs; I've settled on *con-man* and *politician*, which seem to be about equally disreputable in current use.

The students work on the categories in small groups. Each group works on all of the categories but is responsible for reporting on only one of them.

When the groups are ready to report, I write their three choices on the board under the respective category names. Then, the discussion begins: The class proposes other choices, and all choices are considered until a consensus is reached for each category.

I've been conducting this little experiment, in one form or another, for over twenty years. It's a fascinating cultural barometer, both for me and for the students who participate. Over that time, I've seen some interesting changes in social values along with the persistence of certain underlying cultural assumptions. The consensus choices of my most recent class show both changes and traditions:

Scientist: brilliant, ingenious, innovative
Student: bright, brilliant, smart
Politician: shrewd, clever, cunning
Auto mechanic: smart, ingenious, brilliant
Athlete: smart, clever, crafty
Grandmother: wise, shrewd, astute

I use these lists as illustrations as I run through the rest of the inquiry. Once the groups have reported, and consensus choices have been reached, the analysis can begin. Which categories get which metaphors, and why? That's the obvious first question. A look at the category lists ought to provide some answers. In the results from my recent class, the cutting adjectives dominate the lists for the politician, the con-man, the mechanic, and the athlete, while the light adjectives are clustered around the scientist and the student. Why? What do these groups have in common, and how do they differ from each other? Why do the two groups get different metaphors? These questions are, of course, at the very heart of this inquiry, and I'm willing to wait a very long time for a class to work out some answers to them.

Most of my classes have eventually come up with some good answers, which I summarize for you here. The core distinction seems to be between practical and theoretical intelligence, between applied and pure intelligence, if you like. Cutting is a decisive action; it gets something done, often quickly. Con-men, politicians, auto mechanics, and athletes all deal with immediate, practical problems, and produce tangible results. A sharp con-man out-smarts a sucker and gets the sucker's money. A shrewd politician sizes up a situation and takes advantage of it, winning a key vote or an election. A smart auto mechanic finds the source of the strange noise and fixes the car, quickly. A smart basketball player makes the right split-second decision on the fast break, every time.

If cutting is our image for intelligence in the practical sphere, light is our image for pure or theoretical intelligence. In the category lists, the light images are clustered around the scientist and the student. I sense a certain traditional idealism operating here: Both the scientist and the student are perceived as having higher, perhaps nobler concerns. They are pursuing knowledge in the broadest sense, general principles, abstract theories; they are seeking to learn and understand, not to solve practical problems or to gain some immediate advantage. It would be absurd to call Albert Einstein *smart*, *sharp*, or *clever*; he was a theoretical physicist, concerned with the very nature of the universe. As such, he can only be called *brilliant*. Very intelligent students can be called *smart* or *clever*, but only as a form of academic understatement. The highest praise words teachers use for their students are *bright* and *brilliant*. *Brilliant* is the highest praise word in the academic sphere, the only one that doesn't need a *very* in front of it.

After a class has worked out the major distinctions, they might want to look at some of the overlaps on the category lists. There will, it is hoped, always be some, and they'll be interesting to discuss. In the list from my recent class, it's quite fascinating to see both the scientist and the auto mechanic described as "brilliant" and "ingenious." The word *brilliant* isn't, of course, always connected with intelligence; it can be just a general praise word meaning "dazzling." Thus, a "brilliant play" in sports does not necessarily involve intelligence. I suspect, though, that calling a mechanic *brilliant* probably does refer to intelligence, to a special talent for understanding the nature of automobiles. I hadn't had a class describe an auto mechanic *brilliant* before. This might be a sign of a cultural shift toward greater respect for so-called menial occupations. I hope so!

Another fascinating overlap on my class' lists involves the last category, *grandmother*. It appears that Granny and the politician are both called *shrewd* and *astute*. What could they have in common? I suppose the answer is worldly wisdom, knowledge of how people act, and how to get them to do what you want. Grandmothers, like politicians, can be pretty shrewd in the practical sphere. Grandmothers are more than just shrewd, though; they are the only people my recent class called *wise*. The native word *wise* is a word of very high status in our current culture. It has, in fact, been the highest English praise word for mental ability ever since Old English times. What does *wise* mean today? Over the years, various classes have given some very rich responses to that question, and those responses have represented, for me, the kind of high-level thinking that this whole inquiry can generate.

I'll try to summarize some of their thinking here. The word *wise* combines both kinds of intelligence—practical and theoretical. A *wise* grandmother may be *shrewd*, but her thoughts will extend beyond practical and immediate concerns to general principles of human nature itself. She's a natural philosopher, with a "philosophy of life" derived from long experience in actual living. She's too philosophical to be simply *shrewd*, yet too grounded in real experience to be *brilliant*. There's only one word that can describe her: She is *wise*.

There are lots of other issues to consider. Some of my classes have explored the question of why the cutting words seem to pick up negative connotations. They've noticed that *shrewd* can shade easily into *cunning*, *crafty*, or *sly*. If they happened to check the third edition of the AHD, they even found out (in the Word History, after *clever*) that the word *clever* was first applied to the Devil! If asked, students should be able to come up with some other words or phrases that express a negative view of practical intelligence: *too clever by half*, *card-sharp*, *sharper*, or *sharpie*. Clearly, there is a deep-seated suspicion of practical intelligence embodied in our language. Part of the reason probably stems from a normal fear of being taken advantage of, being *outsmarted*. There is also, I think, something more to it. Practical intelligence is seen as an amoral or immoral force, something unguided by any principle beyond selfish interest.

By contrast, pure intelligence, the intelligence expressed by light images, seems to be regarded as moral and good. "How come?" a class might ask. One answer has to do with respect for the unselfish pursuit of truth. A deeper answer may have to do with the associations of light itself. Ask your class to jot down some free associations with light, and I'll bet you get something like this: images of safety and protection against the dark, such as home, night-lights, campfires, flashlights, and lighthouses; and images or ideas of religion, such as candles, menorahs, spiritual (versus physical), and God. I'm usually wary of religious associations from students, but here I welcome them. Light is, in fact, an ancient symbol of divinity and spiritual truth in many of the world's religions, including Christianity, Judaism, Buddhism, and Islamic. Prior to the Renaissance, most of the English *light* words discussed in this chapter were used with God, not the human mind, as the source of truth: The mind was *illuminated* or *enlightened* by God. Although this image was later secularized, with the mind as the discoverer of the truths of nature, the earlier religious associations persist in the English language even today. If your students look up *light*, *illumination*, and *enlighten(ment)* in the AHD, they'll find religious or spiritual definitions listed for each of these words, often right beside the secular definitions: *Illumination*, for instance, is defined as "spiritual or intellectual enlightenment." It's highly likely that the positive, spiritual associations of light, still present in the language and religions of today, are a major reason why pure intelligence, associated with light, is regarded so favorably in our current culture.

Once again, this inquiry can shoot off in surprising directions—so much the better! There is, of course, no one set route for every class to follow; every class should find its own route. I've tried to present this inquiry as a series of possibilities, not as a tightly unified structure. Part One—identifying the metaphors—could be done by itself. Part Two—applying the metaphors—could be done in all sorts of different ways, with different categories and different questions. This area of inquiry is so rich that the possibilities are almost endless; I've included some others in the Applications section. However your class chooses to explore this area, your students will learn a great deal about the language they use and the culture in which they live.

Applications

1. A common metaphor for understanding is a light bulb suddenly popping on over one's head. Consider the conception of the mind embodied in this metaphor. Is the mind active or passive or a combination of the two? In the popular image, a person says, "Eureka!" when the light bulb pops on. Look up the word *eureka*. Does it shed any more light on the issue?

2. The polarities *quick/slow*, *sharp/dull*, and *light/dark* are all commonly applied to intelligence. How about *hot/cold*? We can speak of a brilliant mind penetrating the dark of ignorance. Can we also speak of a hot mind melting the ice of ignorance? Would a hot mind, or a cold mind, be a likely image in our language? Why, or why not ?

3. What conception of intelligence is embodied in the word itself? Look up the root meaning of *intelligence* in the *AHD* or in any dictionary that has etymological information. Also, look up the meanings of the Latin sources of the word in a Latin dictionary. On the basis of what you find, write a personal definition of the root meaning of the word *intelligence*. Your definition could take one sentence, one paragraph, or a whole essay.

4. Compare and contrast the meanings of *intelligence*, *intuition*, *instinct*, and *genius*. Do these concepts differ in kind or just in degree? Could

you arrange them in a spectrum? Discuss these questions in a small group. Then, work out your answers in writing.

5. Come up with as many substitutes as you can for *understand* in "I understand (it)" and "I don't understand (it)." Identify and discuss any metaphors you find. Looking up root meanings might uncover some hidden metaphors.

6. Trace the etymology of the word *deity*. What light does this etymology shed on common conceptions of truth and the mind?

7. Explore the words used for *intelligence* in various categories. List three synonyms for *intelligent* for each word in each category; then, interpret the results. Here are some possible categories:

   a. A set of professions: doctor, lawyer, teacher, minister, architect, engineer, police chief, and so on

   b. Family members distinguished by gender and age: mother, father, grandmother, grandfather, child, and teen-ager

   c. A group of animals: cat, dog, horse, raccoon, dolphin, fox, chimpanzee, turkey, and so on

8. The stereotype of the "big, dumb jock" is very common in our culture. Behind it is the belief that playing a sport need not require much intelligence. Yet, people who know and respect athletes and sports frequently use terms for mental ability; they speak of "smart" or "intelligent" players and plays. In professional sports, rookies generally need a year or two to "learn" the game, no matter how physically talented they may be.

   Analyze in detail how much and what kind of intelligence is required to play a specific sport, or a specific role within a sport. If you don't have first-hand knowledge, you might want to interview someone who does. Possible examples are a basketball player, a tennis player, a baseball/softball pitcher, a baseball/softball hitter, a football interior lineman, a football quarterback.

9. Some tasks—dishwashing, for example—really do seem mechanical and mindless, yet apparently simple and straightforward tasks often require much more intelligence than we might think. Investigate a job or task that seems to involve very little use of the mind: Interview someone who does it well; ask that person about techniques, problems, and tricks of the trade. Do you still think the job or task is as simple and mindless as you originally thought? Write up your findings and conclusions.

10. Rightly or wrongly, people tend to equate intelligence with the

ability to use language well. Thus, someone who doesn't speak very well is often considered unintelligent, while someone who speaks smoothly is usually assumed to be intelligent and knowledgeable. What is the relationship between intelligence and the ability to express one's self in language? Obviously, it's possible to talk without thinking—we see examples all around us—but is it possible to have profound or complex ideas without being able to put them into words? Do people really "have a lot to say" if they can't manage to say it? To explore these questions and some of our common cultural answers to them, work through the following activities.

a. Look up the root and current meanings of *dumb* and *stupid*. What common conception of intelligence seems to underlie the history of each word?

b. The words *wise* and *witty* were synonymous in Old English, and people addressed prayers to "Witty God." It's hard to imagine such a prayer today. What does *witty* mean now, and why do you think the words *witty* and *wise* have grown apart in meaning?

c. Do we expect a wise person to be highly verbal? What forms do "words of wisdom" often take? Consider this well-known saying of Benjamin Franklin's: "A word to the wise is enough, and many words won't fill a bushel."

11. Which do you think is more useful: intelligence without knowledge or knowledge without intelligence? Which is more dangerous? Develop your answers in essay form.

13
Familiar Quotations
Exploring Concepts in Depth

I *have* been a fan of Bartlett's *Familiar Quotations* for a long, long time. I've been known to pluck juicy quotes from it and use them on final exams. I also like to collect quotes that use the same word. When I ponder these collections, I find my understanding of the concept expressed in the word becoming broader and deeper as I explore how others have defined it. I also discover significant connections between different people in different periods, and I understand the history of Anglo-American culture a little better. If given the chance to work with collections of related quotations, students can experience these effects, too: They can understand complex concepts more deeply, and they can acquire and interpret a wealth of culturally significant information. In this chapter, I illustrate and suggest some ways that you might use groups of related quotations to help your students achieve these two goals.

A Literature Unit on Courage

I began experimenting with groups of related quotes several years ago when I was assigned to teach a unit on Courage. I like to develop thematic units, and, like many teachers, I like to start them with some kind of vocabulary work as a prereading activity, to get the class thinking about the key words and concepts. In the past, I would merely have students write and share brief paragraphs defining and illustrating the word or words in question. For the class on Courage, though, I decided to try something different. I combed through my *Bartlett's*, collecting interesting quotes with the word *courage* in them. I put a list of them on a handout and distributed it at the first class. This handout seemed to work wonders.

The five-week unit on *courage* was part of a college freshman Humanities course. The class of thirty students met twice a week for ninety minutes. I

FIGURE 13.1

Selections from *Bartlett's Familiar Quotations:*
Courage, Bravery, Cowardice

1. One man with courage is a majority.
   —Andrew Jackson (1767–1845) (369.13)
2. Two o'clock in the morning courage: I mean unprepared courage.
   —Napoleon, 1815 (370.21)
3. The fate of unborn millions will now depend, under God, on the courage and conduct of this army. Our cruel and unrelenting enemy leaves us only the choice of brave resistance, or the most abject submission. We have, therefore, to resolve to conquer or die.
   —George Washington, 1776 (336.14)
4. What we really need the poet's and orator's help to keep alive in us is not . . . the common and gregarious courage which Robert Shaw showed when he marched with you, men of the Seventh Regiment. It is that more lonely courage which he showed when he dropped his warm commission in the glorious Second to head your dubious fortunes, Negroes of the Fifty-fourth. That lonely kind of courage (civic courage, as we call it in times of peace) is the kind of valor to which the monuments of nations should most of all be reared.
   —William James, at the unveiling of the Shaw Monument in Boston on May 31, 1897. (795b)
5. Familiarity with danger makes a brave man braver, but less daring.
   —Herman Melville, 1850 (695b)
6. Courage is resistance to fear, mastery of fear, not absence of fear.
   —Mark Twain, 1894 (762a)
7. You gain strength, courage, and confidence by every experience in which you really stop to look fear in the face. You are able to say to yourself, "I lived through this horror. I can take the next thing that comes along." —Eleanor Roosevelt, 1960 (654.14)
8. The courage of New England was "the courage of conscience." It did not rise to that insane and awful passion, the love of war for itself. —Rufus Choate, 1834 (422.16)
9. O God, give us serenity to accept what cannot be changed, courage to change what should be changed, and wisdom to distinguish one from the other. —Reinhold Niebuhr, 1934 (1024a)

10. However highly you are appraised, always have the courage to say to yourself, "I am ignorant." —Ivan Pavlov, 1936 (819a)

11. Those who won our independence believed that the final end of the State was to make men free to develop their faculties; and that in its government the deliberative forces should prevail over the arbitrary. They valued liberty both as an end and as a means. They believed liberty to be the secret of happiness and courage to be the secret of liberty. —Louis Brandeis, 1927 (568.14)

12. For without belittling the courage with which men have died, we should not forget those acts of courage with which men have lived. The courage of life is often a less dramatic spectacle than the courage of a final moment; but it is no less a magnificent mixture of triumph and tragedy. A man does what he must—in spite of personal consequences, in spite of obstacles and dangers and pressures—and that is the basis of all human morality.
    —John F. Kennedy, 1956 (1072a)

13. Fortune favors the brave. —Virgil (70–19 B.C.) (94.25)

14. Cowards die many times before their deaths;
    The valiant never taste of death but once.
    —Shakespeare, *Julius Caesar*, II. ii. 32 (188.11)

15. He wished that he, too, had a wound, a red badge of courage.
    —Stephen Crane, 1895 (611.2)

16. Cowardice . . . is almost always simply a lack of ability to suspend the functioning of the imagination.
    —Ernest Hemingway, 1942 (702.7)

17. Courage is the price that life exacts for granting peace.
    The soul that knows it not, knows no release
    From little things;
    Knows not the livid loneliness of fear,
    Nor mountain heights where bitter joy can hear
    The sound of wings.
    —Amelia Earhart (1898–1937) (700.7)

18. There are several good protections against temptations, but the surest is cowardice. —Mark Twain, 1894 (763a)

---

selected five texts, one for each week. We started with Robert Bolt's play about Thomas More, *A Man for All Seasons*. Next, we read *Murder in the Cathedral*, T. S. Eliot's play about another religious martyr, Thomas Beckett. Then, we read the three Theban plays by Sophocles, in this order: *Oedipus the King*, *Antigone*, and *Oedipus at Colonus*. I had taught this course many times, each time with a different theme and different texts—and no time with any great success. I had always assigned the kinds of texts I believe a college Humanities course should include, and then watched the students struggle to make sense of them. This time, though, the course went better than it ever had. Class discussions were lively and productive, and the papers and exams were pretty darn good. Maybe it was just a good class, but I tried the unit again the following semester, and it went just as well. I think one of the main reasons it went so well was the list of quotes.

In Figure 13.1, with a few minor changes, is the list of *courage* quotes I gave to the class. I was using the fourteenth edition of *Bartlett's*, which I'd had around the house for years, when I made this list, and some of the quotes on it do not appear in the sixteenth edition, or they appear there in different forms. Therefore, the quotes from the fourteenth edition are designated by a page number and column letter, as in *795b*; the quotes from the sixteenth edition are designated by a page and an item number, as in *369.13*.

At the first class meeting, I passed out this sheet, put the students in small working groups, and they just started talking. For the full ninety minutes, those groups—students who had never before met each other—poured over these quotes, comparing and connecting them, and developing their own conceptions of courage in the process. I may be idealizing the scenario a bit, but I can't remember doing anything more myself than circulating among the groups, listening and answering an occasional question. I do remember that we never did reconvene as a whole class during the entire ninety-minute period.

Interpreting and discussing these passages with their peers got the students actively thinking about the issues on which the unit would focus: What does courage involve? Can there be true courage without fear? Are there different kinds of courage? Are some types of courage higher than others? Does the highest courage have to involve some larger cause? The discussion begun in this first session continued for all five weeks, and it was conducted at quite a high level. As the students analyzed and discussed each text in class, they continued to refer to the list of quotes, considering each new character in terms of the various definitions stated there. As I listened to them, I heard a process of mutual adjustment: The students' views of the characters were influenced by their concepts of courage, but those concepts were, in turn, evolving and deepening as the students applied them to each new character. At the conclusion of the unit, each student had to produce a five-page paper. The following section described the way in which I set it up.

Unit paper. Write a paper on one of the following topics. In writing this paper, you will need a clearly defined conception of courage. You might want to check the handout of quotations given to you at the first class as you formulate your criteria.

1. Compare Thomas More and Antigone in terms of courage.
2. Compare Thomas Beckett and Antigone in terms of martyrdom, pride, and courage.
3. Discuss Oedipus, Thomas Beckett, and/or Thomas More in terms of intellectual courage.
4. Discuss the relationship of suicide and courage in *Antigone* and *Oedipus the King*.
5. Do Thomas Beckett and Oedipus (in *Oedipus at Colonus*) display courage at their deaths, or are their final states of mind "beyond courage?" Discuss.

Because I returned all of the papers, I can't quote from them here. I can, however, share the detailed notes I made about the papers I liked. In their papers on the first topic, the students were quite divided in their assessments of Antigone. Some felt she has no real interest in living and no real fear of dying, that she almost wants to die a glorious martyr's death to be free of a wretched existence. Those students felt she is being more arrogant and self-serving than truly courageous. Others saw Antigone as facing certain death for the sake of a large and just cause: loyalty to her family and to the gods. They, of course, argued that Antigone is highly courageous, although many of them did acknowledge some of the opposing arguments. All of the students saw Thomas More as courageous, citing his love of life, his fear of dying, and his willingness to die for a larger cause. From the very first week, More became the epitome of courage for many students in the class, the touchstone by which to judge the other characters. The same conflicting assessments of Antigone appeared in the essays on question 2. The views of Beckett in those essays were interesting in that students saw him as a proud person who has to subdue his own pride before choosing martyrdom in the proper spirit; most felt that he does, finally, become a true martyr to a larger cause. In the papers on topic 3, students saw all three characters as embodiments of intellectual courage: Oedipus, by staying alive and seeking further understanding; Beckett, by honestly examining his own motives; and More, by brilliantly defending his own position and never compromising it. In writing on topic 4, the students saw Oedipus as courageous for not choosing suicide, for not taking the easy way out, as they saw Jocasta doing; they saw Antigone's suicide as part of a larger action of courageous defiance, but they viewed the suicides of Haimon and Eurydice as not motivated by any higher principle. Finally, the students who wrote on topic 5 saw both Oedipus and Beckett as reaching a state of mind that is beyond human fear and courage, one that is in harmony with some kind of divine will.

Not all of the papers were successful, by any means, and the preceding comments are, frankly, summaries of only the better ones. Still, I remember being pleasantly surprised by how well developed many of the arguments were; quite a few of the students had developed clear criteria for defining courage, and they had used those criteria in assessing the characters. I attribute much of this intellectual depth to the influence of the quotation sheet, both in the opening class and throughout the course.

Talking About Ideas

A group of related quotations can be useful by itself, without serving as a lead-in to a reading unit. It can generate a lot of good thinking and good talk, as illustrated by the following description of a visit to Donna Bakke's ninth-grade English class one recent spring. I had visited her class during the previous fall and had spent a week working on word clusters with them (see Chapter 2). Because I knew these students were good at talking about words, I decided I'd see what they might do with the list of *courage* quotes. I passed it out, and we had a fine conversation for a full ninety-minute period.

Some of the quotes were difficult for the students to understand, and Donna and I had to provide a good deal of help. Still, it was a real conversation, with students asking questions and volunteering information, just as we were. The class worked through the first three quotes in order, and then things began to jump around. The third quote, from George Washington, defines courage in terms of facing death in warfare. This is, of course, the way courage is most commonly regarded, and I decided to probe it a little. I asked the students to look at quote number 8, in which Choate speaks of "that insane and awful passion, the love of war for itself." We discussed why someone might love war and whether such a person could be considered truly courageous. We delved into death wishes, berserk frenzies, and love of risk-taking for its own sake. The students saw all these things as contrary to genuine courage.

Someone mentioned the word *fear* and that led the class to focus on quote 6: "Courage is resistance to fear, mastery of fear, not absence of fear." Everyone found this to be a most valuable definition, and they seemed to agree that there could be no courage without some degree of fear. "Does it have to be fear of death?" someone asked, and the class came up with some other things it might take courage to overcome: fear of shame or embarrassment, fear of loss of reputation or status, and fear of loss of security. The word *fearless* came up, and the class discussed it for a while. They came up with examples of fearless people: a child who sticks a hand over a candle, and a daredevil type. They decided that neither the child nor the daredevil should be considered courageous. They dismissed the child as simply ignorant of the danger, but they struggled to find a term for the daredevil, the person who takes unreasonable risks. Through a little prodding, they eventually settled on *reckless*.

The class now had some criteria, which they went on to apply to the other quotes. In discussing quote 4, they decided that Colonel Shaw was courageous by risking his social status and his very life in order to lead a company of inexperienced Black soldiers. In discussing number 10, they saw the scientist as courageous for risking his high reputation. In discussing quote 9, they saw that pushing for changes requires the courage to face social disapproval or loss of personal comfort. And so it went for most of the period.

Some of the quotes proved too hard for any of the students to crack, particularly numbers 14, 16, and 17. I ended up having to lead them through the first two. As I see it, "Cowards die many times before their deaths" because their fear leads them to keep imagining how they might die. Their cowardice results from "a lack of ability to suspend the functioning of the imagination." Even after I explained it, the students couldn't really figure out what Hemingway is saying in number 16. This quote is certainly not up to Hemingway's clear and concise standard, and I think I'll drop it from the list before trying this handout again. The students seemed to enjoy number 17. They knew who Amelia Earhart was and how she died, and the poem allowed them into the mind of a glamorous and mysterious figure. I had to help them with the opening metaphor, which I take to mean something like this: Life will sell us peace, but we must give up our courage to get it. Once the first line was cleared up, the class could see how the rest of the poem, with its reference to "fear" and "bitter joy," is a vivid description of a courageous state of mind, with perhaps a hint of the daredevil in it.

FIGURE 13.2

Quotations Involving *Moderation, Excess,* or *Extreme*

CLASSICAL

1. "Moderation in all things." —Terence (c. 190–159 B.C.) (85.12)
2. "Extreme law is often extreme injustice." —Terence (86.1)
3. "Nothing in excess." —Anonymous Latin (119.15)

EARLY BRITISH

4. "In charity there is no excess." —Francis Bacon, 1625 (159.14)
5. "The desire for power in excess caused the angels to fall; the desire of knowledge in excess caused man to fall." —Francis Bacon, 1625 (159.16)
6. "Therefore love moderately; long love doth so;
   Too swift arrives as tardy as too slow."
   —Shakespeare, *Romeo and Juliet* II, vi, 14 (175.24)

AMERICAN

7. "A thing moderately good is not so good as it ought to be. Moderation in temper is always a virtue; but moderation in principle is always a vice." —Thomas Paine, 1792 (341.8)
8. "We are now forming a republican government. Real liberty is neither found in despotism or the extremes of democracy, but in moderate governments." —Alexander Hamilton, 1787 (355.2)
9. "I will be as harsh as truth and as uncompromising as justice. On this subject I do not wish to think, or speak, or write, with modera-

---

This conversation was valuable in several ways. It encouraged some serious thinking about important ideas. It also provided the students with practice in speaking and listening, and in reading, because the conversation was based on close readings of the quotes. What struck me even more, though, was the great wealth of cultural information that was exchanged. I say "exchanged" because the students contributed quite a bit of it. Some of them had seen the movie *Glory*, which involves Colonel Shaw and his company, and they described it to their classmates. Some of them knew that quote number 9, the prayer by Reinhold Niebuhr, is frequently used in Alcoholics Anonymous. Some of them had even heard of Pavlov's salivating dogs. Donna and I got the chance to tell them things, too: about Melville and *Moby Dick*, about Kennedy's *Profiles in Courage*,

tion. No! No! Tell a man whose house is on fire to give a moderate alarm; tell him to moderately rescue his wife from the hands of the ravisher; tell the mother to gradually extricate her babe from the fire into which it has fallen; but urge me not to use moderation. —William Lloyd Garrison, 1831 (437.14)

10. "This much I think I do know—that a society so riven that the spirit of moderation is gone, no court *can* save; that a society where that spirit flourishes, no court *need* save; that in a society which evades its responsibility by thrusting upon the courts the nurture of that spirit, that spirit in the end will perish." —Judge Learned Hand, 1942 (615.3)

11. "The Negro's great stumblingblock is not the White Citizen's Counciler or the Ku Klux Klanner, but the white moderate who is more devoted to 'order' than to justice . . ." —Martin Luther King, Jr., 1963 (760.16)

12. "Extremism in the defense of liberty is no vice. And . . . Moderation in the pursuit of justice is no virtue." —Barry Goldwater, 1964 (341 n.1)

OTHERS

13. "All government—indeed, every human benefit and enjoyment, every virtue and every prudent act—is founded on compromise and barter." —Edmund Burke, 1775 (331.20)

14. "The best is the enemy of the good." —Voltaire, 1764 (306.19)

---

about Justice Brandeis and Brandeis University, about what a great book *The Red Badge of Courage* is, and about Mark Twain's sense of humor (as shown in quote 18). Working with these quotes gave us all an occasion to share information about a whole host of historically significant figures, authors, and books, and to see them all as contributors to our common culture.

Stimulated by this conversation, I returned to my trusty *Bartlett's* to find some other words that might be especially valuable to explore with students. I also relied on two other sources, *The Barnes and Noble Book of Quotations*, edited by Robert I. Fitzhenry (New York: Barnes & Noble Books, 1987), and *Popular Proverbs and Sayings*, by Gregory Y. Titleman (New York: Gramercy Books, 1997). I looked for words that will lead students to explore important concepts in depth and expose students to a rich variety of culturally significant figures.

After testing more than a few words, I found several that students could learn from studying in depth. In Figure 13.2, you will find a collection of quotes involving *moderation* and its opposites, *excess* or *extreme*. Two quotes involve the concepts but not the actual words. All are from the sixteenth edition of *Bartlett's* and are identified by page and item number there.

If I were exploring the list of Figure 13.2 with a class, one thing I'd want to do is get the students to put the pro-moderation and anti-moderation quotes into two groups, and then explore the attitudes of each group. I'd focus on the more modern quotes, because the concept of moderation doesn't seem to become controversial until the late eighteenth century. Those speaking favorably of moderation include Hamilton (no. 8), Judge Hand (no. 10), and Burke (no. 13), who praises the inherently moderate concept of *compromise*. I'd try to unpack Hamilton's statement first: As I see it, Hamilton is interested in "forming" a "government," an institution midway between the extremes of "despotism," where the people have no power, and "the excesses of democracy," where, in Hamilton's view, the people have too much power. Hamilton wants a "republican" government, a government with established forms and laws, to provide a "moderate" force to counteract popular enthusiasms. Hamilton's wary attitude toward pure democracy was shared by many of the founders of our democracy. They wanted the people to have power, but they also wanted the stability and order that institutions could provide. One could see all three of the pro-moderation statements as motivated by a strong desire for order: Hand sees "the spirit of moderation" as essential to society's survival, while Burke sees "compromise" as the key to "government" and "every human benefit."

If the pro-moderation voices value order and, in Burke's word, "prudent" action, those who speak against moderation want radical change and speak in highly moral terms. I'd put Paine (no. 7), Garrison (no. 9), King (no. 11), and Goldwater (no. 12) in this group. A focus on words makes strange bedfellows, as students will learn when they look at this group. These are four people with different causes but sharing a common attitude: an early American patriot, a nineteenth-century abolitionist, a Black civil rights leader, and a conservative Republican. I'd start exploring this attitude by looking at Paine's statement that "moderation in principle is always a vice" (no. 7). Paine sees moderation in moral "principle" as a "vice" because he sees principles as absolute goods that should not be "compromised" away. The three other speakers also speak in terms of absolute moral standards: "I will be as harsh as truth and as uncompromising as justice" (no. 9); "The Negro's great stumbling block is . . . the white moderate who is more devoted to 'order' than to justice" (no. 11); "Moderation in the pursuit of justice is no virtue" (no. 12). Goldwater's comment is especially interesting because it takes *extremism*, a term with highly negative connotations, and turns it into a moral virtue: "Extremism in the defense of liberty is no vice."

I added Voltaire's "The best is the enemy of the good" (no. 14) to this collection because it's a fairly common statement that goes right to the heart of the controversy raised by all of these quotes. I am curious to see how students might interpret it. I've heard this quote used in praise of moderation and compromise: Holding out for the "best" solution in a controversial matter can prevent a political group from arriving at a "good" solution acceptable to all parties. I can see, though, how it might be interpreted the other way. There's no way to resolve the conflict between moderation and devotion to principle. It's the eternal conflict between the pragmatic and the ideal. It arises between people, and within each person, whenever a difficult decision must be made. Students could learn a lot about politics and morality by exploring the concept of moderation.

I found another interesting collection of quotations involving the concept of patriotism. While the quotes for moderation can lead students into a discussion of profound moral and philosophical issues, this group is perhaps more interesting for the people it involves than for the issues it raises. Hence, I think I would try a different tack in exploring these quotes with a class. I would assign each quote to a different student and ask that student to comment on the quote and provide information about the person who said it. This task wouldn't involve a great deal of research. It could be done quickly by use of the Internet or by consulting an encyclopedia in the school library. I would save the Samuel Johnson quote (no. 1) for class discussion at the end. With the exception of quote number 7, I would assign each of the others to individual students, who would be expected to report briefly on the author and to comment on the quote. I would assign quote number 7 to two students: One would be asked to report on Robert Gould Shaw, the other on the Shaw monument in Boston; the two could collaborate in talking about the quote. All of the quotations in Figure 13.3 are identified by page and item number in the sixteenth edition of Bartlett's *Familiar Quotations*.

The following is what I'd hope to see students get from each quote, and what I might do to help them. For number 2, I'd want students to learn why Thomas Paine was important and to recognize this famous statement. I'd also expect a student reporter to be able to explain what a "sunshine patri-

FIGURE 13.3
Quotations About Patriotism

1. "Patriotism is the last refuge of a scoundrel." —Samuel Johnson, 1775 (316.25)
2. "These are the times that try men's souls. The summer soldier and the sunshine patriot will, in this crisis, shrink from the service of their country; but he that stands it *now*, deserves the thanks of man and woman . . ." —Thomas Paine, 1776 (340.22)
3. "I only regret that I have but one life to lose for my country." —Nathan Hale, 1776 (354.16)
4. "Patriotism in the female sex is the most disinterested of virtues. Excluded from honors and from offices, we cannot attach ourselves to the State or Government from having held a place of eminence. Even in the freest countries our property is subject to the control and disposal of our partners, to whom the laws have given sovereign authority. Deprived of a voice in legislation, obliged to submit to those laws imposed upon us, is it not sufficient to make us indifferent to the public welfare? Yet all history and every age exhibit instances of patriotic virtue in the female sex; which considering our situation equals the most heroic of yours."
—Abigail Adams, 1782 (347.11)
5 "Our country! In her intercourse with foreign nations may she always be in the right; but our country, right or wrong." —Stephen Decatur, 1816 (390.22)
6. "I can never join with my voice in the toast which I see in the papers attributed to one of our gallant naval heroes. I cannot ask of

ot" might be. Quote number 3 is perhaps *the* classic expression of American patriotism. I'd expect students to remember it better when they learned that these were Hale's last words just before being hanged, at age twenty-one, by the British. Students could learn a lot from the remarkable statement by Abigail Adams (no. 4); they could learn how few rights women used to have in the United States, and they could learn that early American women could be eloquent and forceful reasoners, despite their lack of formal education. Students might also ponder why any person should be patriotic toward a country in which they are denied basic rights and opportunities—this is an issue that African Americans are discussing this very day.

heaven success, even for my country, in a cause where she should be in the wrong. . . . My toast would be, may our country be always successful, but, whether successful or otherwise, always right."
—John Q. Adams, 1816 (368.14)

7. Inscription on the Robert Gould Shaw Monument by Augustus Saint-Gaudends, Boston Common, Boston, Massachusetts.

   To the Fifty-fourth Regiment of Massachusetts Infantry:

   The white officers, taking life and honor in their hands, cast in their lot with men of a despised race unproved in war, and risked death as inciters of servile insurrection if taken prisoners, besides encountering all the common perils of camp march and battle.

   The black rank and file volunteered when disaster clouded the Union cause, served without pay for eighteen months till given that of white troops, faced threatened enslavement if captured, were brave in action, patient under heavy and dangerous labors, and cheerful amid hardships and privations.

   Together they gave to the nation and the world undying proof that Americans of African descent possess the pride, courage, and devotion of the patriot soldier. One hundred and eighty thousand such Americans enlisted under the Union flag in 1863–1865.
   —Charles William Eliot, 1897 (522.13)

8. "Our country, right or wrong. When right, to be kept right; when wrong, to be put right." —Carl Schurz, 1899 (510.18)

9 "I realize that patriotism is not enough. I must have no hatred or bitterness towards anyone." —Edith Cavell, 1915 (590.8)

Stephen Decatur was a naval hero celebrated for his boldness in the War of 1812, and his brash speech (no. 5) was delivered as a toast. It has echoed through American history ever since. Students might be asked to discuss it in connection with the revisions to it made by John Quincy Adams, the future sixth president, in 1816 (no. 6) and by the German-born senator and American patriot, Carl Schurz, in 1899 (no. 8). Quote number 7 is important for the well-known story of the White officer Robert Gould Shaw and his all-Black regiment, and for the little-known information it also provides. Students should know that 180,000 Black Americans fought for the Union in the Civil War; the one thousand soldiers in Shaw's regiment were not the only ones to do so. I would hope that student reporters would have access to the Internet for this one; there's a lot of good material there on Shaw and on the Shaw monument in Boston. It's not hard to find websites that offer color pictures of the monument; on the site I found, I was able to get an enlargement of any detail in the picture simply by clicking on it. While students might know of Shaw's regiment from the movie *Glory*, they certainly wouldn't know who Edith Cavell was. They would be impressed by quote number 9 when they learned her story: She was a British nurse in Belgium during World War I, and she was executed by the Germans for sheltering Allied soldiers. Quote number 9 contains her last words, spoken just before she was shot to death. This quote is well worth discussing because Cavell, who was certainly loyal to her country, recognizes a higher value than patriotism. Students might want to explore her attitude and compare this quote with quote number 3, the last words of Nathan Hale.

Students might also be invited to discuss quote number 1, the other statement that appears to question the value of patriotism. In calling patriotism "the last refuge of a scoundrel," Samuel Johnson is not, however, attacking patriotism itself, but the phoney patriotism of hypocritical "scoundrels." Students might be advised to keep Johnson's statement in mind as they watch political campaigns. Johnson was actually very respectful of sincere patriotism, as I discovered when I checked out the *Samuel Johnson Sound Bite Page* (http.//www.Samueljohnson.com/) on the Internet. Students who access this site out can find at least twenty positive quotes from Johnson on the topic of patriotism.

A Unit on Violence and Nonviolence

Exploring the concept of patriotism led me to the larger, philosophical issue of the proper use of force. I collected quotations involving the word *violence* and its close synonyms *force* and *might*, as well as famous quotations related to the concept of violence, such as Patrick Henry's "Give me liberty or give me death." As I was exploring words for violence, the term *nonviolence* began to crop up as well. In fact, I found a remarkable constellation of quotes containing the word *nonviolence*. The resulting collection of quotations for and against violence provides a view of American and European history during the past three centuries.

Obviously, the collection of quotes in Figure 13.4 on page 204 could be used to introduce a whole course on the topic of violence versus nonviolence, complete with reading selections from key figures. I could see such a course as a Humanities offering or as an advanced English course. Likewise, I could see this collection being used as a lead-in to history courses of various kinds: a course in nonviolent protest in the twentieth century or, more narrowly, in twentieth-century America. Such courses could easily be interdisciplinary, involving faculty from English and Social Studies.

If I were to use this list as a unit in an English or Humanities course, I'd want to do two things. I'd want to explore the quotations in depth, to define and analyze the various attitudes expressed in them. At the same time, I'd want to be sure that the class knew who all these people were, so that the students could see these statements in their historical contexts. The discussion would be much more meaningful to the students if they could see that these statements led to action in the real world.

In dealing with the quotations, I would begin by asking the class to sort the quotations into groups and then analyze each group in depth. At the start, I'd sort the students themselves into small groups. Then, I'd give each group a different quote, ask them to define the attitude toward violence that it expresses, and then find other quotes that seem to express the same attitude. I'd give each group one of these four quotes: Trotsky's comment about force and gravitation (no. 11), Washington's "conquer or die" speech (no. 6), Gandhi's definition of *Satyagraha* (no. 10), and Emerson's statement that "thoughts rule the world" (no. 9). As I see them, these quotes express at least three different attitudes toward violence: (1) a pro-force position, which accepts force as an effective means of achieving one's ends and which displays no moral scruples about using it; (2) a pro-force with reluctance position, which supports violence as a last resort, and only in a just or moral cause; and (3) a nonviolent position, which rejects any use of force and views force as incompatible with a just and moral cause. Closely allied with this third position is the belief that, in Emerson's words, "spiritual is stronger than any material force." If, in fact, the students did understand the four quotes in this way, I'd expect them to group all of the quotes more or less like this. Placed in the pro-force position would be Trotsky (nos. 10 and 11), Mussolini (no. 14), Mao Tse-Tung (nos. 15 and 16), and probably "Might Makes Right" (no. 3). Placed in the reluctant position would be Henry (no. 4), Washington (no. 6), and Lincoln (no. 8). Placed in the nonviolent position would be Gandhi (nos. 12 and 13), King (nos. 17 and 18), Chavez (no. 20), and perhaps Solzhenitsyn (no. 19). Placed with Emerson would be Hugo (no. 7) and perhaps Burke (no. 5). The biblical reference to the sword (nos. 1 and 2) might be placed with either position three or four.

I have no idea how long all this process of classifying the quotes might

FIGURE 13.4
Quotations Involving the Concepts of Violence and Nonviolence

---

TRADITIONAL

1. "All they that take the sword shall perish with the sword." —The *Bible*: Matthew 26:52 (37.1)
2. "He who lives by the sword dies by the sword." —Popular American saying (Titelman, G. Y., *Popular Proverbs and Sayings*, 1997, 131)
3. "Might makes right." —Traditional saying (Titelman, G. Y., *Popular Proverbs and Sayings*, 1997, 232)

EIGHTEENTH CENTURY

4. "The war has actually begun! . . . Our brethren are already in the field! Why stand we here idle? . . . Is life so dear or peace so sweet as to be purchased at the price of chains or liberty? Forbid it, Almighty God. I know not what course others may take, but as for me, give me liberty or give me death!" —Patrick Henry, 1775 (339.10)
5. "The use of force alone is but *temporary*. It may subdue for a moment; but it does not remove the necessity of subduing again; and a nation is not governed, which is perpetually to be conquered." —Edmund Burke, 1775 (331.11)
6. "Our cruel and unrelenting enemy leaves us only the choice of brave resistance, or the most abject submission. We have, therefore, to resolve to conquer or die." —George Washington, 1776 (336.14)

NINETEENTH CENTURY

7. "An invasion of armies can be resisted, but not an idea whose time has come." —Victor Hugo, 1852 (427.18)
8. "Let us have faith that right makes might, and in that faith let us to the end dare to do our duty as we understand it." —Abraham Lincoln, 1860 (448.15)
9. "Great men are they who see that spiritual is stronger than any material force, that thoughts rule the world." —Ralph W. Emerson, 1876 (433.18)

TWENTIETH CENTURY

10. "The dictatorship of the Communist Party is maintained by recourse to every form of violence." —Leon Trotsky (1879–1940) (641.3)
11. "Not believing in force is the same as not believing in gravitation." —Leon Trotsky (*Barnes and Noble Book of Quotations*, 1987, 288)

---

take. I'd expect disagreements about what certain quotes mean and where they should be classified. I'd also expect, sooner or later, some healthy skepticism about position four: How, exactly, can nonviolence resist or defeat violence? A close scrutiny of the quotes from Gandhi and King can lead stu-

12. "The term *Satyagraha* was coined by me . . . in order to distinguish it from the movement then going on . . . under the name of Passive Resistance.

    Its root meaning is 'holding on to truth,' hence 'force of righteousness.' I have also called it love force or soul force. In the application of *Sayagraha*, I discovered in the earliest stages that pursuit of truth did not permit violence being inflicted on one's opponent, but that he must be weaned from error by patience and sympathy. For what appears truth to the one may appear error to the other. And patience means self-suffering. So the doctrine came to mean vindication of truth, not by the infliction of suffering on others, but on one's self." —Ghandi, 1922 (606.13)

13. "Nonviolence and truth (*Satya*) are inseparable and presuppose one another. There is no god higher than truth." —Ghandi, 1939 (607.1)

14. "You know what I think about violence. For me it is profoundly moral— more moral than compromises and transactions." —Benito Mussolini (1883–1945) (*Barnes and Noble Book of Quotations*, 1987, 358)

15. "A revolution is not the same as inviting people to dinner, or writing and essay, or painting a picture . . . A revolution is an insurrection, an act of violence by which one class overthrows another." —Mao Tse-Tung (1891–1976) (686.11)

16. "Every Communist must grasp the truth: Political power grows out of the barrel of a gun." —Mao Tse-Tung (686.12)

17. "Nonviolence is the answer to the crucial political and moral questions of our time; the need for man to overcome oppression and violence without resorting to oppression and violence.

    Man must evolve for all human conflict a method which rejects revenge, aggression, and retaliation. The foundation of such a method is love." —Martin Luther King, Jr., 1964 (761.4)

18. "The Negro was willing to risk martyrdom in order to move and stir the social conscience of his community and the nation . . . He would force his oppressor to commit his brutality openly, with the rest of the world looking on . . . Nonviolent resistance paralyzed and confused the power structure against which it was directed." —Martin Luther King, Jr., 1964 (761.8)

19. "Violence does not and cannot exist by itself; it is invariably intertwined with *the lie*." —Alexander Solzhenitsyn, 1972 (746.5)

20. "In some cases non-violence requires more militancy than violence." —Cesar Chavez (1927–1993) (*Barnes and Noble Book of Quotations*, 1987, 358)

©2001 by Thomas Carnicelli from *Words Work*. Portsmouth, NH: Heinemann.

dents to the answers those two men determined. I'd ask students to start with Gandhi's statement that "Nonviolence and truth (*Satya*) are inseparable" (no. 13). If nonviolence is the same as truth, then a nonviolent person must be a truth-seeker, someone who has some idea what truth is, while a violent person is in error. Hence, the way to defeat violence must involve showing violent people the error of their ways. How can this be done? Students could search the speeches of Gandhi and King for answers: "one's opponent . . . must be weaned from error by patience and sympathy" (no. 10); "The foundation of such a method is love" (no. 17); "to risk martyrdom in order to move and stir the social conscience of his (the Negro's) community and the nation" (no. 18). If and when students found these answers, I'd want to pose one more question: On what common belief are these answers based? It seems to me that they're based on the belief that all people have some good in them, some capacity to respond to the truth if they can come to see it. It's this belief that inspired both Gandhi and King to believe that nonviolence can overcome the forces of violence and ignorance within other people.

That's how I like to imagine I'd deal with my first objective, getting the students to explore the quotes in depth. As for my second objective—getting students to know the historical contexts of these quotes—I'd have students do research on many of the quotes, either on the Internet or in a school encyclopedia. This collection contains quotes from a great many people that students need to know about in order to understand their own culture and the world around them. Students could be asked to make reports on any number of important figures: Edmund Burke, Ralph Waldo Emerson, Leon Trotsky, Gandhi, Mussolini, Mao Tse-Tung, Martin Luther King, Jr., Alexander Solzhenitsyn, Cesar Chavez. In the course of these reports, a lot of complex issues would arise, and I'd want to help students avoid oversimplifying them. For instance, the pro-force comments by Mussolini, Trotsky, and Mao Tse-Tung might lead students to see America's two great twentieth-century adversaries, the fascists and the communists, as nothing more than thugs. Mussolini was a thug, and I wouldn't attempt to defend him, but I would certainly tell students that the leaders of the Russian and Chinese communist revolutions believed they were pursuing a just cause, even though they were willing to use force against all who opposed them. In general, I'd steer students away from making moral judgments about complex historical movements and events; I'd focus their attention on trying to *understand* various attitudes. To understand the attitudes of Gandhi and King, students need to know that both men based their philosophies on values taken from both Western and Eastern religions; their belief that all people can recognize the truth came from their religious belief that all are created "in the image of God." After learning this information, students might be tempted to generalize, to equate religion and nonviolence. If they did, I'd want to step in again, to remind them that religion has been a major cause of violence throughout human history, and that religious warfare is still going on in the world today.

In preparing these last three collections of quotations, I started with *Bartlett's* but I also did a great deal of research on the Internet, so that I could get a better sense of the historical contexts in which these various statements were made. I've been a most reluctant computer-user in the past, but this experience has convinced me of the enormous educational value of the Internet. I got so much information, so quickly and so easily! I simply typed the name of an historical figure into my search engine and within minutes I had all the information I needed, and then some. I typed in *Edmund Burke* and got a capsule biography, along with the full texts of several of his key speeches; I was, thus, able to read his comments about the ineffectiveness of force and the necessity of compromise as part of an effort to get the British government to reconcile with the American colonists. I found a site filled with quotes from Gandhi, typed in key words, and got his thoughts on any topic I wished. I read several full speeches and sermons from Martin Luther King, Jr., and also found that he had spent a year in India, studying the work of Gandhi. I had only a vague recollection of Cesar Chavez, but my Internet search quickly provided me with plenty of material about him: a picture, a biography, and selections from his speeches. As I was reading about the United Farm Workers, which Chavez founded, I read that the union took a pledge of nonviolence, in accordance with the principles of Gandhi. So, through the Internet, I discovered that Gandhi had influenced both the Black Civil Rights Movement in the American South and the effort to obtain bargaining rights for farm workers in California and other states. This information led me to give Gandhi a prominent position in my collection of quotes.

All this will seem like belaboring the obvious to veteran Internet users, but not all teachers are, and not all teachers have found ways to use the Internet with their students. Having students give reports on the contexts of important quotations is an excellent way to give the Internet a valuable role in instruction. A quotation means more to students if they have some sense of the person who said it and of the historical context in which it was said. Searching the Internet is the quickest way for students to acquire that information, which they can then pass on to their peers.

To summarize this long and diverse chapter, I will simply repeat that groups of related quotations provide students with an excellent vehicle for exploring concepts in depth. Such groups can be used as a means to stimulate serious class conversations about significant ideas and issues. They can also be used to help students acquire culturally valuable information and develop their research skills. Finally, such groups are especially valuable as lead-ins to reading units devoted to a common theme.

REFERENCES

The American Heritage Dictionary of the English Language (3rd ed.). 1992. Boston: Houghton Mifflin.

The American Heritage Dictionary of the English Language (4th. ed.). 2000. Boston: Houghton Mifflin.

Anon. [Fifteenth Century?] 2000. "Western Wind." In M. H. Abrams, (ed.), *The Norton Anthology of English Literature* (Vol.1, 7th. ed.). New York: W.W. Norton.

Avi. 1993. *Nothing But the Truth.* New York: Avon.

Barnes and Noble Book of Quotations. 1987. Robert I. Fitzhenry (ed.). New York: Barnes and Noble Books.

Bartlett, John. *Familiar Quotations.* (14th ed.). 1968. Emily Morison Beck, ed. Boston: Little, Brown.

———. *Familiar Quotations.* (16th ed.). 1992. Justin Kaplan, ed. Boston: Little, Brown.

Baugh, Albert C., and Thomas Cable. 1993. *A History of the English Language* (4th ed.). Englewood Cliffs, NJ: Prentice-Hall.

Baumann, James F., and Edward J. Kameenui. 1991. "Research on Vocabulary Instruction: Ode to Voltaire." In James Flood, Julie M. Jensen, Diane Lapp, and James R. Squire (eds.), *Handbook on Teaching the English Language Arts*, 604–632. New York: MacMillan.

Beck, Isabel L., Margaret G. McKeown, and Richard C. Omanson, 1987. "The Effects and Use of Diverse Vocabulary Techniques." In Margaret G. McKeown and Mary E. Curtis (eds.), *The Nature of Vocabulary Acquisition,* 147–163. Hillsdale, NJ: Lawrence Erlbaum.

Bede. [731] 1990. *An Ecclesiastical History of the English People.* London: Penguin.

Bolt, Thomas. [1960] 1990. *A Man for All Seasons: A Play in Two Acts.* New York: Bantam.

Burke, Jim. 1999. *The English Teacher's Companion.* Portsmouth, NH: Boynton/Cook.

Chapman, Robert. 1991. *Thesaurus of American Slang.* New York: HarperCollins.

Churchill, Winston. 1940. "We Shall Fight in the Fields and in the Streets." Address to Parliament, June 4, 1940. In William Bennett, *The Book of Virtues.* 1993. New York: Simon and Schuster.

Coghlan, Jean. 1985. "Backward Boy." In David A. Sohn (ed.), *Ten Top Stories.* New York: Bantam.

Crane, Stephen. [1895] 1976. *Red Badge of Courage.* New York: Bantam.

Crutcher, Chris. 1995. *Staying Fat for Sarah Byrnes.* New York: Laurel Leaf.

Dickinson, Emily. [1890] 1979. "These Are the Days When Birds Come Back." In Thomas H. Johnson (ed.), *The Poems of Emily Dickinson.* 3 vols. Cambridge, MA: Belknap Press (Harvard University Press).

Dieterich, Daniel (ed.). 1976. *Teaching About Doublespeak.* Urbana, IL: NCTE.

Dubois, W. E. B. [1903] 1994. *The Souls of Black Folk.* New York: Dover Publications.

Eliot, Thomas Stearns. [1935] 1963. *Murder in the Cathedral.* New York: Harcourt Brace Jovanovich.

Frost, Robert. [1923] 1979. "Fire and Ice." In Edward Connery Lathem (ed.), *The Poetry of Robert Frost: The Collected Poems, Complete and Unabridged.* New York: Henry Holt.

Gig: Americans Talk about Their Jobs at the Turn of the Millenium. 2000. John Bowe, Marissa Bowe, and Sabin Streeter (eds.). New York: Crown.

Graves, Michael F. 1987. "The Roles of Instruction in Fostering Vocabulary Development." In Margaret G. McKeown and Mary E. Curtis (eds.), *The Nature of Vocabulary Acquisition*, 165–184. Hillsdale, NJ: Lawrence Erlbaum.

Hemingway, Ernest. [1938] 1995. "In Another Country," "Big Two-Hearted River: Part One," and "Big Two-Hearted River: Part Two." In *The Short Stories.* New York: Scribner.

Hillocks, George, Jr. 1986. *Research on Written Composition: New Directions for Teaching.* Urbana, IL: ERIC Clearinghouse on Reading and Composition Skills and the National Conference on Research in English. Distributed by NCTE.

Hinton, S. E. [1967] 1997. *The Outsiders.* New York: Puffin (Penguin USA).

Hirsch, E. D., Jr. 1987. *Cultural Literacy: What Every American Needs to Know.* Boston: Houghton Mifflin.

Melville, Herman. [1856] 1989. "Bartleby the Scrivener." In *Billy Budd and Other Stories.* New York: Penguin.

Millward, C. M. 1989. *A Biography of the English Language.* New York: Holt, Rinehart and Winston.

The Oxford English Dictionary. (2nd. ed.). 1989. London: Oxford UP.

Orwell, George. [1946] 1970. "Politics and the English Language." In *A Collection of Essays.* New York: Harcourt Brace Jovanovich.

Pyles, Thomas, and John Algeo. 1993. *The Origins and Development of the English Language.* (4th. ed.). Orlando, FL: Harcourt Brace Jovanovich.

Roget's International Thesaurus (4th. ed.), rev. by Robert Chapman. 1977. New York: Harper & Row.

Samuel Johnson Sound Bite Page (http.//www.Samueljohnson.com/)

Sophocles. 1984. *The Theban Plays.* Robert Fagles, trans. New York: Penguin.

Stotsky, Sandra. 1997. *State English Standards: An Appraisal of English/Language Arts Standards in 28 States.* Washington, DC: Thomas B. Fordham Foundation.

Titelman, Gregory Y. 1997. *Popular Proverbs and Sayings.* New York: Gramercy Books.

Thoreau, Henry David. [1854] 1983. *Walden and Civil Disobedience.* New York: Penguin.

Wordsworth, William. [1800] 1993. "A Slumber Did My Spirit Seal." In *Selected Poetry.* New York: Penguin.